W9-ACT-733

CONTINENTAL, LATIN-AMERICAN AND FRANCOPHONE WOMEN WRITERS

Volume III

Edited by

Ginette Adamson
Eunice Myers

University Press of America,® Inc.
Lanham • New York • Oxford

University Press of America,® Inc.
4720 Boston Way
Lanham, Maryland 20706

12 Hid's Copse Rd.
Cummor Hill, Oxford OX2 9JJ

Printed in the United States of America
British Library Cataloguing in Publication Information Available

Library of Congress Cataloging-in-Publication Data

Wichita State University Conference on Foreign Literature (lst : 1984)
Continental, Latin-American, and Francophone women writers.
Bibliography: p.
l. Literature--Women authors--History and criticism--Congresses. I. Wichita State University Conference on Foreign Literature (2nd : 1985) II. Myers, Eunice. III. Adamson, Ginette. IV. Title.
PN471.W5 1984 809'89287 87-8105 CIP

ISBN 0-7618-0856-6 (cloth: alk. ppr.)

The paper used in this publication meets the minimum requirements of American National Standard for information Sciences—Permanence of Paper for Printed Library Materials, ANSI Z39.48—1984

TO THE MEMORY OF

Marie Susini (1920 - 1993)
Rosa Chacel (1898 - 1994)

CONTINENTAL, LATIN-AMERICAN AND FRANCOPHONE WOMEN WRITERS, VOL.III

EDITORS

Ginette Adamson
Eunice Myers

ACKNOWLEDGMENTS

Successful conferences and the publication of selected papers from them are only possible as a collaborative effort. Therefore, we have the pleasure and obligation to thank several people and organizations who facilitated our work. First, our special appreciation to the enthusiastic scholarly participants. Our gratitude to our keynote speakers and invited writers: Madeleine Ouellette-Michalska, Madeleine Monette and the Délégation du Québec (Chicago) for their continued support; Paule Constant, the Ministère des Affaires Étrangères (Paris), and the Service Culturel de France; Magaly Alabau (Cuba), Yolanda Rosas (Ecuador), Lisa Kahn (Germany), and Christiane Seiler (Germany). We also thank the editorial board who often put aside other pressing matters to review manuscripts.

Our gratitude goes also to our colleagues in the Department of Modern and Classical Languages and Literatures, to the Deans in the College of Liberal Arts and Sciences and to the Vice-President for Academic Affairs, for their financial help and encouragement; to other colleagues at Wichita State University who contributed their time to the success of our conferences. Special thanks to Carl Adamson and Robert Phillips for providing technical assistance and to our assistants Elena Dreisziger and Melissa Beckloff.

The following contributors will retain copyright privileges:

Roseanna Lewis Dufault and Obioma Nnaemeka.

The editors gratefully acknowledge permission from the following authors and their publishers to quote from their works: Andrée Chedid, Annie Ernaux, Eulalia Galvarriato, Susan Griffin, Cristina Lacasa, Luise Rinser, Marie Susini, Christa Wolf; from Malou Woehrling for the inclusion of her poem "Errance"; from Gaëtan Brulotte and the *Revue des sciences humaines* for allowing the reprint of his article, which first appeared in that journal's number 217 (jan-mar 1990), and from Frédérique Chevillot and her publisher Anma Libri for the reprint of pages 120-24, 129-35, from *La réouverture du texte*.

TABLE OF CONTENTS

INTRODUCTION

ERRANCES

Envie de dire des souffrances
envie de dire des joies
d'espérer
les idées se bousculent
et se confondent
cris larmes appels au secours
résignation révolte
acceptation comment dire
les pensées dansent la sarabande
orchestre sans chef
je me sens soliste
ne connaissant pas ma partition
les mots se taisent
tristesse obsession
promenade solitaire dans la nuit
angoisse agacement
poème abandonné pensées vagabondes
résignation
paix retrouvée...

Malou Woehrling
Jan. 1993
Strasbourg
(Unpublished)

Among the purposes of both the Wichita State University Annual International Conference on Continental, Latin-American and Francophone Women Writers and this publication stands the desire to introduce to the participants and readers, unknown women writers. We include the poem "Errances" by Malou Woehrling, placed as incipit of this volume, with this in mind. Its title ("Wanderings") traces its author's search for words to express her pain, joy and hope, the resulting solitude and resignation before regaining peacefulness. "Wanderings" may also symbolize the history of many women.

"Errances" also echoes the whispers Eunice Myers and I heard incessantly, whispers which led us to the creation of the Wichita State University Annual Conference. It responds to the concern among several colleagues who noted the lack of channels to exchange ideas on non-Anglophone women writers in a receptive setting devoted entirely to such activity. For Eunice Myers and for me this desire to speak, "envie de dire," began in 1984 and continued for twelve years. The closing of "Errances" ("paix retrouvée") also suggests the outcome of our professional gatherings: a friendly and peaceful atmosphere for the pursuit of common goals. We learn and share knowledge on women writers and their works in the light of current critical feminist theories applicable to each author's textual orientation.

The articles included here, because of their diversity, merit a brief presentation at the least. They offer new opportunities for reflection on issues concerning women's writings and writings about women.

I. About German-Speaking Women Writers:

Tiiu V. Laane deals with Louise von François's principal concern, namely, the education of women. Von François was influenced by the educator, Johann Friedrich Herbart, a disciple of Pestalozzi. Inspired by Herbart's ideal of 'inner freedom,' her concept of educating women concentrated on the person, rather than the feminine aspect. A fervent supporter of democratic precepts, von François promoted critical thinking by women over their use of imagination, a trait traditionally perceived to be the prerogative of the female mind.

According to Mary Seager, it is symptomatic of Christa Wolf's vision of the Cassandra myth that she surrounds the heroine's prophecies with an aura of silence. In so doing, Wolf denies Cassandra's public voice and rejects the transformational capacity of both *logos* and *eros*. In this way, reason as the dominant force takes precedence over prophecy and passion as cathartic and redemptive experiences.

In Hanna B. Lewis's account of Fanny Lewald's role in the Bismarckian era, the writer emerges as an incisive commentator. However, she is less interested in women's emancipation in the contemporary sense of the term than in exploring social issues affecting women. Thus, her heroines tend to pursue conventional careers. Lewald's treatment of her subject is comprehensive, for her writings encompass women of lower social rank, as well as female protagonists of the middle and upper social strata.

Luise Rinser, as viewed by Iman Khalil, depicts truly emancipated women in her novel *Mitte des Lebens* (1950) as being truly emancipated at a time when feminism was still a relatively unfamiliar concept. A complete reversal of her position takes place in *Abenteuer der Tugend* (1957). A third work, *Geh fort, wenn du kannst* (1959), is representative of Rinser's metaphysical and religious phase. In later years, the author became actively involved in the peace movement and endeavored to serve as a bridge between East and West.

As Uta Liebmann Schaub emphasizes, Irmtraud Morgner and Heide Göttner-Abendroth represent the ideological division between East and West Germany in their respective discussions of feminist concerns. Göttner-Abendroth, unlike Morgner, places matriarchy at the very inception of history. She espouses an ideal *Urgemeinschaft* in the romantic tradition. Both authors share an unequivocal rejection of patriarchy.

II. About Spanish and Latin-American Women Writers:

Concha Alborg's article rescues Eulalia Galvarriato from virtual anonymity, offering interesting insights into the novel *Cinco sombras*. Until now, she has been known mostly as the wife (now widow) of famed critic and poet Dámaso Alonso. The five shadows of the book's title, the repressed daughters of a traditional household, are analyzed by Alborg in their relationship and similarity to their father's caged birds.

Herlinda Charpentier Saitz also focuses attention on a writer who was virtually forgotten until recently. While most critics concentrate on Carolina Coronado's biography and social circumstances, Saitz prefers a theoretical analysis of her works.

Catherine Bellver incorporates contemporary feminist theory into a cogent analysis of Martín Gaite's masterpiece, *El cuarto de atrás*. She examines the role of writing in Martín Gaite's life, synthesizing earlier critical studies and making important new observations on the metafictional aspects of this work.

Barbara May's study applies Susan Griffin's feminist ecological observations to Cristina Lacasa's latest poetry. Lacasa's poetry and May's reading of it call into question supposedly objective patriarchal voices.

Rosa Montero also questions and subverts the male view. Mary C. Harges's study of *Te trataré como a una reina* shows how Montero dismantles both patriarchal journalism and paternalistic male-female relationships.

III. About Francophone Women Writers:

Frédérique Chevillot presents a well-argued analysis of the "incipits" and "clôtures" as narrative techniques in two of Anne Hébert's novels. Chevillot demonstrates an impressive command of pertinent scholarship devoted to the opening and the closure of literary texts. She also addresses the phenomenon of the "réouverture narrative qui y est lié." This circular movement, so ingeniously used in the sixties by playwrights of the theater of the absurd, especially by Ionesco and Beckett, is a stimulating technique practiced by Hébert in *Les fous de Bassans*, as shown by Chevillot.

Victor-Laurent Tremblay seeks to determine and understand the specific circumstances which may have led to Blais' preoccupation with three elements repeated throughout her writings: obsession with the mother figure, the fight against social oppression, and the search for artistic pleasure. Trembly proposes that her early works offer the source of these obsessions, indicating Blais' preference for the privileged moment of fusion between mother and daughter. The methodology of "psycho-critique" is used convincingly. This is a valuable contribution to Marie-Claire Blais studies for the attention it pays to her lesbianism in the pre-oedipal context.

Roseanna Lewis Dufault analyzes the role of mothers in two of Gabrielle Roy's novels in which "fathers play only a minor role" while "mothers set an example of relative independence by testing the limit of their traditional roles, undertaking ambitious projects that set them apart from their peers." Contrary to Roy's own upbringing the mothers in these novels adopt an attitude of rearing their children to become more independent. This and other considerations lead Dufault to conclude that Roy "distinguishes herself as a feminist foremother by portraying a strong mother-daughter relationship comparable to those developed in English-Canadian and Québécois women's writing more than a decade ago."

Claire-Lise Tondeur presents the double alienation of language for Annie Ernaux: the familiar language of her childhood being that of the working class, as opposed to the one she learns in school, a language which closes the possibility of communication with her parents. Her new social milieu of the intellectual clashes with the reality of her childhood. Later, the discovery of her sexual difference adds to her alienation. Writing, as a substitute, can alleviate her tension stemming from being an unfulfilled person.

Marcelle Tinayre is virtually unknown today, although her novels in the 1900's put her on a par with the male author Romain Rolland. Marie-France Hilgar characterizes Tinayre as a "romancière de la passion" who creates pathological characters, victims of their passion and envy, who become vengeful and cultivate feelings of hatred leading to brutal death. Their imagination evokes the era of Madame Bovary, evading reality by superimposing a fictional life. This article forces the reader to go back to a little-known writer whose work may cast new light on the entire literature of an era of the "prise de conscience féminine" by both female and male writers.

Georgiana Colvile brings to our attention the treatment of the corsican woman in the works of Marie Susini, a native of Corsica who died in 1993. Much appreciated in France and other countries, Susini remained obscure in the United States until Colvile brought her to light here. Colvile describes the love-hate relationship of Susini with Corsica. She also evokes the solitude which Susini embodies in her all-female cast of characters. These women are imprisoned by the mother (la mère), just as the land is surrounded by the sea (la mer). Susini's only escape, explains Colvile, was writing or fleeing.

Claudine Fisher engages the reader in a sensitive study of works by Paule Constant, a writer who is becoming increasingly known since I first introduced her on the American continent at the WSU conference in 1987.[1] Tiffany (the main character) in *Propriété privée* spends her life between the reassuring and comforting "propriété" of her grandmother and the boarding school of the "Dames Sanguinaires." Fisher focuses her study around the circular movement of the story as Tiffany travels from one place to the other. Fisher explores Constant's play with the mythical and realistic dimension of Tiffany's state of mind. This study also sheds light on the intertextuality between Constant's novels.

Obioma Nnaemeka's study on "marriage as institution and as experience" in the writings of Mariama Bâ is a provocative and controversial essay. Nnaemeka speaks as an African woman who refuses to define—and dismisses—all feminist thought as *a priori* "western." She establishes an interesting textual relationship between social reality and fiction. The author demonstrates through a lucid analysis of Bâ's novels that it is not the notion of polygamy in itself that is rejected by the writer's female characters, but rather the way it is put into practice by African men. These concerns about abuses of polygamy, brought to attention in the seventies by Sembène Ousmane in his novel/film *Xala*, merit the new look, offered in this volume, by a female critique.

Sally Kitch analyzes the phenomenon of "the hom(m)osexual economy" in three of Yourcenar's novels. In describing the novel's economy of the Same the author of this article, in light of Irigaray's theory on this subject, situates Yourcenar's treatment of female characters in the context of the western cultural heritage. Kitch explores, on one hand, the contradiction of Yourcenar's acclaimed brilliance, her election as the only woman to the all male membership at the Académie Française, and, on the other hand, the criticism to which she is subjected concerning her treatment of gender. The reader is offered, supported by a solid theoretical framework of gender issues and literary analysis, several convincing interpretations.

Drawing from recent studies in anthropology on the subject of corporal manifestations (gestures) of human beings, Gaëtan Brulotte analyzes the use and meaning of gestures in the novels of Nathalie Sarraute. Gesture, Brulotte explains, is for Sarraute, the best access to an individual, and to his or her imaginary universe. From an anthropological point of view one can distinguish within

Sarraute's fictional writings five axes of her "gestuaire." Brulotte takes care in analyzing each one, always keeping Sarraute's texts in mind, making this an informative study of one of the most respected women writers of France.

Judy Cochran gives insight into the poetry and prose of the Egyptian-born author Andrée Chedid whose reputation is well-established in France, where she lives. Cochran analyzes the theme of liberation for women in the poetry of Chedid. After presenting images of repression, imprisonment, physical and mental confinement, and silence in the author's prose, she turns to the poetic works in which Chedid evokes the theme of liberation for women, leading to her ability to transcend time and space.

In the same vein, Katharine Conley studies another important woman poet. Although almost completely ignored, Joyce Mansour may be the most significant woman surrealist poet in France. Conley impels readers, male and female, to look into the female poet's work and evaluate its qualities in the context of the well-known male surrealist poet Robert Desnos. In this comparative analysis the feminine approach prevails and specific differences are established between the treatment of common themes by both poets.

The last two contributions on Francophone women poets, along with Barbara May's study of Cristina Lacasa's latest poetry (described earlier), help fill the lack of critical texts in the body of current publication on women poets in particular, and on poetry in general.

We hope that the "envie de dire" (desire to speak) which motivated each of the contributors to this volume will lead to an "envie de lire" (desire to read) what we believe to be a very informative and stimulating collection of articles about women writers. Malou Woehrling's poem "Errances" is an invitation to every reader to wander through each text included in this volume.

Ginette Adamson

Notes

[1] Several colleagues have contacted me requesting information concerning my work on Paule Constant. With this in mind I am adding the following, begining with my first presentation "Paule Constant," Latin American and Francophone Women Writers, Wichita State University, April 1987.

"Paule Constant" in *Dictionnaire littéraire et répertoire des femmes de langue française de Marie de France à Marie NDiaye* . Ed. Christine Makward et Madeleine Hage. Paris: Éditions Karthala, 1996.

Constant. *White spirit.* Paris: Gallimard, 1989. The French Review. 64. 2 (1990).

Paule Constant. *Un monde à l'usage des Demoiselles.* Paris: Gallimard, 1987. *Rocky Mountain Review* 63.1-2 (1989).

"La fonction de l'exil dans l'oeuvre de Paule Constant." Annual meeting of The Pacific Ancient and Modern Language Association, Santa Barbara, Nov. 1995.

"L'exil chez Paule Constant." L'exil au XVIIème siècle et de nos jours, Centre Méridional de Rencontres sur le XVIème siècle, Marseille, 30 octobre 1993.

"Toiles peintes, toiles à tisser: création romanesque de Paule Constant." Eighteenth Annual Colloquium on Literature and Film, West Virginia University, Morgantown, September 9-11, 1993.

"L'écriture de la peinture: *Le grand Ghâpal* de Paule Constant." Thenth Annual International Conference on Continental, Latin American and Francophone Women Writers, Wichita State University, April 1-3, 1993.

"Ambiguité du fantastique chez Paule Constant." Rocky Mountain Modern Language Association, Tempe, Arizona, October 17-19, 1991.

"Le fantastique dans l'oeuvre de Paule Constant." International Convention of the American Associatin of Teachers of French, Paris, July 10-14, 1989.

"Impressions d'Afrique: l'imaginaire et le vécu. Raymond Roussel et Paule Constant." Colloque de la Société des Professeurs Français et Francophones d'Amérique, Midwest Modern Language Association, St. Louis, November 3-5, 1988.

Louise von François and the Education of Women

Tiiu V. Laane
Texas A&M University

In his first letter to the German novelist Louise von François (1817-1893), in what was to become a long and heartfelt correspondence, Conrad Ferdinand Meyer summed up François's works as an "eigentümliche Mischung von conservativen Überlieferungen und freien Standpunkten" (*Briefwechsel* 1). His words pinpoint the source from which François's narratives derive their elusive character. They offer the reason why François, until recently, has seldom been mentioned in feminist analyses of nineteenth-century women writers.[1] Louise von François was an idealist, moralist and positivist who advocated conventional bourgeois values: the importance of the home, the sacrosanct role of the woman as wife and mother. At the same time, her narratives carry an undercurrent of progressive social thinking which reflects the mind and character of an intelligent and independent thinker. François's views about the education of women reveal similar conservative and liberal philosophical patterns. She regarded education as the force which developed the moral values of the nation. The ethics of the family, she argued, were to set the tone for the proper education of children. At the same time, François advocated education as the means to eradicate the gulf between the lower and upper ranks of society and called into question the sharp disparity between educational opportunities for men and women. She challenged the stereotypical image of women as intellectually inferior beings in no less radical terms than leaders of the nineteenth-century women's education movement such as Louise Otto-Peters, Luise Büchner, Malvida von Meysenberg, Henriette Schrader-Breymann, and Helene Lange.

In order to put Louise von François's views on the education of women into historical perspective, it would seem most informative to begin with the education of François herself, for there can be no clearer example of the limitations of women's education in nineteenth-century Germany. Born in Herzberg in the province of Saxony in 1817, François grew up in the little town of Weissenfels in Prussia as a member of a well-to-do middle-class family. François's home, Prussia, was on the forefront of educational reform in Germany. As the result of the French Revolution, rising industrialization and the effects of the Enlightenment, there was a growing interest in literacy and education, for men and for women, throughout all of Germany.[2] Like all women in nineteenth-century Germany, however, François was imprisoned in a patriarchal society which strictly defined the roles of men and women and which adapted their respective educations accordingly. Notable thinkers like Rousseau and Humboldt had defined the sexes according to their supposed "inner" natures and social responsibilities. Women were regarded as the tender, sensitive, soft, and weak pole of human existence, emotional and given to fits of hysteria due to their hormones. Men were the rational, productive members of society, capable of higher reasoning and abstract thinking.[3] François's early education was commensurate with her expected role in society: to become a wife and mother. Typically, middle-class girls were prepared in school to run a household, to care for children and to do "Handarbeit." Since women were believed to possess a smaller brain and therefore to be capable primarily of "mechanical" thinking—as exhibited in girls by their repetitive and "gedankenarme Spiele" like playing with dolls ("Pädagogische Briefe" 422)—subject matter was minimal and was addressed to the "aesthetic" and "emotional" side of womanly nature.[4] Girls were taught religion, reading and writing, French, rudimentary history and geography, natural history, music, drawing, simple arithmetic and "Handarbeit." A bright and mercurial child, François received private education, an alternative to public elementary school, in the company of a few children. She quickly acquired the title "Fräulein Grundtext" because of her endless questions (Enz 7). With this, François's formal education came to an end. Middle and upper-class girls could attend a "Mädchenschule" or "Töchterschule" in the nineteenth century where they were divided according to social class and basically retaught the elementary curriculum in an unsystematic manner. François did not even receive such rudimentary instruction. Painfully aware of the poverty of her education, François augmented her learning by reading everything in print that she could get her hands on (Schwartzkoppen 194). She delved throughout her life into readings in history, philosophy and literature and took delight in subjects far beyond the norm of typical nineteenth-century women who were discouraged from serious thinking (Cocalis and Goodman 6).[5] Her lifelong ambition was to conquer the precepts of Kant. "Lese in Kant und koche Rindfleisch mit grünen Kartoffeln," she wrote laconically to her friend Marie von Ebner-Eschenbach (Ebner-Eschenbach, "François" 1). At age fifty-eight she professed to have mastered him (*Briefwechsel* 58). Cheated out of her inheritance by an unscrupulous guardian and abandoned by a weak-willed fiancé, François spent a life of severe hardship in the little town of Weissenfels taking care of sick and dying relatives. She turned to writing in secret—and at first anonymously—to support her family.

Her ardent wish was to become a physician, but she was thwarted by a society which did not permit women to study at a university until the first decade of the 1900s.

François's concern about the education of women shimmers from the pages of her narratives. They span the years 1855-1881 and thus encompass the years when the nascent women's movement in Germany was at its low point in the 1850s and came to new life in the 1860s and 1870s. The majority of François's works were written in the 1850s after Louise Otto-Peter's *Frauen-Zeitung* with its advocacy for meaningful women's education had been forced to close down, and political and social repression had stilled the voices of liberal thinkers.[6] Published primarily in *Das Morgenblatt für gebildete Stände*, side by side with vitriolic attacks on advanced women's education, François's narratives serve as a steady and progressive voice to counter the shrill voices which condemned women's intellectual development. They witness the new surge of interest in women's education with the creation of the *Allgemeiner Deutscher Frauenverein* of 1865 in Leipzig, the *Lette-Verein* of 1866 in Berlin, and stand in harmony with the resolutions of the Weimar Conference of 1872 which demanded advanced education for girls. The reclusive and painfully shy François was foremost an artist and avoided overtly tendentious literature. Many of her comments on women's education are couched in irony or veiled as statements of "bizarre" aunts or of men.[7] Social concerns, however, clearly form the core of her intricately interwoven and complex narratives. The theme of education of women, an issue of central importance to the feminist movement, runs like a colored thread throughout her works, emphasizing again and again that the dependent status of women in society and the emptiness of their lives derive primarily from their lack of education.[8] The topic is given most systematic treatment in the short story "Eine Gouvernante" (1859) and in her last novel, a "Bildungsroman" entitled *Die Stufenjahre eines Glücklichen* (1877). Education also becomes the subject of lengthy discussion in every narrative. No female character is introduced without some description of her degree of erudition or lack of it.

Like other moderate feminist thinkers, Louise Otto-Peters, Luise Büchner, and even the resolute Helene Lange who was to later stand at the heart of the women's education movement, François believed that men and women had indeed different characters because of their sexes. Her letters and narratives repeatedly speak of "womanly" intuition and "womanly" tenderness, of "womanly" heart or even "womanly" fussiness.[9] The gentler side of women, however, did not exclude women from a capacity to learn or to act with "Vernunft." Firmness of mind characterizes François's letters to Conrad Ferdinand Meyer. Here she reaffirms the ability and right of women to learn and to be treated as responsible and intelligent beings. François believed in the inborn capacity of women to study and to study thoroughly (*Briefwechsel* 20). She condemned Schiller's "Frauenideal," embedded deep in nineteenth-century society:

> Noch gilt in Deutschland das Schillersche Frauenideal und vom Standpunkte des Geschlechtes Nummero Eins aus betrachtet, gewiss mit Recht. Nur dass den vielen Unbegehrten und den wenigen nicht Begehrenden nicht der Raum versperrt werden darf, auf eigenen Füssen zu einem würdigen, menschlichen Ziele zu gelangen. (*Briefwechsel* 27)

François was well aware of the hopeless plight of the unmarried and widowed women in Germany. Nearly half of all women were not married at mid-century (Weber-Kellermann 140). Crippled by their lack of knowledge, untrained for meaningful work, and caught up by their own stereotypical thinking about the nature of "correct" female activities, they were forced to live at the mercy of relatives. At best they could seek employment as low-paid governesses, teachers, or piano teachers, the only acceptable occupations open to middle-class women. Sharp voices condemned even such activity.[10] Education of women was perceived to be the first step to the dissolution of the family ("Über weibliche Bestimmung" 495). Rousseau's *Emile* (1762), with its views that women be given a natural, practical education so that they would "please their husbands," cast a long shadow over the nineteenth century. Late in life François confessed to Meyer that Rousseau had "repulsed" her when she was young (*Briefwechsel* 168). François's narratives express concern for women trapped in their roles as inferior beings. Motifs of autonomy and subordination echo through the voices of her female characters who must come to grips with nineteenth-century concepts of womanhood.

A picture of the oppressive reality of women's education emerges. In the story "Phosphorus Hollunder" (1857) a perceptive aristocratic widow sums up the painful options for her uneducated and penniless daughter Blanka:

> Eine günstige Heirat für eine unvermögende Tochter der gebildeten Stände wird heutzutage je mehr und mehr zu einer Chance wie das grosse Los, und auf bisher noch wenig gebrochener Bahn selbstständig durch die Welt zu dringen, bedingt für uns Frauen einen harten Kampf.

> Glaubst du dich solchen Kampfes fähig, Blanka? (*Werke* 4: 406)

The "Last ihrer Hülflosigkeit" overwhelms Blanka (*Werke* 4: 420). Like an "Opferlamm" she enters a loveless marriage (*Werke* 4: 430). Christian Klösterley, the narrator of the novella "Der Katzenjunker" (1879), throws a particularly probing and ironic light on the educational constraints placed on women. He recounts the plight of a widowed baroness who must endure the humiliation of eking out a miserable existence by peddling finely embroidered slippers, the only acceptable means of earning money for impoverished aristocratic women (*Werke* 5: 53). Brought up on a steady diet of "Schäferspiele," the baroness yawns through her days, succumbs to melancholy and falls prey to attacks of nerves (*Werke* 5: 78).[11] Uneducated herself, she neglects the education of her daughter Lori, who learns "[e]in bisschen Französisch plappern . . . von eigentlichem Unterricht war keine Rede" (*Werke* 5: 57). Klösterley takes Lori's education under his own care and considers the options available for her, either life at a pedantic cloister school or instruction by one of the vain governesses, "diese geschminkten, geschnörkelten, tänzelnden, näselnden Französinnen" (*Werke* 5: 103). François devotes pages to the consideration of Lori's education (102-10). She peppers her narratives with statements which satirize the stereotypical precepts about women's education. Her voice ranges from bitter irony to wry humor:

> Mit Addieren und Multiplizieren hat das klügste Frauenköpfchen ja auch für seine Lebenszeit mehr als genug getan, während, wenn möglich, noch ein Dutzend weitere Spezies erfunden werden müsste, um diesem oder jenem männlichen Schädel sein Gnügen zu tun. (*Werke* 3: 118)

The spry and well-educated Hanna Blümel, a former governess and the mother of seven daughters, gives a tongue-in-cheek explanation why her daughters cannot learn serious subjects like the classics. When her husband, the kindly pedagogue Pastor Blümel, sighs that he has no son to whom to teach "die alten Heiden," Hanna sympathizes. After all, he only has "sieben nichtsnutzige Mädchen, die von alten Heiden den Kuckuck verstehen, menschliche Wesen zweiter Klasse, Mitteldinger zwischen Aff und Mann" (*Werke* 3: 13).[12] In "Die Geschichte eines Hässlichen" (1858), François's emotionally gripping story about social misfits, she draws the portrait of a draconian father, the epitome of male arrogance, who feels threatened by intelligent women. A weakling himself, he is terrified of the "superkluge Frau" Sophie, who is capable of running his entire estate, though he blames his dislike for her on her red hair (*Erzählungen* 1: 24). Education is clearly a threat to female subservience and delicate character.

François refutes such stereotypical thinking through the creation of strong female protagonists—she terms them "manly"—guided by reason, and capable of productive activity. Tall, healthy, and strong—they frequently tower over men—they are calm and self-possessed and have an iron will.[13] All have an education which surpasses the norm. As François points out, it is the source of their independent thinking and fulfillment as individuals. François's concept of education derives from the humanist tradition which gives high priority to the development of the individual personality. Her mentor, as she confessed to Conrad Ferdinand Meyer, was Heinrich Pestalozzi (1746-1827) who advocated the natural, progressive and harmonious development of the total individual (*Briefwechsel* 243). François makes Pestalozzi's ideal binding also for women: ". . . sich selber fertigbringen, soweit die eingeborene Gestaltungskraft reicht, ist des Menschen oberstes zeitliches Gesetz, denn nur nach dem Masse seiner Fertigkeit wirkt er" (*Werke* 3: 341). The concept of "innere Freiheit" proposed by Pestalozzi's follower, the prominent educator Johann Friedrich Herbart (1776-1841),[14] recurs in François's narratives to describe the spiritual state achieved by her best educated heroines. The intelligent Katharine in the story "Glück" (1871), having received a "freie Entwicklung bei sorgfältiger Bildung" (*Erzählungen* 1: 224) achieves "Ruhe der Seele, diese einfache Harmonie, diese Wahrheit und Freiheit der ganzen Organisation" (*Erzählungen* 1: 188). Her education is broadly humanistic in nature and is the source of her independence. She is the center of a literary circle which includes brilliant men and in which discussion dips into "Kunst, Literatur, Politik, in gewissem Sinne Philosophie selbst" (*Erzählungen* 1: 210). Luitgard in "Der Erbe von Saldeck" (1856) is given an "ernsten Bildungsgang" by her father which has a "sinnende Richtung" (*Erzählungen* 2: 96). She is praised for the "Freiheit ihres geistigen Aufschwungs" (*Erzählungen* 1: 93). Important to note is that François does not neglect Luitgard's "feminine" education. She points out carefully that Luitgard does not fail in her "weibliche Entwicklung." Luitgard retains her caring nature, her "Zartsinn," and does not flag in her womanly desire to help others (*Erzählungen* 2: 97).[15] Karoline Rudolphi's concept of "noble femininity" forms an integral part of François's thinking as it did for most moderate women activists (Weber-Kellermann 147). What is significant, however, is that François demands that a woman be educated first as a person, and secondly as a female. Her thoughts match those of the most progressive feminist thinkers, Mary Wollstonecraft, Theodor Gottlieb von Hippel, and Betty Gleim, who insisted that women be regarded as spiritually independent beings (Bäumer, *Frauenbildung* 83).

A basic premise of François's views on the education of women is that women are intelligent beings, capable of learning. Like men, they have a drive to learn and are able to think rationally. The fearsomely intelligent Brigitte von Mehlborn in *Die Stufenjahre eines Glücklichen* has an "eingeborenen Bildungstrieb" (*Werke* 3: 128). She is the first daughter of a farmer to attend an "elegant institute of learning" in the capital (*Werke* 3: 58). Her passion for philosophy is boundless. She publishes pedagogical tracts and spends her life reading Kant. "Merkwürdigerweise," notes François ironically, "hat [sie] die Kritik der reinen Vernunft verstanden" (*Werke* 3: 66). The "superkluge" Sophie manages a huge estate with the astuteness of the finest lawyer. Frequently François's female characters outstrip their male study companions (*Werke* 1: 72). They read and refuse to knit. Repeatedly, François demands an education commensurate with women's capability to learn. Women, like men, must be guided through their educational process with a steady and calm hand, and not be submitted to emotional whims ("Gouvernante" 228). Women must be taught how to think, not memorize and "plappern" like children. François spells out the proper program for education most systematically in "Eine Gouvernante" where Cornelia Wille clarifies the principles used by her own father in her education. Cornelia's father, an educator schooled in Pestalozzian thinking,[16] insists first that children be only taught by natives of Germany ("Gouvernante" 243). Here François joins efforts with the most prominent nineteenth-century educators who believed that excessive French influence on German education was harmful to the German national character.[17] Cornelia's father purposefully refrains from using modern languages, the most traditional subjects taught to girls, as an educational tool. He considers "die modernen Sprachen" to be a "Gedächtnisübung" instead of a "Denkübung" ("Gouvernante" 243). Cornelia remains grateful to him that he teaches her "den innerlichen Bildungsprozess alter wie neuer Sprachen . . . . Es wurde dadurch ein Grund gelegt, auf dem sich weiterbauen lässt . . . " ("Gouvernante" 244). In refuting memorization as an educational tool, Cornelia's father suggests that the education of women should promote rigorous critical thought. He reiterates here one of the main platforms of the women's education movement.[18] François warns against an overemphasis on the development of imagination, widely accepted as the domain of women. The reading of "verwogene Ritterromane" and "süssliche Liebesgeschichten," reminiscent of the immensely popular romantic novels of Eugenie Marlitt (1825-1887), is seen as an unfruitful activity damaging to women. Dorl in *Die letzte*

Reckenburgerin (1871) wastes her days in such frivolity and never develops serious purpose (*Werke* l: 149). The intelligent Lydia quickly wearies of the "modern" books sent to her by her fiancé and turns to Dante (*Werke* 3: 343). François emphasizes the need for women to study serious literature. The dowager in *Die letzte Reckenburgerin*, an independent free-thinker, opens the "Schlossbibliothek" to her niece Eberhardine and explicitly explains that serious novels offer no danger to women as was commonly felt in the nineteenth century (*Werke* l: 149).[19]

At the heart of François's educational program lie firmly rooted democratic principles. She expresses them most movingly in *Die Stufenjahre eines Glücklichen*, the summation of her idealistic ethical precepts. The novel traces the development of Dezimus Frey, the son of the lowest of low peasants on his path to becoming a famous astronomer. François's moral voice is Pastor Blümel, the gentle teacher who guides Dezimus on his way to learning. Blümel reiterates Pestalozzi[20] who called for the rejuvenation of a nation through the education of all classes (Downs 96). The pastor bitterly condemns the social structures and constraints placed on persons of low-class origins who consequently lack the opportunity for self-fulfillment. They are refused education and are forced to squander their abilities (*Werke* 3: 431). Blümel speaks implicitly also for the rights of women. Lydia reiterates these ideas later in the novel when she is told that her desire to become a doctor is "unsuitable" for a woman:

> Warum . . . soll dem Weibe nicht naturgemäss sein, was es dem Manne doch ist? Oder nennen Sie den Beruf des Arztes auch einen ungemeinen? Es müssen mehr solche allgemeine Aufgaben uns erschlossen werden. Die Erfüllung, die Sie zu meinen scheinen, liegt nicht in unserer Gewalt; wofür wir aber die zulängliche Kraft des Organs in uns erkennen, müssen wir auch das Recht haben, uns auszubilden und das Ausgebildete zu verwerten. (*Werke* 3: 440)

François's heroines chafe not only at their watered-down curriculum, but at their limitations for advanced study. Again and again they must stop their studies when the subject matter gets challenging. Lydia goes to school as the companion to her brother and masters "die alten Heiden" which were thought to be too "taxing" for the female brain. When they reach the "rigorous subjects," however, she must step aside in favor of a male study companion (*Werke* 3: 239). Erdmuthe in the novel *Frau Erdmuthens Zwillingssöhne* similarly learns together with a boy. Yet, when she and her male study companion reach the time when he begins higher learning, Erdmuthe must stay behind. "Solch ein wohlbestallter Untersekundaner könnte mein Fräulein Erdmuthe nun auch sein," sighs the young man. "Ach wäre sie doch ein Junker und noch mein Kamerad!" (*Zwillingssöhne* 50).

François's call for the free determination of the course of one's life is given most heartrending treatment in "Glück." Here she explores the plight of the female artist whose creative urge is shackled by taboos. Ulrike, the daughter of an aristocrat, is possessed by the desire to sing. When a well-meaning friend advises her to "protect" her talent from the world, Ulrike insists that she needs a "lauteres Echo, eine andere Welt" for her gift (*Erzählungen* 1: 191). She knows her calling:

> Schon als Kind habe ich ihn [meinen Beruf] gefühlt, bewusstlos zwar, aber tief und deutlich. O, lassen Sie es mich einmal an den Tag bringen, was die Qual meiner ganzen Jungend gewesen ist, was mir noch heute die Brust zu sprengen droht. (*Erzählungen* 1: 191)

Ulrike is forbidden to follow her inner urge by her father who considers singing a disgraceful profession. Her torment ends only when her father dies and releases her from his "wohlmeinende Absurdität" (*Erzählungen* 1: 197). Ulrike goes to Paris to "test out" her talent (*Erzählungen* 1: 253). François's phraseology is of importance, for her concept of education does not tolerate dilettantism, either for men or for women. Floundering in dillydallying or in a field for which one has no real aptitude is firmly rebuked (*Erzählungen* 2: 118-19). One must study thoroughly and with purpose to become a useful member of society. Like Herbart, François locates the purpose of education in the development of virtue, "Sitte," which serves as the foundation of society (*Werke* 3: 103-04).[21] Similarly, François condemns the use of education for purposes of self-aggrandizement. "Aesthetic teas" and the snobbery of "Gelehrtentfrauen" receive sharply satirical treatment.[22]

In spite of François's commitment to the education of women, there remains a residue of worry. It becomes evident in her description of Luitgard's education which, as we have seen, instills in Luitgard a "manly" seriousness and ability to reason. François ends her summation with the insistence that Luitgard, nonetheless, has not failed in her "weibliche Entwicklung" (*Erzählungen* 2: 97). Like other moderate women thinkers who believed in the existence of a womanly nature, François seems troubled that women may acquire a hard edge from their intellectual independence. Luitgard is chastised by some for being a "weiblicher Emil" (*Erzählungen* 2:105). The coolly rational and superbly educated aunt in "Die Geschichte eines Hässlichen" is condemned for being "kalt wie Eis" (*Erzählungen* 1:42). François senses a possible conflict between the traditional role of women as wives and mothers and their self-identities as educated women. Reconciliation between accepted modes of female socialization and independence is problematical. Brigitte in *Die Stufenjahre eines Glücklichen,* François's most brilliant female character,"Vernunft" personified, cannot seem to find a comfortable equilibrium. As she plunges into her career, ironically that of an educator, she sends her children away so that she may devote her full energy to her intellectual efforts. Brigitte marches through life with a "Gangart, wie auf hoch gespanntem Seil, Schritt für Schritt, die Balancierstange in der Hand und zwischen den Lippen einen scharf geschliffenen Stahl" (*Werke* 3: 156). Similarly, the highly educated Katharine in "Glück" experiences difficulties. She breaks her engagement when she realizes that the values instilled in her by her learning do not match those of her bigoted fiancé. He wants a marriage based on the "demüthige Beschränkung" of his wife (*Erzählungen*1:213). Katharine is not willing to be humiliated. In the end, she remains independent but alone. François does not condemn nor lecture. She recognizes marriage as a woman's "Bestimmung" and motherhood as the supreme calling. At the same time, she acknowledges that some women are not motherly and prefer independence.[23] All women, nonetheless, have the profound need to fulfill themselves as individuals and need education to achieve personal, social and economic independence.

Dramatic advances in women's education were to be reserved for the latter part of the nineteenth century, to a time when François was no longer writing. Her voice, temperate and tinged with irony, must be regarded as that of a forerunner, of a quiet supporter of the cause of advanced women's education. François was well aware that the road faced by women wanting to expand the parameters of their existence was "steil" (*Briefwechsel* 22) and the existence of an educated woman "sehr zweifelhaft" (*Briefwechsel* 27). Through the example of her intelligent heroines, she offers women hope and encouragement. By recognizing women as rational and intelligent beings, capable of training their mental faculties, François gives them personal dignity. In insisting that women have the right to develop themselves first as individuals, and then as women, she gives them spiritual freedom and offers a vision of true emancipation.

Notes

[1] See Fox and Worley for most recent reevaluations of François's position in the nineteenth-century women's movement.

[2] For historical background to educational reform in the nineteenth century, see Bäumer, *Frauenbildung*, pp. 72-90; Schneider, pp. 1-12; Simmel, pp. 102-10.

[3] Physicians produced numerous biologically-based theories of womanhood. For example, the prominent Rudolf Virchow stated in 1848: "Das Weib ist eben Weib durch seine Generationsdrüse . . . alles, was wir an dem wahren Weibe als Weibliches bewundern und verehren, ist nur eine Dependenz des Eierstocks" (168-69). A discussion of the polarization of sexes in the nineteenth century can be found in Fout, pp. 106-09; Weber-Kellermann, pp. 117-18; Worley, "François," pp. 66-73.

[4] For theories of education of nineteenth-century women, see Gisela Brinkler-Gabler's "Die Frauenbewegung im deutschen Kaiserreich" in Drewitz, pp. 53-84; Joanne Schneider's "Enlightened Reforms and Bavarian Girls' Education" in Fout, pp. 55-71; Juliane Jacobi-Dittrich's "Growing Up Female in the Nineteenth Century" in Fout, pp. 210-17. See also Weber-Kellermann, p. 56.

[5] François's letters to Conrad Ferdinand Meyer are informative sources for the nature of her readings and for her opinions on countless authors, thinkers and philosophers. See also Schwartzkoppen, p. 196.

[6] For historical background, see Drewitz, p. 53; Worley, "François," pp.153-60.

[7] See Worley, "François," p. 93, for François's "masking" techniques.

[8] Although François lived in relative isolation in Weissenfels, she was well aware of social and political issues and was familiar with the works of Fanny Lewald, Countess Ida Hahn-Hahn, and Amalie Bölte. The latter invited François to an "aesthetic tea" when François was eighteen. In 1856 François wrote a compelling bibliographical review of George Sand's *Histoire de ma vie*, published anonymously in the *Deutsches Museum*.

[9] See *Briefwechsel*, pp. 18, 21, 45, 53, 183, 257.

[10] Even democrats like Johannes Scherr criticized any role for women outside the home, especially in political activities. He writes: "You can be sure that the contingent of women who are pushing themselves unasked into public life is made up either of old, ugly, and hysterical spinsters—who might be forgiven for physiological reasons—or else slovenly housewives and mothers who have forgotten their duty . . . and whose children are physically and morally unwashed" (188-89).

[11] The motif of "ennui" recurs in François's narratives to depict the emptiness of women's lives. See *Werke* 1: 148, 149, 159, 160, 331; *Werke* 5: 51, 63, 74, 165, 172; *Erzählungen* 1: 196.

[12] The quote is a direct parody of Schopenhauer who states in his "Über die Weiber" that women are "eine Art Mittelstufe, zwischen Kind und Mann," p. 651. François condemned Schopenhauer and his pessimistic view of life in *Die Stufenjahre eines Glücklichen* (*Werke* 3: 657).

[13] François summed up her reasons for the use of strong female characters to Marie von Ebner-Eschenbach: "Ich war zu alt, um zarte und zärtliche Menschen, zumal Frauen, zu schaffen, hätte es schwerlich auch in der Jugend zu Stande gebracht. Ich bin selbst nicht zart und zärtlich, meine Stoffe handeln von gereiften Menschen und von Kindern, ihr Quellpunkt ist nicht das Herz, sondern das Gewissen" (Ebner-Eschenbach, "François" 1).

[14] See Heigenmooser, pp. 216-17.

[15] François's emphasis on the important role of men in the education of their daughters reflects historical reality. It was the chief means for a woman to break the bonds of restrictive education (Fout 204).

[16] Pestalozzi's theories and those of his school are at the core of François's views on education. Like Pestalozzi she refutes the use of memorization as a pedagogical tool. She insists on the adaptation of education to the inner nature of the child (*Werke* 3: 367; *Werke* 5: 102; *Erzählungen* 1: 105). She subscribes to his theory of "Anschauung" (*Werke* 5: 60). See Downs, pp. 78-86.

[17] See Schneider, pp. 40, 119, 126-27.

[18] See Drewitz, p. 58; Albisetti, pp. 307-08.

[19] Cornelia Wille in "Eine Gouvernante" warns against the

frequent telling of fairy tales because they may overstimulate fantasy (255). See also Renate Möhrmann's "The Reading Habits of Women in the *Vormärz*" in Fout, pp. 104-17.

[20] François makes direct reference to Pestalozzi and to his Gertrud in the novel (*Werke* 3: 30, 36, 175).

[21] For a discussion of Herbart's theories on the purpose of education, see Heigenmooser, pp. 215-33.

[22] François's description of an "aesthetic tea" given by the eccentric harpist Thusnelda von Hartenstein in *Die Stufenjahre eines Glücklichen* is a sample of her fine satire. See also *Erzählungen* 2: 97.

[23] See *Werke* 3: 211-12; *Werke* 1: 122, 320. François herself longed above all for a child (*Briefwechsel* 106). She admits to Clotilde von Schwartzkoppen, however, that "[sie] glücklich nur ganz allein leben könnte. Das Alleinsein zu Zweien ist ein zu seltenes, zu ideales Glück" (198).

Selected Bibliography

Albisetti, James C. "Could Separate Be Equal? Helene Lange and Women's Education in Imperial Germany." *History of Education Quarterly* 22 (1982): 301-17.

Bäumer, Gertrud. "Louise von François: Preussische Typen." *Die Hilfe* 47(1919): 665-68.

______. *Der Stand der Frauenbildung in den Kulturländern.* Berlin S.: W. Moeser, 1902. Vol. 3 of *Handbuch der Frauenbewegung.* Eds. Helene Lange and Gertrud Bäumer. 4 vols. 1902-1906.

Bernstein, George, and Lottelore Bernstein. "The Curriculum for German Girls' Schools 1870-1914." *Paedagogica Historica* 18 (1978): 275-95.

Bettelheim, Anton. "Marie von Ebner-Eschenbach und Louise von François." *Deutsche Rundschau* 27.1 (Oct. 1900): 104-19.

Cocalis, Susan L., and Kay Goodman, eds. *Beyond the Eternal Feminine: Critical Essays on Women and German Literature.* Stuttgarter Arbeiten zur Germanistik 98. Stuttgart: Heinz, 1982.

Downs, Robert B. *Heinrich Pestalozzi: Father of Modern Pedagogy.* Twayne's World Author Series. Boston: G. K. Hall, 1975.

Drewitz, Ingeborg, ed. *Die deutsche Frauenbewegung: Die soziale Rolle der Frau im 19. Jahrhundert und die Emanzipationsbewegung in Deutschland.* Bonn: Hohwacht, 1983.

Ebner-Eschenbach, Marie von. "Louise von François." *Neue Freie Presse* 23 Feb. 1894: 1-3.

______. "Louise von François. Erinnerungsblätter." *Velhagen und Klasings Monatshefte* 8 (March 1894): 18-30.

Enz, Hans. *Louise von François.* Diss. U. Zürich: Rascher, 1918.

Fout, John C., ed. *German Women in the Nineteenth Century: A Social History.* New York: Holmes & Meier, 1984.

Fox, Thomas. "Louise von François: Between *Frauenzimmer* and *A*

Room of One's Own." Diss. Yale U., 1983.

François, Louise von. *Erzählungen*. 2 vols. Braunschweig: Westermann, 1871.

______. *Frau Erdmuthens Zwillingssöhne*. Zürich: Manesse, n.d.

______. *Gesammelte Werke*. 5 vols. Leipzig: Insel, 1918.

______. "Eine Gouvernante." In *Natur und Gnade nebst anderen Erzählungen*. 2 vols. Berlin: Otto Janke, 1876.

______. "Das Leben der George Sand." *Deutsches Museum* 6 (1856): 600-93.

______. *Louise von François und Conrad Ferdinand Meyer: Ein Briefwechsel*. Ed. Anton Bettelheim. Berlin: Georg Reimar, 1905.

Frederiksen, Elke, ed. *Die Frauenfrage in Deutschland. 1865-1915. Texte und Dokumente*. Stuttgart: Reclam, 1981.

Heigenmooser, Joseph, and Alfons Bock, eds. *Geschichte der Pädagogik: Quellen und Überblick der Geschichte der Pädagogik*. München: Seyfried, 1912.

K. L. "Pädagogische Briefe." *Morgenblatt* 18-20 (1860): 418+.

Lange, Helene. *Entwicklung und Stand des höheren Mädchenschulwesens in Deutschland*. Berlin: R. Gaerner, 1893.

Lehmann, Gertrud. *Louise von François: Ihr Roman "Die letzte Reckenburgerin" als Ausdruck ihrer Persönlichkeit*. Diss. U. Greifswald, 1918. Greifswald: Julius Abel, 1918.

Mitterauer, M., and R. Sieder. *Vom Patriarchat zur Partnerschaft*. München, 1977.

Pestalozzi, Johann Heinrich. *Wie Gertrud ihre Kinder lehrt und Ausgewählte Schriften zur Methode, besorgt von Fritz Pfeffer*. Paderborn, 1961.

Scherr, Johannes. *Von Achtundvierzig bis Einundfünfzig. Eine Komödie der Weltgeschichte*. Vol. 2. Leipzig, 1886.

Schneider, Joanne Frances. "An Historical Examination of

Women's Education in Bavaria: *Mädchenschulen* and Contemporary Attitudes about Them." Diss. Brown U., 1977.

Schopenhauer, Arthur. "Ueber die Weiber." *Parerga und Paralipomena. Schopenhauers Sämtliche Werke*. Ed. Arthur Hubscher. Wiesbaden: Brockhaus, 1947. 2: 650-64.

Schwartzkoppen, Clotilde von. "Louise von François: Ein Lebensbild." *Vom Fels zum Meer* 10 (1894): 193-98.

Simmel, Monika. *Erziehung zum Weibe: Mädchenbildung im 19. Jahrhundert*. Frankfurt and New York: Campus Verlag, 1980.

Twellmann-Schepp, Margrit. *Die deutsche Frauenbewegung: Ihre Anfänge und erste Entwicklung 1843-1889*. Meisenheim am Glan: Anton Hain, 1972.

"Über weibliche Bestimmung." *Morgenblatt* 21 (1860): 492-519.

Urech, Till. *Louise von François: Versuch einer künstlerischen Würdigung*. Diss. U. Zürich, 1955. Zürich: Juris, 1955.

Virchow, Rudolf. "Über die puerperalen Krankheiten, l. Der puerperale Zustand, das Weib und die Zelle." *Verhandlungen der Gesellschaft für Geburtshilfe in Berlin* 3 (1848): 151-96.

Weber-Kellermann, Ingeborg. *Frauenleben im 19. Jahrhundert: Empire und Romantik, Biedermeier, Gründerzeit*. Munich: Beck, 1983.

Worley, Linda Kraus. "Louise von François: A Re-Interpretation of Her Life and Her 'Odd-Woman' Fiction." Diss. U. of Cincinnati, 1985.

_______. "The 'Odd' Woman as Heroine in the Fiction of Louise von François." *Women in German Yearbook 4: Feminist Studies and German Culture*. Ed. Marianne Burkhard and Jeanette Clausen. Lanham, New York, London: University Press of America, 1988.

Prophecy Equals Utter Madness in Wolf's *Cassandra*

Mary Seager
Washington University

> I witnessed how a panic rapture spread through me, how it mounted and reached its pinnacle when a voice began to speak:
>
> Aiee! Aieeeee!
> Apollo! Apollo!
>
> Cassandra. I saw her at once. She, the captive, took me captive: herself made an object by others, she took possession of me. Later I would ask when, where, and by whom the pacts were joined that made this magic. It worked at once. I believed every word she said: so there was such a thing as unqualified trust. Three thousand years—melted away. So the gift of prophecy, conferred on her by the god, stood the test of time. Only his verdict that no one would believe her had passed away.
>
> Wolf, *Cassandra* 144-45

Panic, rapture, captivity, possession, magic, trust. belief, prophecy. All are words which form the web and woof of Christa Wolf's novel *Cassandra,* a feminist and Marxist examination of the power of the word to capture, possess, transform, redeem or murder. What is it about that woman's voice echoing across the difference of three thousand years which so engages the emotions of its hearers? Is the distinction, difficult for the contemporary hearer, between true prophetic utterance and the babble of the mad? Is it the fear of the source of the utterance—possession and capture by the Other, whether Apollo, a lover or our own alienated personae—and our own potential response to that occupation? Is it that we suspect that we lack Cassandra's courage to continue an utterance which will cause our exclusion from our communities?

Cassandra, for Christa Wolf, is a voice first which possesses her immediately and passionately. It is this moment of captivity as Wolf reads *The Oresteia* (in German) in the Athens airport from which the novel springs. It is this moment for which she seeks a source simultaneously mythic, historical and fictional. It is this voice, in all of its paradoxes and contradictions, which provides

Wolf with an opening through which to enter the utterances and the silences within her own art. The Cassandra of the Homeric epics and the Aeschylean tragedy is the incarnation of prophecy and madness, inclusion and exclusion, the woman become Other, because she raised her voice in the service of her vision. It is this voice which possessed Wolf that she seeks to possess for herself through her imagination. Her openness to that voice's power also suggests an intuitive leap which Wolf undergirds with research through layers of language and history. She explicates this search in the companion lectures which she presented at the University of Frankfurt, "Conditions of a Narrative":

> To learn to read myth is a special kind of adventure. An art that presupposes a gradual, peculiar transformation: a readiness to give oneself to the seemingly frivolous nexus of fantastic facts, of traditions, desires, and hopes, experiences and techniques of magic adapted to the needs of a particular group—in short, to another sense of the concept "reality." (196)

This "special kind of adventure," which culminates in Cassandra as the protagonist of a modern novel, becomes a threefold archaeology of the imagination: translation, the reconstruction of fragments, and transformation. The "reality" encountered in the ancient fragments (Sappho) is predominantly martial, bloody and male. For example, it is not until Cassandra appears in *The Oresteia* that she is allowed to speak. The Homeric Cassandra, "a girl like Aphrodite the golden," (*Iliad* 493) and "loveliest of his daughters, Kassandra" (280), is merely one of the silent frieze of doomed Trojan women. In *The Odyssey,* through Agamemnon's eyes, we see her as captive and victim, slain by Clytemnestra. There is only the presumptive wordless scream of a victim, still peripheral to the fate of others. It is this Cassandra's voice which Aeschylus amplifies into the ironic oracular madwoman we recognize: the speaker of a remembered future, the voice which collapses time and translates temporal distance into presence. Through the Aeschylean transformation of "the loveliest of Priam's daughters" to "a thing of dreams, a beggar-maid outworn," Cassandra has moved from inclusion to exclusion, from privilege to exile, from life to death.

It is this movement through which Wolf inscribes herself on the ancient image in the opening paragraph of the novel:

> It was here. This is where she stood. These stone lions looked at her; now they no longer have heads. This fortress—once impregnable, now a pile of stones—was the last thing she saw. A long forgotten enemy demolished it, so did the centuries, sun, rain, wind. The sky is still the same, a deep blue block, high, vast. Nearby, the giant fitted-stone walls which, today as in the past, point the way to the gate, where no trace of blood can be seen seeping out from beneath. Point the way into the darkness. Into the slaughterhouse. And alone. Keeping in step with the story, I make my way into death. Here I end my days, helpless, and nothing, nothing I could have done or not done, willed or thought, could have led me to a different goal. (4)

Wolf has transformed herself into Cassandra. With these opening words, she has appropriated the voice which she does not relinquish until the last moment before Cassandra's murder by Clytemnestra at the end of the novel. The story is told as a first person interior monologue, a reminiscence, a recounting of action past. The entire novel is a protracted flashback which explicates: "nothing, nothing I could have done or not done, willed or thought, could have led me to a different goal." Nothing or no-thing uttered as an accomplishment of fate implies some things, some questions for which the reader wants an explanation. What has brought Cassandra to her death at the lion gates? Has the risk Wolf took in transforming *her self* into the Otherness of Cassandra fulfilled itself for the reader?

The "nothing," the "no-thing" prefigures the rejections, the silences, the contradictions contained in the rhetoric of the novel. Shoshana Felman in *Writing and Madness* refers to this kind of self-subversive narrative: "This rhetorical theory looks specifically for the uncanny moment in the theory: it uses logic and the instruments of logic in the aim of finding the aporetic moment at which logic itself falters" (27). When we look at Wolf's text in this way, we see that the aporetic moments and her fictional rhetoric need to be examined.

The search for the "no-things" reveals that Cassandra's primary actions, those on which the forward movement of the narrative turns, are either reflections or involuntary utterances. Her rejections are those connected with the passions of men; she rejects Apollo and Aeneas whose future as a hero she cannot bear to share. Thus, her exile begins early when she eschews what for other women would be an honor. Wolf comments on these rejections:

> Naturally Cassandra loved this god, or whatever he was; for that very reason she had to reject him when he grew obtrusive. Western female logic? More like male logic. Witness Aeschylus. But why did she choose a man's profession when she trained to be a seeress? Why did she want to become like men? Had it always been so? If not, since when? And are those generally the sorts of questions that are able to free Cassandra from myth and literature? (153)

In this passage, we can see some of the contradictions inherent in Wolf's own thinking about her subject. Her historical sense is not particularly accurate; it has long been known that many of the classical oracles were women or servants at the shrines of female deities. And while she chides Aeschylus for presenting male logic, she ignores the fact that it was Aeschylus who endowed Cassandra with the voice which enraptured her. We can also see Wolf's unwillingness to credit the religious context of Cassandra's prophecy and madness, a perfectly acceptable juxtaposition in classical Greece. This produces one of the central contradictions of the novel: Cassandra's faith in the power of Apollo disappears but she retains her prophetic voice.

Similarly, when we look at Wolf's speculations about the type of Cassandra's madness, we see again the inscription of contemporary concerns on the ancient tradition: "Her 'madness' could be real madness, a regression to undifferentiated stages of her personality... triggered... by the demand to break a taboo.... Her inner history: the struggle for autonomy" (264). This is not the ancient madness born of passion nor from holy acquiescence to the gods. This is contemporary madness, a secular madness derived from an excess of self.

There are five incidents of madness clustered in the first half of the novel. The first two initiate Cassandra into madness, into the moment of seizure by Otherness, but no prophetic vision emerges. The third seizure, central to the story in its timing and complexity, is the moment which translates private grief into the prophetic vision of Troy's suicide. It is this third episode which radicalizes Cassandra on the personal level. The last two seizures thrust the radicalized Cassandra into the palace community as prophet and ultimately cause her imprisonment.

What is most strange to realize about this Cassandra is that we never hear her prophecies in the novel. She has been denied her public voice. The voice we hear is a confiding and explaining voice, a muffled private utterance. not the cry of a prophet from the towers of Ilion. Why has Wolf given up the opportunity to explore the sound of an untrammeled female voice, powerful in the truth of its vision? Why does Wolf reject the very aspects of the Aeschylean Cassandra which captured her in "panic rapture?" I suggest that fear, fear of panic and rapture, fear of possession by a voice, caused that rejection. Wolf rejects the transforming power of words (logos) and physical passion (eros) for her Cassandra. In the novel, both prophecy and physical passion remain hidden. Both are presumptive: they remain silent, untranslated and untransforming.

This silence within the novel is less surprising when Wolf's commentary on the novel and her earlier essays are examined. It is clear that Wolf feels a deep sense of loss and impossibility when she confronts what she perceives to be the deformation and perversion of language itself. This loss derives partly from her feminist understanding that Western literature is a male literature without models for women, but also that the "forlorn landscape" is the product of the moral schizophrenia of Western Christian civilization which centers on the double code of "Thou shalt not kill" and the glorification of war. In Wolf's view, this moral split has not only laid waste the language but has also left her with only "the narrow path of reason" as a dialectical way through history (*The Reader and the Writer* 211). While she sees that the male-dominated rationale of science has led to the spectre of a nuclear holocaust, her fear of powerful emotions keeps her on "the narrow path."

Wolf's Marxism intertwines with her feminism to form an analysis of Cassandra which uses her self-knowledge to remove her from the ancient tragic arena and recreate her as a contemporary. This reconstruction of Cassandra is not tragic because self-knowing suppresses much discussion by Greek philosophers about the relationship between mind/body/soul, about the relationship between madness, love, and art, and finally about the poetic and rhetorical uses of language to elucidate those human conjunctions. Once reason becomes the sole rhetoric, the possibility of passion reaching the transforming catharsis is denied.

Intuition suggests that Wolf's translation of Cassandra from an ancient tragic voice to that of a contemporary was more than an exploration of self. It suggests that this work was meant to be simultaneously prophetic and potentially redemptive. It is a present answer to a personal confrontation with the future holocaust and the past Holocaust. Her misunderstanding of the inability of logic to control human passion, to organize life without the irrational moment, was the flaw which allowed the power of Hitler's speech. The size of his vision, which was constructed around a lie greater than the disappearance of Helen from Wolf's Troy, overpowered a nation so starved for a hero that it would not discern the evil energy of that perverted vision, and those who uttered the truth were silenced.

Wolf, in her insistence on reason and prose, in her denial of Cassandra as a classic tragic figure, a woman larger than life and possessed by the Other, denied catharsis and redemption for herself and her readers. Ultimately, Wolf shares her Cassandra's fate. She is not believed, and "her pain will remind us" of the terrible cost of denying the noble rhetoric of madness.

Works Cited

Felman, Shoshana. *Writing and Madness.* Ithaca, NY: Cornell University Press, 1985.

Wolf, Christa. *Cassandra. A Novel and Four Essays.* Trans. Jan van Heurck. NY: Farrar, Strauss, Girou, 1984.

______. *The Reader and the Writer: Essays, Sketches, Memories.* Trans. Joan Becker. Berlin/GDR: Seven Seas Books, 1977.

Fanny Lewald's Emancipatory Writings

Hanna B. Lewis
Sam Houston State University

By the 1860s Fanny Lewald's literary career was progressing very well indeed. Not only was she widely read in Germany, England and America, but she was being paid at the highest per-page rate by her German publishers (Steinhauer 129). Obviously, she was able to give her public what it wanted. Critics may have labelled her a "Tendenzschriftstellerin"—one who wrote on the popular issues of the day—but this was her strength as well as her weakness, since her social commentary was objective and accurate. In the 1860s, women's issues became extremely prominent in a Germany that, under Bismarck, was at last able to realize the prospects of political unity, and could therefore give more attention to social and economic problems. Lewald was able to promulgate ideas that she had had for many years, verifiably since 1843 and her first published essay on the subject of the education of women ("Einige" 380). These ideas were shared by many other prominent German women, notably by Louise Otto-Peters, who had been instrumental in founding the *Allgemeiner Deutscher Frauenverein* (German Women's Federation) in 1865, the first German women's organization concerned with the enfranchisement and education of women, rather than charitable work.

Lewald was traditional enough to regard a happy marriage and a secure family life as the ultimate goal for both men and women. But she felt such a goal could only be reached by choice and free will, not imposed by an authoritarian father or society. The only way to ensure this was to provide financial and social independence for both sexes. While men had opportunities to advance themselves and to make choices in mates, jobs, and leisure-time activities, women were generally denied these rights because of their inadequate education. They had to marry to survive financially, since their training and society did not provide chances to support themselves or their children otherwise. They had no clubs, no restaurants, nothing to entertain them outside the home without great expense or male chaperonage. In two series of essays, first published serially in *Westermanns Monatshefte*, a popular monthly periodical in publication until recently, and then as separate books, Lewald detailed the lack of adequate social services, educational aims and facilities for women, and set forth sensible solutions.

Osterbriefe für die Frauen (Easter Letters for Women, 1863)—Easter letters because they were written before Easter and call for a resurrection of womankind—is a volume of ten letters, incorporating several much earlier essays, dealing with the case of female servants and working-class women. The letters are dedicated to the German Handicraft and Workers Union and addressed to middle- and upper-class women. Lewald points out that good mistresses train good servants and that it is a duty of prosperous women to ensure the upward mobility of their less fortunate sisters by providing lessons in the home, teaching them to work efficiently, and offering them proper recreational opportunities for their leisure time. The middle-class woman should seek to improve her own knowledge so that she can pass it on. Apprenticeships, pension and health benefits, and social clubs should be as readily available for young women as for young men. Lewald appeals to the pride and self-respect of the women reading these letters and hopes that they will want to help, aided by their husbands and fathers.

In the families of small craftsmen and tradesmen, some of these beneficial changes were already occurring with the establishment of Sunday schools, libraries and "Vereine" (clubs or lodges). But Lewald pointed out that poorer women had no such outlets; they sat at home in their miserable lodgings and learned nothing. They could not even help their sons to advance because of their own ignorance.

Ironically enough, the growing civil emancipation of men only served to widen the gender gap. The man's enhanced civil responsibilities threw more duties on his wife and daughters at home. Those who became servants had little concept of the correct performance of household chores, and their mistresses usually complained of their fecklessness rather than setting a good example and training them properly.[1] Instead of criticizing, the mistress of the house must have a more personal relationship with her employees, be a role model and raise the maidservants to her level. On its part, the government could offer better and more advanced public education, though real progress was only possible woman to woman. Lewald's advice was that the woman of the house must consider her servant as a master does an apprentice.

The preferred treatment of servants should begin with decent wages and a raise every year. They should not receive "Kostgeld" (a form of expense account for food, lodgings and incidentals), but decent lodgings and good food within the household's means. Respect was essential—respect between husband and wife, parents and children, and master/mistress and servant—to the extent of addressing the maid as "Sie" rather than "Du."[2] Each member of the household, parents, children, servants, should be basically aware of the financial circumstances of the family, in order to understand why money was spent or economies effected as they were—an idea that would seem revolutionary to some breadwinners even today.

Lewald felt that prosperous women spent too much time in frivolous activities that provided no benefit to themselves or their families. Instead they should set aside regular hours every week to give their servants instruction; two hours late Sunday afternoon would suffice for a small school for four to six girls. The housewife and her friends could take turns teaching this class. The first thirty minutes were to be occupied with copying a dictation into a notebook. Subjects would include keeping accounts, letter writing, Roman numerals (for reading clock faces), thermometer reading, astronomy, a review of their school subjects, and other practical items. The second hour would be devoted to entertainment: the reading aloud of stories or Goethe or Schiller ballads; preparing dramas and acting out different roles; reading anything, including fairy tales that would make the young girls feel that this was an enjoyable activity, not a chore. Pastimes could also include songs, old and new, games, handwork, hobbies (like origami!) and small inexpensive treats, such as those one would give children. Good hygiene and elementary nursing would also be taught. Lewald suggested using Florence Nightingale's books as texts. Instructions should be accompanied by field trips to good day-care centers to teach proper child-care. These visits would serve a second purpose: training the girls for related jobs. Other subjects included good nutrition, housing, heating, and ventilation. A knowledge of political science was necessary as well as instruction in basic insurance, the stock market, interest, and general finance. Lewald realized that the mistress of the house probably was deficient in her own knowledge of such matters, but she could always call in "guest experts" and learn something herself. And even the limited informational resources of the housewife were generally so much greater than her servants that any accurate facts would bring some enlightenment.

After the Sunday afternoon school had gained acceptance, another evening class could be added, and if the number of students became too great for a home, a school classroom could be rented. Lewald realized that young married women usually did not have the time or experience to conduct such classes without neglecting their households or children. But older women or widows did have these assets and unmarried women with a sense of mission could help.

At this time, there were approximately 20,000 female factory workers in Berlin and 10,000 female servants. The girls preferred working in the factories because the hours and tasks were limited, the salaries frequently higher, and the independence greater, although the environment in the factory and the contact with men on leisure hours frequently led to moral decline. Even middle-class girls worked in some of the better factories, since wages were adequate and they could save money toward their dowries.

When innocent country girls came to the city to work in factories, they needed a hostel to live in. Otherwise they often fell prey to white slavers and unscrupulous boarding house owners. These hostels would give the girls peer support and would be similar to the Marthashof hostel just opened in Berlin, which was also a training school and employment agency and offered child care. Such an institution could also be a place for servants to stay while their employers were on vacation and the house closed up. Lewald was unhappy about the religious emphasis of the Marthashof, but admitted its value and felt it should be emulated and improved. In Lewald's next series of letters, she recommended cafeterias for working women, since it was uncomfortable for them to go to a restaurant alone. Even upper- and middle-class women would appreciate ladies' restaurants, cafeterias, or clubs that catered to both sexes, as in England. One good job for women would be running such a club or hotel garni.

Lewald concluded the *Osterbriefe* by declaring that real equality of human beings did not exist. There was no value in equality before the law, if everything else was unequal. Women were considered dependent and their only real legal equality was the right to receive equal punishment for their crimes. The inequity in the setting of moral standards was even more appalling, since it was a class as well as a gender gap. Men seduced women, and only the woman's reputation suffered. Men salved their consciences by denigrating women. The "fallen" woman had few choices: she could become a wet nurse, go to the poorhouse, or kill herself.

Six years later, Lewald published a follow-up volume, *Für und wider die Frauen* (For and against Women). It consisted of fourteen letters, six of them already published in *Westermanns Monatshefte* from April to September of 1869 under the title "Für die Gewerbtätigkeit der Frauen" ("For the Employment of Women") and an additional eight in response to the massive correspondence received for the former and the *Osterbriefe*. These letters are dedicated to John Stuart Mill, whose *On the Subjugation Of Women* had just been published (1869) in London; for its first German edition (1872) Lewald wrote the introduction. In contrast to the

Osterbriefe, which dealt with the education of lower-class women, *Für und wider die Frauen* treated the education of the middle- and upper-class women of Lewald's own circle. Again, emancipation meant freedom of women to work outside the home for their own and their family's benefit.

Most of the correspondence Lewald had received was from "alte Mädchen"—unmarried women of good family, who had become governesses or companions to support themselves, but found their dependence on their employers and their position depressing and without a future. Many of them felt they could be writers like Lewald; she dryly commented on the confidence they felt in their own ability and the already overcrowded market for such authors.[3] The skills they had been taught were negligible—a smattering of English or French, piano playing, handwork. Still they felt offended at her suggestions that they should seek employment as saleswomen or waitresses and thought such jobs demeaning.

What kind of education, then, would be a practical one for educating women to earn their own living and not to be dependent upon marriage or a demeaning job to support themselves? Lewald had just returned from a conference of the German Women's Federation in Berlin with the feeling that what women lacked was not a good general education (now available) but scientific and technological training. Before university there must be the equivalent of a high school education, either a vocational or an academic one. In 1864, Lewald had visited an "école professionnelle pour femmes" in France which emphasized trade skills and singing, and had heard that a similar one was planned in Leipzig. She felt that this was an impractical combination, since the best training for women would feature office and business skills.

There were two basic problems in employing women in shops, as managers of small businesses, as bookkeepers or in similar jobs. First, men were frequently unwilling to accept women in these situations, and their reasons were "benevolent"—or so they thought: a patriarchal protectiveness to shield the ladies from unwanted intimacies. Secondly and more seriously, few women were trained for such positions. The daughters of small tradesmen and handworkers were often taught good skills and were able to earn their own living. But middle-class women found the same prejudices that sons of professors or professional men (not to mention the sons of the aristocracy) encountered when they wanted to go into a trade. Women had finally gained acceptance as school teachers for the lower grades, and Lewald hoped the same acceptance would follow for businesswomen when the income advantages were clearly seen. In reiterating her rallying cry of "the emancipation of women to work," Lewald made the following points.

Wealth is not in itself honorable and the lack of it is no disgrace. Work, on the other hand, is honorable for men *and* women, and any kind of productive labor is worthwhile. Women's natural sense of honor has been suppressed by the burden of dependency. They want to protect and help those they love as much as men do; therefore, both sons and daughters should work for the benefit of the family. For the daughters to sit around, waiting only for marriage, was bad for their health and led to the hypochondria and reliance on doctors and drugs so prevalent in the middle and upper classes. Lewald's concept of the highest happiness for women (marriage to a husband of one's own choosing and a comfortable existence) was too traditional to find the idea of working wives attractive, but there was no doubt in her mind about the advantages of such careers before marriage or instead of an undesired marriage. Training for such work would also be insurance in the case of widowhood or divorce, or for highly motivated childless women, such as herself. And women with the requisite intelligence, drive, and good secondary education should certainly be permitted in the universities to study law or medicine without any fear of being contaminated by the curriculum or contact with male colleagues.

Surprisingly, Lewald was not very concerned with women's suffrage. In a third work "Die Frauen und das allgemeine Wahlrecht" ("Women and Universal Suffrage"), published in *Westermanns Monatshefte* in 1870 in response to a letter written to the German-language newspaper in St. Louis, the *Westliche Post*, about her views on this subject, she stated that too many unqualified men who did not understand the issues were already voting. To add unqualified women voters who would generally vote as their husbands did or on appearance or whim was no improvement. Instead, better education for all men and women was necessary before universal suffrage should be implemented.[4] In the meantime, the right to vote should be based on education, not gender, and those women who were qualified and *who really wanted to vote* should have this privilege.

Regula Venske and Renate Möhrmann have pointed out that Lewald's working heroines pursue very traditional feminine careers. The eponymous *Adele* writes only to support herself and her mother until a suitable husband arrives. She is one of the writers of whom Lewald is so scornful. A more happy and successful example of a writer and far more autobiographical is

Cornelie in *Wandlungen* (Changes). Here the heroine develops her talents because of her marriage to a supportive, intellectual, liberal Jewish doctor. Her sister becomes an important painter. There are performing artists both happy and unhappy: the actresses, Hulda in *Die Erlöserin* (The Redeemer), who immediately gives up a successful career when her noble lover finally decides to marry her, and Sophie Harcourt, a true professional, who dies when her lover forsakes her in *Eine Lebensfrage* (A Vital Question). Since Lewald had had some bad experiences with music,[5] musicians usually do not fare well in her novels. Regine, the poor seamstress, who becomes a famous opera singer in *Wandlungen* only does so because of unrequited love, and the pianist Leontine in *Die Reisegefährten* (The Travel Companions) comes to an untimely end (a probable suicide) because she is emotionally unstable.[6]

There are, of course, any number of women characters who act as companions, governesses and assistant teachers, occupations which offered perfectly acceptable solutions for the unmarried women of the nineteenth century. In response to the criticism that her characters usually pursue only the traditional careers for women, I would like to mention a short novel, "Mamsell Philippinens Philipp," (Mademoiselle Philippine's Philipp), in which a widow successfully runs her deceased husband's bakery—admittedly, only until she remarries.

Obviously, Lewald was far too pragmatic to allow her female characters to have careers that would have been impossible in her society. How could a woman who had no legal right to attend a university become a doctor or a lawyer? What woman, perhaps inheriting a factory or business from her father or husband, could get bank loans or sign contracts, even if she had been trained to continue the work? Where could a disenfranchised female find civil service or elective positions? These are the injustices that Lewald was trying to correct in her emancipatory works. Education is the key to everything, including professional or business employment or government service. At every level of society women should help their sisters and be helped by their brothers to achieve this education. If Lewald still considered marriage the ultimate good, it was not just any marriage, but a marriage of choice between two equals who loved and respected each other and who could support their mate if necessary. That is what Lewald achieved for herself.

Lewald has been seen as a feminist writer by some critics and attacked as not being feminist enough by others. In actuality, she was a hard-headed, pragmatic, self-made woman, who had little patience with those who did not work as diligently as she did. If women did not work and study like men, they did not deserve the privileges of men, just as the freed slaves of America and the serfs of Russia did not deserve any rights solely because of their previous oppression. It was her opinion that the state and more privileged women should provide education and social services to enable women to work to raise their social and economic status and that of their families. In the majority of her fictional works—*Von Geschlecht zu Geschlecht* (From Generation to Generation, 1864-1865), *Stella* (1883) and *Die Familie Darner* (The Darners, 1887), to mention only a few examples— upward mobility is the dominant theme for Lewald; for both women and men, this can be achieved by a good marriage and/or by hard work, combined with the best utilization of one's native talents. And both sexes should have equal opportunity and education to achieve their goals.

Notes

[1] A current analogy would be those employers of unskilled household workers from Central America, who are annoyed when their new maids are unacquainted with modern electrical appliances or cleaning methods.

[2] As in many European languages, there is a formal and informal pronoun for expressing the word "you." Using "Sie" instead of "Du" would be paying a servant the respect due an equal.

[3] Lewald herself derived much pleasure from writing, but wrote in her memoirs in 1875 that she thought she would have made an excellent physician (*Gefühltes* 200). Indeed, it was the lack of scientific training she most regretted in her own life. She commented that the amount of money spent on her piano lessons would have been far better employed in teaching her drawing, foreign languages—which, incidentally, her father was happy to pay for—and instruction in natural sciences, "which to be sure, were not included then in the area of general education" (*Lebensgeschichte* I: 207).

[4] Lewald was thinking to some extent of the recently emancipated and enfranchised black men, whose education was as poor or poorer than the majority of white women, but who had been given the vote solely on basis of their sex.

[5] Her inability to escape the hated piano lessons imposed by her father are an almost comic leitmotif of her autobiography.

[6] Lewald blames part of Leontine's instability on the fact that she is half Spanish—sometimes Lewald's Prussian prejudices show. However, her fondness for the Italians exempts them from such censure.

Works Cited

Primary Sources by Fanny Lewald in chronological order:

"Einige Gedanken über Mädchenerziehung" and "Andeutungen über die Lage der weiblichen Dienstboten." *Archiv für vaterländische Interessen oder Preußische Provinzialblätter.* Ed. O. W. L. Richter. Königsberg, 1843: 380-89, 421-33.

Eine Lebensfrage. Leipzig: Brockhaus, 1845.

Wandlungen. Berlin: Janke, 1853.

Adele. Braunschweig: Vieweg, 1855.

Die Reisegefährten. Berlin: J. Guttentag, 1858.

Meine Lebensgeschichte. Berlin: Janke, 1861.

Osterbriefe für die Frauen. Berlin: Janke, 1863.

"Mamsell Philippinens Philipp." *Neue Romane*, v. 5. Berlin: Janke, 1864.

Für und wider die Frauen. Berlin: Janke, 1870.

"Die Frauen und das allgemeine Wahlrecht." *Westermanns Monatshefte* 28 (1870): 97-103.

"Und was nun?" *Der Frauenanwalt* 1 (1871): 1-18.

Gefühltes und Gedachtes. Dresden u. Leipzig: Minden, 1900.

Secondary Sources:

Bell, Susan Groag, and Karen M. Offen, eds. *Women, the Family and Freedom* , I. Stanford: Stanford University Press, 1983.

Brinker-Gabler, Gisela. "Die Schriftstellerin in der deutschen Literaturwissenschaft: Aspekte ihrer Rezeption von 1835 bis 1910." *Die Unterrichtspraxis* 9.1 (Spring 1976): 15-29.

Fout, John C., ed. *German Women in the Nineteenth Century: A Social History*. New York: Holmes & Meier, 1984.

Gosche, Agnes. *Die organisierte Frauenbewegung*, II. Berlin: Herbig, 1927.

Herminghouse, Patricia. "Women and the Literary Enterprise in Nineteenth-Century Germany." *German Women in the Eighteenth and Nineteenth Centuries*. Eds. Ruth-Ellen B. Joeres and Mary Jo Maynes. Bloomington: Indiana UP, 1986. 78-93.

Möhrmann, Renate. *Die andere Frau. Emanzipationsansätze deutscher Schriftstellerinnen im Vorfeld der Achtundvierzig Revolution*. Stuttgart: Metzler, 1977.

______. "Women's Work as Portrayed in Women's Literature." *German Women in the Eighteenth and Nineteenth Centuries*. 51-77.

Steinhauer, Marielouise. *Fanny Lewald, die deutsche George Sand. Ein Kapitel aus der Geschichte des Frauenromans im 19. Jahrhundert*. Diss. Berlin, 1937.

Venske, Regula. "Alltag und Emanzipation. Eine Untersuchung über die Romanautorin Fanny Lewald." M.A. Thesis Hamburg, 1981.

______. "Discipline and Daydreaming in the Works of a Nineteenth Century Woman Author: Fanny Lewald." *German Women in the Eighteenth and Nineteenth Centuries*. 175-92.

Luise Rinsers Frauenbild

Iman Khalil
University of Missouri at Kansas City

Das Frauenbild der Schriftstellerin Luise Rinser, geboren 1911, läßt sich auf zwei Ebenen verfolgen: auf einer realen, nämlich Luise Rinser selbst, und einer fiktiven Ebene, die sich aus ihrem literarischen Werk herauskristallisiert.

Rinsers berühmteste Frauengestalt ist ohne Zweifel Nina Buschmann, die Heldin beider Erfolgsromane der 50er Jahre: *Mitte des Lebens* (1950) und *Abenteuer der Tugend* (1957). *Mitte des Lebens* zeigt uns eine im wahrsten Sinne des Wortes emanzipierte Frauenpersönlichkeit, zudem in einer Zeit, in der von Frauenemanzipation und Feminismus im allgmeinen Bewußtsein kaum die Rede war. Ninas emanzipatorisches Aufbegehren, ihre Ansichten und Ansprüche an sich selbst und an das Leben stehen denen der heutigen feministischen Bestrebungen in nichts nach. Es scheint, als wollte hier die damals 38jährige Autorin ein literarisches Modell der emanzipierten Frau errichten. Insofern wird Nina mit Recht als ein "neuer Frauentypus" (Lennartz 1424) bezeichnet. In diesem ersten Nina-Roman verfolgt die Autorin den Werdegang einer mutigen Person, die es als ihre innere Bestimmung und Lebensaufgabe auffaßt, sich als Frau in der Welt zu behaupten. Um ihrer Selbständigkeit und geistigen Freiheit willen scheut Nina kein Risiko. In verschiedenen Lebensstationen wird sie mit harten Bewährungsproben konfrontiert: als Studentin in der Hitler-Zeit, als Verkäuferin in einem kleinen Laden auf dem Lande, als aktive Nazi-Gegnerin, die im Konzentrationslager landet, als Ehefrau und Mutter von zwei Kindern, als geschiedene und auf sich selbst angewiesene Frau, als erfolgreiche Schriftstellerin und Redakteurin einer angesehenen Zeitung, die schließlich, um einer unglückseligen Liebe zu einem verheirateten Künstler aus dem Wege zu gehen, den resoluten Entschluß faßt, nach England zu übersiedeln. Ninas starkes Selbstbewußtsein und ihr ungebrochener Drang nach Unabhängigkeit und Selbstverwirklichung geben ihr die innere und äußere Widerstandskraft und den Mut, die Hindernisse, die ihr das Leben in den Weg legt, zu überwinden. In gefährlichen Situationen exzellieren ihre Kühnheit, Tatkraft und Resolutheit. Dieser außerordentlichen Frau ist der große Durchbruch durchaus gelungen.

Umso befremdender wirkt Rinsers Roman *Abenteuer der Tugend*, der sich als Fortsetzung des ersten versteht. Wider Erwarten wird in diesem zweiten Nina-Roman die schwer erkämpfte Unabhängigkeit der Protagonistin zurückgenommen. Die Bekehrung der "aufsässigen Nina" (*Im Dunkeln singen* 150) findet statt. *Abenteuer der Tugend* besteht ausschließlich aus Briefen der Heldin, in denen der äußere wie innere Verlauf ihres weiteren Schicksals seit der Übersiedlung nach England erzählt wird. Gegen besseres Wissen und Gewissen willigt sie bald doch in die Ehe mit dem inzwischen geschiedenen Künstler ein, gibt ihre Karriere auf und lebt nur noch für ihn, um den nunmehr ihr ganzes Leben kreist. Die rebellische, tatkräftige Nina des ersten Romans wird im zweiten zu einer passiv leidenden Frau, die ihr "Schicksal" (*Abenteuer der Tugend* 174) erduldet. Der schwermütige, egozentrische, kaum von seiner Drogensucht geheilte Künstler verfällt nun dem Alkoholismus. Ein unerträgliches Leben zu zweit endet mit seinem Tode durch einen Autounfall. Nina, die inzwischen heftig mit dem Katholizismus gerungen hat, öffnet sich mit voller Einsicht dem Glauben und der göttlichen Gnade und wendet sich nun ganz der katholischen Kirche zu.

Die ganze Perspektive des Romans ist einerseits auf den Künstler-Ehemann reduziert, andererseits auf den inneren Kampf Ninas um den Katholizismus, den sie in ihren Briefen minuziös beschreibt. Die Briefe sind ihrerseits mit psychologischen, theologischen und philosophischen Reflexionen überfrachtet. Von der Außenwelt, von Zeitbezügen, ist keine Spur, als lebte Nina in einem Vakuum, das nur noch ihr Innenleben gelten läßt. Diese Wandlung ihrer Persönlichkeit löst die Frage aus, was wohl Luise Rinser zu dieser radikalen Änderung ihres Frauenbildes bewogen haben mag. Um diese Frage zu beantworten, werden hier zwei außerliterarische Aspekte bemüht: ein zeithistorischer und ein persönlicher. Der zeithistorische Aspekt erklärt diesen Rückzug ins Innere als einen charakteristischen Trend der Literatur der 50er Jahre. Auf die erste Phase westdeutscher Nachkriegsliteratur, die unmittelbar nach 1945 die Katastrophe literarisch zu verarbeiten suchte, folgt eine Abkehr der AutorInnen von der politisch-gesellschaftlichen Wirklichkeit. Auch das Lesepublikum zeigt ein auffallendes Desinteresse an der aktuellen Wirklichkeit und der politischen Thematik und mehr Interesse für Innerlichkeit und Subjektivität. Während dieser apolitischen Phase bundesdeutscher Literatur ist der Roman *Abenteuer der Tugend* entstanden. Als geistiges Produkt seiner Zeit, also auch als ihr Spiegelbild, entsprach er den Publikumserwartungen. Eine Rezension vom 18. Januar 1958 konstatiert, daß "Luise Rinsers Buch zu Weihnachten viel gekauft wurde" (Sturm, FAZ). Eine andere Besprechung aus derselben Zeit rühmt die Technik der Briefmontage, da sie die Möglichkeit biete, "vom Realen und

Banalen, vom Handgreiflichen äußerer Vorgänge (...) frei zu bleiben und alles Gewicht dem inneren, dem geistig-seelischen Erleben (...) zuzuwenden." Dies, so heißt es weiter, "kommt dem Bedürfnis des heutigen Menschen entgegen," der "die Werte, die Position erst einmal monologisch oder (...) grübelnd, reflektierend zu erkennen und zu benennen sucht" (Wilk 1033).[1]

Der persönliche Aspekt leitet sich aus Luise Rinsers Leben ab. Der Roman *Abenteuer der Tugend* erzählt von der schwierigen Ehe einer begabten Schriftstellerin mit einem Künstler, dem Opernsänger Maurice. Die Entstehungszeit dieses Romans fällt in die Zeit, in der die Erfolgsautorin Luise Rinser selber mit einem Künstler, dem Komponisten Carl Orff, verheiratet war. Daß es sich dabei keineswegs um eine glückliche Verbindung handelte, beweist die nach fünf Jahren erfolgte Scheidung, genau zwei Jahre nach der Veröffentlichung des Romans. So läßt sich annehmen, daß Luise Rinser in diesem monologischen Werk persönlich "erlittene" (*Im Dunkeln singen* 121) Realitäten literarisch verarbeitet hat. Durch die "Konversion" der Heldin transzendiert sie im Kunstwerk das Geschehen um eine gescheiterte Ehe in höhere Regionen.[2]

In zwei späteren Romanen um Frauenschicksale, *Geh fort, wenn du kannst* (1959) und *Die vollkommene Freude* (1962), betont Luise Rinser weiterhin das Metaphysische und Religiöse. So wird diese literarische Phase als ihre "'katholisierende' Phase" bezeichnet (Weigel 8). In den folgenden Jahren, bis 1983, hat Luise Rinser wenig Literatur geschrieben, dafür aber eine beachtliche Zahl sozialkritischer Essays, Tagebücher, Reisebeschreibungen und eine Autobiographie. Diese "nicht-belletristische Phase" (Weigel 2) hat einen fundamentalen Wandel in ihrer Haltung hervorgebracht. Ihr Interesse am Metaphysischen und Religiösen vertiefte sich, um das soziale und politische Engagement einzuschließen. Darin spiegelt sich auch der Geist der 60er Jahre wider.

Scheint die Nina des zweiten Romans mit der nonkonformistischen Nina des ersten nur noch den Namen gemeinsam zu haben, so findet man, wenn man vom literarischen Werk absieht und sich der Autorin als Privatperson zuwendet, daß sich das frühe Frauenbild der Nina nahtlos in das Modell einer modernen emanzipierten Frau einfügen läßt, das Luise Rinser als Frau unserer Gegenwart leibhaftig verkörpert. Im Alter distanziert sie sich denn auch von ihrem Konzept im zweiten Roman und schreibt: "Das war FRÜHER" (*Im Dunkeln singen* 150).

Das Frauenbild, das die Autorin verkörpert, ist das Produkt eines kritischen Geistes, der sich nicht durch vorgegebene Ideale manipulieren läßt. Im Gegensatz zur allgemein herrschenden Meinung mag sie z.B. Raphaels Sixtinische Madonna "ganz und gar nicht"; sie begreife nicht, wie man von dieser "glatten banalen Schönheit hingerissen sein kann. Vielleicht entspricht diese Darstellung der Weiblichkeit dem Ideal des Mannes. Will der Mann die Frau so? Möchten Frauen so sein, so gesehen werden?" (*Im Dunkeln singen* 177). Ihrer Meinung nach sollten sich Frauen in einer immer noch vom Mann dominierten Welt nicht durch männliche Vorbilder beirren lassen und keineswegs in die Fußstapfen des Mannes treten. So attackiert sie den latenten Wunsch mancher Frauen: "Wir wollen Männer sein" (*ebenda* 168) und kritisiert die Einstellung junger Bundesbürgerinnen, die im Namen der Gleichberechtigung für die Aufnahme von Frauen in die Bundeswehr eintreten. Sie fragt polemisch, ob die Gleichberechtigung darin bestünde, daß die Frau "töten darf wie der Mann?" (*ebenda* 167). Daß Männer den Wehrdienst verweigern, dagegen aber "Frauen sich begeistert in diese Lücke werfen, Männer sein wollend", veranlaßt sie, Freuds Wort vom "Penis-Neid" umzumodeln in "Das Gewehr als Penis" (*ebenda* 168). Die Gestaltung der "Zukunft der Menschheit" will sie folglich nicht einer männlich orientierten Geisteshaltung anvertrauen. Denn die Zukunft soll "radikal anders" sein als die Vergangenheit, d.h.

> nicht mehr männer-bestimmt, nicht vom männlichen Ehrbegriff (...), nicht mehr vom Willen zur Gewalt, nicht mehr von der Bereitschaft zum Töten. Die Zukunft muß "weiblich" bestimmt sein, das heißt: völlige Ablehnung von Gewalt und Krieg, friedliche Neutralität, Abschaffung des Militärs; also weder Frauen noch Männer zum Morden bereit. "Frauen ans Gewehr" oder auch nur "Frauen zum Militär" ist schlimmste Reaktion; ein Rückfall ins alte Männer-Denken. (*ebenda* 167)

Seit 1961 lebt Luise Rinser in einem ruhigen Ort bei Rom. Dennoch ist sie mit dem Weltgeschehen aufs engste verwoben: "Ich suche hier keinen Frieden, (...) ich lasse nicht 'die Welt' draußen vor der Tür (...); ich nehme vielmehr entschlossen die Unruhe der Welt mit hinein" (*Septembertag* 19). In der Tat ist sie politisch äußerst aktiv. Die Tendenzwende der 70er Jahre zur erneuten Abkehr von der politischen Arena macht sie nicht mit. Statt dessen pocht sie unerbittlich auf die Notwendigkeit des politischen Engagements der Schriftsteller: "Ein Schriftsteller an hoher Stelle" würde positive Änderungen herbeiführen. "Ein Schriftsteller, der zugleich eine Frau ist, vermöchte vielleicht sogar die beschämend rüde, männlich aggressive Sprache der Politiker zu verändern in eine von gegenseitigem Respekt und von Herzenshöflichkeit getragene" (*Im Dunkeln singen* 162). Ihren eigenen politischen

Einsatz versteht sie als die Verpflichtung eines verantwortungsbewußten Menschen seinen Mitmenschen gegenüber. Den scharfen Tadel seitens der Leserschaft ihres politischen Engagements wegen beantwortet sie mit der Frage: "Gibt es etwas, das NICHT politisch wäre? (...) Was ist denn Politik? Sorge um den Mitmenschen" (*ebenda* 57). Ihr Selbstverständnis als engagierte Autorin drängt sie zu intensiver Aktivität in politischer und sozialer Hinsicht. 1971/72 bereist sie die Bundesrepublik als Wahlhelferin der SPD. Seit vielen Jahren ist sie eine prominente Unterstützerin der Grünen[3] und widmet viel Zeit und Energie der Friedensbewegung. Unermüdlich nimmt sie an Friedenstagungen und Friedensdemonstrationen teil und läßt sich nicht durch Feindseligkeiten ihrer konservativen Gegner einschüchtern.[4] Luise Rinsers politischer Einsatz und persönliche Hilfeleistungen in Wort und Tat gelten ferner den benachteiligten Randgruppen der Gesellschaft. Dazu gehören die deutschen Zigeuner, die Behinderten und Rentner, die Ausländer im Land, die Strafgefangenen.[5] Als eine der wenigen namhaften weiblichen Repräsentanten bundesdeutscher Gegenwartsliteratur kam sie durch Lesereisen in verschiedene Länder in Ost und West. Noch stärker brachte sie ihre Friedensarbeit mit der ganzen Welt in Berührung, nämlich als Teilnehmerin an vielen internationalen Friedenskongressen.

Luise Rinser, Mitglied der West-Berliner Akademie der Künste und des PEN-Zentrums der BRD, Beratungsmitglied der deutsch-polnischen Gesellschaft, mit zahlreichen Kultur- und Literaturpreisen ausgezeichnet, freute sich insbesondere über die DDR-Bobrowski-Medaille: "Es war nicht nur ein 'Literaturpreis', es war weit mehr: eine Anerkennung für meine stille, beständige Arbeit des Brückenbauens zwischen Ost und West" (*ebenda* 177). Ihre Hoffnung ist "eine neue Ära des Friedens auf dieser Erde" (*ebenda* 48). Für diese Aufgabe würden sich Frauen gut eignen: Frauen seien "besser geeignet, Frieden zu stiften und Leben zu hüten" (*Mirjam* 81). Auf dieses Frauenbild macht sie 1982 eine Germanistinnen-Tagung in Boston aufmerksam: "Für mich, an Arbeit mit Männern gewöhnt, ein neues Erlebnis: (...) In meinem langen Leben habe ich keinen Kongreß erlebt, der so wie dieser hier den Geschmack von Frieden und Glück gehabt hätte" (*Im Dunkeln singen* 44). Auch in Japan sei die Friedensbewegung von Frauen ausgegangen, von Frauen getragen. Jedoch zeigt 1984 ein Friedenskongreß in Tokyo, daß weltweit Frauen politisch nicht ins Gewicht fallen: "Laßt sie reden, diese Weiber!" Luise Rinser resigniert aber nicht vor derartigen Parolen, sondern ist voller Zuversicht in bezug auf das, was japanische Frauen alles leisten könnten, wenn sie sich mit den Frauen anderer Länder verbündeten (*ebenda* 207). Den Frieden erwartet sie "von der Basis her" (*ebenda* 186). Dabei baut sie auf eine signifikante Rolle der Frauen, zumal in Verbindung mit der Jugend: "Jugend der Welt zusammen mit den Frauen: was für eine Macht kann das sein!" (*ebenda* 211). Diese Erwartung entspringt ihrem modifizierten Frauenbild, das zum humanen Wirken unbedingt das soziale und politische Engagement zählt. Friede, Gewaltlosigkeit, Seelenheil lassen sich demnach nicht kontemplativ verwirklichen, sondern aktiv, d.h. durch mutige Stellungnahmen und energisches Handeln, durch ein kühnes Hinaustreten aus der Isolation in die reale Welt, jedoch ohne dabei ins "alte Männer-Denken" zurückzufallen. Letzteres attackiert sie vehement am Beispiel der britischen Ministerpräsidentin, die "aus supermännlichem Ehrgeiz" Engländer und Argentinier "kaltschnauzig in den Heldentod" schickte. Die politisch engagierte Autorin richtet sich, "von Frau zu Frau", an die Berufspolitikerin mit scharfen Worten: "Mrs. Thatcher, eiserne Lady, stolz auf diesen makabren Titel, Mörderin auch Sie (....), werden Sie wieder eine Frau, statt ein verdorbener Mann zu sein" ("Redeentwurf zur Wahl des Bundespräsidenten" 56).[6]

Ferner prangert Luise Rinser als unmittelbar Betroffene die geistige Unterdrückung der Frau durch den Mann an: "Was haben uns die Männer angetan seit Jahrhunderten! Sie ließen uns nicht hochkommen und sagten dann, es gebe unter uns keine Talente, die mit ihnen konkurrieren könnten!" Bislang dominierte der Mann auf allen Gebieten. Auch die Germanistik sei von Männern besetzt, die die von Frauen geschriebene Literatur für "zweitrangig" hielten; nach "Männer-Urteil" also "Weiberkram" bzw. "Weibersachen, die keinen Mann interessieren" (*ebenda* 43f.). Auch das Frauenbild in der Männerliteratur wird bloßgestellt: "Da hatten wir Frauen die obligate Rolle als Geliebte, als Mutter, als Hure, als Spionin allenfalls" (*ebenda* 44).[7] Schließlich rüttelt sie auch an der patriarchalischen Überlieferung: "Es ist Gottes Wille, daß Frauen ihren Ehemännern untertan sind." Sie fragt: "Wessen Gottes? (...) Wir kennen nur kultur-, zeit-, räumlich bedingte Gottes-Bilder" (*ebenda* 107). Sie weist den "Mythos der Frau als verführerischer Evagestalt" (Frederiksen 134) zurück und wirft unkonventionelle Fragen auf, die das tradierte Gotteskonzept auf den Kopf stellen: "Wenn Adonai (Gott) nicht einen Mann, sondern eine Frau als Messias geschickt hätte? Wenn der Christos bei der Wiederkehr am Ende der Zeiten als Frau erschiene? Wenn die Aufgabe der Erlösung der Madonna verbliebe, der großen Mutter?" (*ebenda* 140). Diese Gedanken notiert sich Luise Rinser während der Arbeit an ihrem Roman *Mirjam* (1983), den sie wiederholt als "politisch" (*Im Dunkeln singen* 45, 150) bezeichnet hat und in dem sie Maria Magdalena als "emanzipierte jüdische Frau" (*ebenda* 45) darstellt. So läßt sie Mirjam ähnliche Bedenken äußern, z.B. bezüglich des

Jesuskindes: warum die Astrologen annahmen, "das vorhergesagte Kind sei ein männliches? Warum muß der Messias ein Mann sein?" Sie geht einen Schritt weiter und fragt nach dem "Höchsten" und ob sich je einer vorstellte, "dieser ewige ER konnte (!) eine Frau sein?" (*Mirjam* 80). Mirjams Antwort ist eine Synthese, die Rinsers Beschäftigung mit fernöstlichen Religionen manifestiert: "Das Unnennbare, das ALLES war: Mann und Frau" (*ebenda* 81).

In zwei Essays, "Zölibat und Frau" (1967) und "Unterentwickeltes Land Frau" (1970), befaßt sich Luise Rinser mit der "Frauenfrage als Teil eines umfassenden Problems, das die Benachteiligung aller Unterdrückten, Schwachen und Armen einschließt" (Frederiksen 134). Über die Frau sprechen, heiße immer, über die Gesellschaft sprechen, d.h. "über das Verhältnis von Autorität und Freiheit reflektieren" (zit. n. Frederiksen 134). Frederiksen bemerkt, daß Rinser hier "die Frau selbst zum großen Teil für ihre Unfreiheit verantwortlich macht", wenn ihr "ein emanzipatorisches Bewußtsein fehlt", daß sie der Frau "Angst vor dem Erwachsenwerden" vorwirft und von ihr eine "Infragestellung" der bisherigen "Identität mit sich" fordert, um ihre als selbstverständlich hingenommenene Lage zu verändern (Frederiksen 134f.).

Was den literarischen Stellenwert der Autorin betrifft, so steht außer Frage, daß sie zu lange zu Unrecht kurzerhand als "Erbauungsschriftstellerin" oder als "Frauenschriftstellerin" (Weigel 2) abgetan wurde. Ihre Nina galt als "suffragettenhaft" (Sturm, FAZ); und lobende Worte schmälerten ihre geistige Begabung als Frau, indem hier "von einem fast männlichen Geist" gesprochen wurde (Wilk 1033). Im Zuge einer Neuorientierung der Literaturkritik, zumal unter Heranziehung feministischer Kriterien, kann heute das Rinsersche Werk zu einer adäquaten Würdigung gelangen. Nach Änderung der höchst fragwürdigen und unzeitgemäßen Einstufung der "Frauenliteratur" als "zweitrangig" könnte man ohne Vorbehalte die "international angesehene" ("Redeentwurf" 56) Luise Rinser, die inzwischen schon mit Frankreichs Simone de Beauvoir verglichen worden ist (Anz, FAZ), die "First Lady des gehobenen deutschsprachigen Frauenromans" (Weigel, zit. n. Lennartz, 1422) nennen.

Anmerkungen

[1] Auch formal wird diese Tendenz in *Abenteuer der Tugend* durch die Rückkehr zur Tradition des Briefromans unterstrichen.

[2] Nach Vilma Sturm, die 1958 den Roman scharf kritisiert, hat Luise Rinser durch die Verflechtung der Geschichte einer Ehe mit der Geschichte einer Konversion "die Sache (...) in die letzten Bereiche vorgetragen und dort zur Entscheidung gebracht." Eben darin liege "die wirkliche Qualität des Buches" (FAZ 1958).

[3] Luise Rinser wurde 1984 von den Grünen als Gegenkandidatin zu Richard von Weizsäcker zum Amt des Bundespräsidenten nominiert.

[4] Sie wurde u.a. der kommunistischen Ideologie sowie der "Terrorismus-Sympathie verdächtigt" (*Im Dunkeln singen* 211). Sie und die Teilnehmer an einer Friedenstagung in Fulda wurden 1984 als "Randalierer und Kriminelle" diffamiert (*ebenda* 184).

[5] Zu diesen Fragen äußert sie sich mehrfach in ihren Aufzeichnungen *Im Dunkeln singen*; auch nennt sie sie als Teil ihres politischen Programms für das Bundespräsidentenamt.

[6] Anläßlich ihrer Nominierung durch die Grünen zum Amt des Bundespräsidenten schrieb Luise Rinser 1984 den erwähnten Entwurf zu einer eventuellen Rede vor dem Deutschen Bundestag.

[7] Hier heißt es weiter über das von Männern suggerierte Frauenbild: "Von Männeraugen gesehen, von Männerwünschen und Männerängsten geprägt, so lange uns vorgesagt, bis wirs selber glaubten und uns in unsre Rollen fügten" (*Im Dunkeln singen* 44).

Zitierte Literatur

Anz, Thomas. "Eine streitbare Volksschriftstellerin: Luise Rinser wird siebzig". In *Frankfurter Allgemeine Zeitung* (30. April 1981).

Frederiksen, Elke. "Luise Rinser". In *Luise Rinser. Materialien zu Leben und Werk*. Hrsg. Hans-Rüdiger Schwab. Frankfurt: Fischer Taschenbuch Verlag, 1986. 131-37.

Lennartz, Franz. "Luise Rinser." In *Deutsche Schriftsteller des 20.*

Jahrhunderts im Spiegel der Kritik. Stuttgart: Kröner, 1984.

Rinser, Luise. *Abenteuer der Tugend.* Frankfurt: Fischer Taschenbuch Verlag, 1979.

_____. *Im Dunkeln singen.* 1982-1985. Frankfurt: Fischer, 1985.

_____. *Mirjam.* Frankfurt: Fischer, 1983.

_____. "Redeentwurf zur Bundespräsidentenwahl am 23. Mai 1984." In *Luise Rinser. Materialien zu Leben und Werk.* Hrsg. Hans-Rüdiger Schwab. Frankfurt: Fischer Taschenbuch Verlag, 1986. 55-59.

_____. *Septembertag.* Frankfurt: Fischer, 1964.

Sturm, Vilma. "Weibliche Lebenskunde." In *Frankfurter Allgemeine Zeitung* (18. Januar 1958).

Weigel, Sigrid. "Luise Rinser." In *Kritisches Lexikon zur deutschsprachigen Gegenwartsliteratur.* Hrsg. Heinz Ludwig Arnold. München: Stand 1982.

Wilk, Werner. "Häresie und Unterwerfung." In *Neue Deutsche Hefte* 43 (1958): 1032-33.

Frauenkunst als Hexenkunst: Irmtraud Morgner und Heide Göttner-Abendroth

Uta Liebmann Schaub
University of Toledo

Das Phantastische und Magische erfreut sich neuer Beliebtheit in der internationalen Literatur der Gegenwart, entweder als gelegentliches Stilmittel oder als Strukturprinzip erzählender Prosa. Aber nur in der Literatur und Theorie von Frauen ist der Rückgriff auf archaische Magie und Mythologie zu einem Mittel geschlechtsspezifischer Selbstdarstellung und zu einer Kategorie feministischer Ästhetik geworden. Zwei interessante Beispiele sind die Erzählprosa von Irmtraud Morgner und die Theorie und erzieherische Praxis von Heide Göttner-Abendroth.

Diese beiden deutschen Schriftstellerinnen sind in den achziger Jahren einem breiteren Publikum bekanntgeworden: die 1933 in Chemnitz geborene und kurz nach Öffnung der deutsch-deutschen Grenzen viel zu früh verstorbene DDR-Autorin Morgner durch die Veröffentlichung ihrer Romane im west-deutschen Luchterhand Verlag; die 1941 in Thüringen geborene, aber in der BRD lebende Heide Göttner-Abendroth, nachdem sie ihren Lehrstuhl für Philosophie an der Universität München aufgegeben hatte und als freie Schriftstellerin ihre Arbeiten über das Matriarchat zu publizieren begann. Beide Autorinnen verwerten, wiewohl in verschiedener Absicht, Motive und Vorstellungen aus dem Umkreis älterer Matriarchatstheorien. Beide greifen außerdem auf eine Tradition zurück, in der Frauen als Hexen und Frauenbünde als Hexenverschwörungen oder “Coven” erscheinen. Beide etablieren damit einen subversiven Diskurs. Heide Göttner-Abendroth tat mit ihren Schriften zum Matriarchat ganz bewußt den Schritt aus dem akademisch anerkannten, offiziellen philosophischen Diskurs, den sie selbst während ihrer Lehrtätigkeit an der Universität durch vielbeachtete wissenschaftliche Arbeiten unterstützt und fortgeschrieben hatte, in die Marginalität eines Gegen-Diskurses, der dem offiziellen Diskurs als Ausdruck eines reduktionistischen, defizienten und dabei zugleich gefährlichen Wissens gilt. Nachdem sie zu Beginn der achziger Jahre in ihren Büchern *Die Göttin und ihr Heros* und *Die tanzende Göttin* eine Theorie des Matriarchats entwickelt hatte, gründete sie 1986 eine Schule für die praktische Anwendung ihres Programms. Dieses Institut und sein Programm nennen sich *Hagia: Akademie und Coven für kritische matriarchale Forschung und Erfahrung*. Das Zentrum dieser Frauen-Akademie ist ein Bauernhof in Bayern, wo Seminare, Mysterienspiele und andere rituelle Zeremonien stattfinden.

Irmtraud Morgners Hexendarstellungen sind integrale Bestandteile ihres poetischen Genres, des Romans und seiner Tradition, an die sie ausdrücklich anknüpfen. Innerhalb der DDR-Literatur allerdings waren auch sie ein Stein des Anstoßes. Der Appell von Morgners Protagonistin Laura an die philosophischen Sachwalter des offiziellen marxistischen Diskurses artikuliert die Forderung nach philosophischer Lebenshilfe "für Nichtfachleute," also nach einem anderen Diskurs als dem offiziellen (*Amanda* 123-24). Morgners Appell ist zwar nicht antimarxistisch, zeigt aber die Grenzen des marxistischen Diskurses auf. Göttner-Abendroth hat sich aus der westdeutschen Schulphilosophie freiwillig zurückgezogen. Morgner hat indessen versucht, auf die Schulphilosophie der DDR reformierend einzuwirken. Ihr Ausschluß aus diesem Diskurs und der Versuch, sie in die Marginalität abzudrängen, erfolgte gegen ihren Willen durch Erschwernisse bei der Drucklegung ihrer Bücher in der DDR (*Hexe* 79). Die Erzählsprache ihrer Romane wurde so auf andere Weise als die Theoriensprache Göttners zu einem Gegen-Diskurs.

Morgner hat ihrem Roman *Amanda* den Untertitel *Ein Hexenroman* gegeben. Eine Dichterlesung Morgners in Solothurn wurde 1986 unter dem Titel *Die Hexe im Landhaus* veröffentlicht. Aber auch ihr früherer Roman *Leben und Abenteuer der Trobadora Beatriz* sei, so sagt Morgner im Solothurner Gespräch, schon ein "Hexenroman" und die Trobadora Beatriz "eine Hexe" (*Hexe* 17). Der Roman *Amanda* stellt dann das Hexen-Thema in den Vordergrund.

Amanda ist die "hexische Hälfte" von Laura Amanda Salman. Laura Amanda Salman kommt 1933, im Geburtsjahr der Romanautorin Morgner, zur Welt. Daß die Laura-Handlung auch autobiographische Details verarbeitet, hat Morgner im Solothurner Gespräch bezeugt (*Hexe* 74, 82-87). Sie sind in die vielschichtige, phantastisch-pikareske Bildlichkeit des Romans eingefügt. Astrologische Voraussagen, eine fünffache Taufe, und die Erscheinung einer besenreitenden Zauberfrau Isebel, die der Großmutter eine Phiole mit Hexenbeschwörungselixir übergibt, zeigen die Geburt eines "weiblichen Querkopfs" an (*Amanda* 34). Das Querköpfige, Ketzerische ist das eigentlich "Hexische" an Laura Amanda. Im Solothurner Gespräch hat Morgner klar definiert: "Der Name des weiblichen Ketzers ist Hexe," und die Ketzerin ist immer zugleich "Grenzüberschreiterin" (*Hexe* 17; cf. auch 55-65). Auf Anpassung an Konventionen bedacht vernichtet die Großmutter die Phiole, aber Laura wird bald selbst nach Ersatz für das verlorene Elixir Isebels suchen. Einstweilen ist die Welt der

Wirklichkeit für das Kind Laura der "alltägliche" Faschismus, Krieg und Nachkrieg. Als junges Mädchen wird Laura Zeugin patriarchalischer Verhaltensstrukturen in klassenbewußten Proletarierfamilien. Als sie auf einem Fest einen Toast "auf die Mütter" ausbringen möchte, wird ihr das mit der Bemerkung eines Altsozialisten verwehrt, die Frau sei "das Hinterland des Soldaten" (*Amanda* 112). Empört beginnt Laura noch am selben Abend mit "alchemistischen Versuchen" (112). Das markiert ihre nun bewußte "Hexwerdung" (Kap. 34). Sie formuliert die Sentenz des chauvinistischen Genossen um und sagt stattdessen: "Die Insel ist das Hinterland der Frau." Die Insel ist hier zugleich Topos und Utopie eines ungefährdet ganzheitlichen Lebens der Frau. Die alchemistischen Experimente gelten zunächst der Suche nach dem Elixir, das es vermag, dahin zu entrücken und unteilbar oder wieder ungeteilt zu machen.

Indessen kann sich Laura Amanda ihre ganzheitliche Persönlichkeit bis in ihre Studentinnenzeit hinein bewahren. Zwar wirken Familie und Gesellschaft auf Anpassung und Emanzipationsverzicht hin, aber Widerstand ist einstweilen noch möglich. Unter den Männern, die sie kennenlernt, sind solche, die das Querköpfige an ihr lieben. Die Spaltung ihrer Person geschieht dann ganz plötzlich durch schwarze Magie: Vom Brocken, aus der hexisch-teuflischen Unterwelt, kommt der Oberteufel Kolbuk und schlägt Laura Amanda mit dem Richtschwert in zwei Teile (Kap. 37). Lauras hexische Hälfte Amanda, ihr *alter ego*, wird in den Hörselberg im Harz versetzt, in das Domizil der Hexen in der Nähe des Brockens. Der Vorgang der Teilung oder Persönlichkeitsspaltung läßt die gesellschaftlich angepaßte DDR-Bürgerin und Berliner Triebwagenfahrerin Laura Salman, Mutter des kleinen Sohnes Wesselin, in ihrer Alltagsexistenz zurück, eine Frau, die indessen ihre ursprüngliche Ganzheit nie völlig vergißt.

Individualpsychologische Deutungen dieser Persönlichkeits- spaltung scheinen sich anzubieten, werden aber dadurch ergänzt und entkräftet, daß Morgner auf gesellschaftliche Ursachen hinweist. Die Misere eines einzelnen Menschen ist bei Morgner immer auch hervorgerufen durch eine defiziente Gesellschaft, die den Einzelnen vernachlässigt und vergewaltigt. Das zeigt der Roman mit der Darstellung des Lebens und der Erfahrungen der alleinstehenden berufstätigen Mutter Laura Salman in der Wirklichkeit des DDR-Alltags. Es ist die Geschichte der modernen Frau in der patriarchalisch-technokratisch strukturierten Welt überhaupt, eine erschütternde Geschichte ständiger physisch-psychischer Überforderung. Bei der S-Bahn fährt Laura die Nachtschicht, um sich tags ihrem Sohn widmen zu können. Der Schlafrhythmus ist gestört, die nötige "Reproduktion der Arbeitskraft" wird immer schwerer. Laura nähert sich dem physisch-psychischen Zusammenbruch. Ihre alchemistischen Experimente dienen nun vor allem der Suche nach einem "Schlafersatzelixir" (135). Der Roman bleibt dabei trotzdem die Geschichte einer fortschrittlichen, in vernünftigen Grenzen anpassungsbereiten Frau, die sich aber von einer immer weiter sich verfremdenden Umwelt im Stich gelassen sieht. Den einzigen Rückhalt bilden Frauenfreundschaften aus dem Umkreis des hexisch-närrischen "Unsinnskollegiums" im Hugenottendom, einer Art von "Coven," von dem individuelle Hilfsaktionen ausgehen, die sogenannten "närrischen Dienste." Im Vordergrund der Kritik steht nun nicht mehr der individuelle Mann, der die Frauen unterdrückt, sondern ein historisch gewordenes System, dessen immer noch fortdauernde patriarchalische Struktur inzwischen nicht nur Frauen, sondern auch Männer und vor allem Kinder bedroht. Szientistischer Fanatismus erscheint als Fortsetzung männlicher Orientierung auf Kampf und Wettbewerb hin, der anhält, obwohl er Abgründen der Selbst- und Menschheitszerstörung entgegenführt. Über dem Fanatismus dieses Wettbewerbs ist ein anderes, das matriarchalische oder, wie Morgner lieber sagt, matristische Verhaltensmuster fast verloren gegangen: das Hegen des Gewachsenen und Gewordenen. Im Solothurner Gespräch hat Morgner diesen Verlust ganz offen als ein Defizit auch des Sozialismus angeprangert. Morgner setzt hier die zusätzliche unbezahlte Mehrarbeit der Frau mit dem Marxschen Mehrwert gleich und damit mit dem Erbübel der Ausbeutung, auf dessen Abschaffung sich sozialistische Staaten so viel zugute hielten. Staat und Gesellschaft insgesamt profitieren von der Doppelbelastung der Frau (*Hexe* 49-58). Morgner sagt damit, daß der ungleiche Profit aus dem Mehrwert noch keineswegs abgeschafft ist, sondern als Ausbeutung der Frau fortexistiert. Zum Kronzeugen beruft sie Marx selbst, der die gesellschaftliche Stellung der Frau zum Maßstab des gesamtgesellschaftlichen Fortschritts erhoben hatte (*Hexe* 90).

Aber die Flucht in eine magische Welt wird von Morgner nicht empfohlen. Die Erfolge der alchemistischen Versuche bleiben höchst zweifelhaft, und im Verlauf der Romanhandlung hat sich überdies gezeigt, daß die hexisch-teuflische Brockengesellschaft ein grelles Duplikat der Menschengesellschaft der Oberwelt ist. Die Unterwelt spiegelt, vielfach vergröbert, die geschlechtsbestimmte Ungleichheit und Hierarchie der Oberwelt. Dissidenz unter den Hexen wird vom Oberteufel streng geahndet. Er ist es ja auch, der die "unbrauchbaren" Hälften querdenkender Frauen in der Oberwelt abschneidet und einsammelt, um sie auf den Hörselberg zu verbannen. Er leistet damit den Mächten der Oberwelt Anpassungshilfe. Auch herrscht unter den Hexen selber keine

Solidarität. An ihren Fraktionskämpfen kritisiert Morgner einen Feminismus, der sich an männlichen Denk- und Kampfstrategien orientiert. Nach zwei magischen Rettungen Lauras durch Amanda ist es am Ende Laura, die der Hörselberg-Dissidentin Amanda im Brocken-Sperrgebiet zu Hilfe eilt.

In Morgners Verwirrspiel der Bedeutungen hat das Hexen-Thema eine doppelte Funktion: Die Hexe verkörpert den Traum einer Freiheit, Unangepaßtheit, Macht und Erotik, die dem reduzierten Alltagsleben der modernen Frau mangeln. Aber bei Morgner wird die Kehrseite mitgesehen. Das Hexische, Ketzerische ist nur in Ausbeutergesellschaften notwendig. Die wilden Walpurgisfeste sind, wie die römischen Saturnalien oder die Karnevalskultur des Mittelalters, nur eine ephemere, zeitlich begrenzte, offiziell sanktionierte Befreiung der extrem Unterdrückten. Ähnliches gilt von Jahrmärkten, Weinfesten, Mirakel- und Mysterienspielen. Für Morgner sind sie nur Ventile für ein Übermaß an Unterdrückung, angeordnet von den Machthabern zur Aufrechterhaltung der Unterdrückungsmechanismen (*Amanda* 414-15).

Ganz anders Heide Göttner-Abendroth. In ihrer Theorie sind magisch-ekstatische Tanzzeremonien und rituelle Mysterienspiele ästhetisch vollendete Gesamtkunstwerke der von ihr beschriebenen matriarchalen Kulturen. In der Praxis ihrer Arbeit mit Frauen im Rahmen der von ihr gegründeten Akademie bilden rituelle Tänze und Mysterienspiele die Schwerpunkte des erzieherischen Programms, das darauf abzielt, diejenigen Kräfte der Frauen neu zu aktivieren, die vom Patriarchat unterdrückt, disqualifiziert und geschwächt worden sind. In ihrem Buch *Die tanzende Göttin*, in dem sie *Prinzipien einer matriarchalen Ästhetik* entwickelt hat (und dem die folgende Dokumentation entnommen ist), fordert sie eine Frauenkunst der Gegenwart, die "Hexenkunst" sein soll (113-208). Es ist klar, daß hier ein archaischer Kunsttypus als Urbild und Präfiguration einer ganz neuen, feministischen Kunst der Gegenwart geltend gemacht wird. Diese Kunst ist ursprünglich Magie, die erst das sich etablierende Patriarchat als "Hexenkunst" verschrieen hat (70). Solche Kunst ist nicht eigentlich Kunst im traditionellen, also patriarchalischen Sinne, sondern sie ist direkter Lebensausdruck und kosmische Feier im Einklang mit den natürlichen Lebenszyklen des irdischen Jahres und mit den astronomischen Gegebenheiten. Der Mond, dem Göttner-Abendroth mit ihrem Neologismus "die Mondin" die ihm in mediterranen Kulturen eignende Weiblichkeit zurückgibt, spielt dabei eine besonders wichtige Rolle, weil sein Zyklus mit den Zyklen des Meeres und des weiblichen Körpers in anscheinend unabweislichem Zusammenhang steht. Mondtänze sind deshalb bei Göttner die Urform aller rituellen Ausdrucksformen. "Hexe" ist der Name, mit dem das Patriarchat die in ihrer matriarchalen Macht wunderbar starke, ungeteilte, der Natur nicht entfremdete Frau diskriminiert und kriminalisiert hat. Indem die moderne Frau diesen Namen annimmt, entwirft sie die Genealogie und zugleich die Strategie ihrer heutigen Situation.

Göttner unterscheidet zwischen einfachen und hochentwickelten matriarchalen Gesellschaften und ordnet ihnen mehr oder weniger hochentwickelte Formen der Ritualkunst zu. Mit ihrem Postulat der Geschichtlichkeit des Matriarchats setzt sie sich über die neuerlich wieder vorgetragene Kritik an diesem Postulat hinweg, wie z.B. über Uwe Wesels Abhandlung von 1980, *Der Mythos vom Matriarchat.* So wird denn auch den neun Musen der griechischen Mythologie bei Göttner ein Platz in der Geschichte des Matriarchats eingeräumt. Göttner denkt sie sich als Weiterentwicklung eines frühen "Priesterinnenkollegiums" und kann so zugleich allen Künsten und Wissenschaften, die ja von den Musen des griechischen Parnaß vertreten werden, matriarchalen Ursprung zuweisen. Noch älter ist die Verehrung der als Gottheit gedachten Mutter Erde oder Gaia, die auch in Morgners Mythologie-Exkursen vorkommt.

Die rituellen Feiern fanden nicht nur zu bestimmten Zeiten statt, vor allem während der Äquinoktien und der Sonnenwenden, sondern auch an bestimmten astronomisch genau bestimmten Plätzen. Stonehenge ist für Göttner das "herrlichste Exemplar" eines solchen Platzes (52), aber auch andere Reste von Megalith-Architekturen gelten als heilige Stätten matriarchaler Kulturen, und Göttners Hagia-Akademie bietet Gruppenreisen zu manchen dieser Stätten an.

Die Verdrängung des Matriarchats brachte dann, Göttner zufolge, durch Einsetzung des "Fiktionalitätsprinzips" eine vom Leben abgelöste, spezialisierte, patriarchalische Kunst hervor. Der rituelle Ernst der Mysterienspiele verkam zur Imitation, zur bloßen Schauspielerei (59). Aristoteles habe mit seiner *Poetik* an diesem Zerstörungswerk maßgeblich teilgenommen. Erst die Kunst des Patriarchats wurde Ware und Fetisch, an Objekte, Autoren, Rezipienten und an einen Kunstmarkt gebunden. Die neue feministische Kunst soll all dies nicht mehr sein. Sie soll wieder ganzheitliche Lebensform werden. In der unmittelbaren Zukunft, die noch im Zeichen des Patriarchats stehen wird, soll Frauenkunst als subversive "Gegenpraxis" wirken, nicht indem sie angreift, sondern indem sie sich dem Zugriff der patriarchalen Gesellschaft entzieht (88) und sich "Inseln" alternativen Lebens schafft (267). Der von Göttner-Abendroth gegründete Weghof in Bayern will eine solche Insel sein.

Englischsprachige feministische Zeitschriften haben inzwischen auch Leserinnen und Leser in den USA mit Göttners Matriarchatstheorien bekannt gemacht, so z.B. *Trivia.* In Westdeutschland ist die Auseinandersetzung schon älter, und dort wird sie vehement geführt. Das zeigt schon das umfangreiche Nachwort der Autorin zur erweiterten Neuauflage ihres Buches *Die tanzende Göttin.* Hier sucht Göttner sich gegen die Vorwürfe des Irrationalismus, des Okkultismus, des Neobiologismus und sogar des Neonazismus zu verteidigen.

Göttners Unternehmen ist sicherlich in größerer Nähe zur Alternativkultur der Lebensreform- und Jugendbewegung angesiedelt als zum linken Diskurs. Indessen hat auch dieser lange Zeit die Idee eines urgesellschaftlichen Matriarchats vertreten. Die Symbiose zwischen Marx und Bachofen geht bekanntlich auf Friedrich Engels' Diktum im *Ursprung der Familie* zurück, wonach die erste Klassenunterdrückung mit der des weiblichen Geschlechts durch das männliche zusammengefallen sei. Uwe Wesel gibt eine Darstellung der Zusammenhänge (26). Die westliche Linke hat dann mit Simone de Beauvoir (79) von dieser Hypothese Abschied genommen. Morgner greift, wie wir gesehen haben, die alte Marx-Engelssche These modifizierend wieder auf. Göttner-Abendroth andererseits stellt vorbehaltlos und mit programmatischer Absicht das Matriarchat an den Anfang aller Geschichte. Sie folgt damit einem schon etablierten, in der romantischen Tradition verankerten Geschichtsdenken, das eine ideale Urgemeinschaft als Präfiguration für eine zukünftige vollkommene Gesellschaft einsetzt. Was immer man von Göttners Thesen halten mag, die heftige Reaktion darauf hat das subversive Potential der Matriarchats-Idee von neuem aufgezeigt.

Die Strategien der Subversion sind verschieden. Göttner empfiehlt und praktiziert die aktive Verweigerung und inselhafte Absonderung gegenüber der etablierten Gesellschaft. Dies entspricht einer verbreiteten Tendenz innerhalb der westdeutschen Alternativkultur. Morgner andererseits wollte verfestigte Denk- und Handlungsmuster der sie umgebenden Gesellschaft von innen her aufbrechen, um sie zu reformieren und zu humanisieren. Ihre Idealfigur ist nicht der weibliche Eremit, sondern der weibliche Ketzer. Der Ketzer verwirft die offiziell für wahr gehaltene Lehre nicht, er hat vielmehr das bessere Wissen von ihr, das er gegen Verfälschungen zu verteidigen sucht. Dies wiederum entsprach dem Selbstverständnis vieler DDR-Schriftsteller. Morgner und Göttner-Abendroth erweisen sich so auch als Exponenten der jeweiligen Gesellschaften, die ihre Lebenswelt geprägt haben. Gemeinsam ist beiden Frauen die Erkenntnis und Ablehnung patriarchalischer Strukturen in ihren jeweiligen Gesellschaften, die Berufung auf archaische Mythen und Rituale und die Hoffnung auf Reproduktion einer originären weiblichen Verhaltensform, die im Verlauf von Millennien männlicher Hegemonie verschüttet worden ist. Wege und Ziele der reformerischen Anstrengungen dieser beiden Schriftstellerinnen sind indessen sehr verschieden. Sie repräsentieren zwei gegensätzliche Denktraditionen der Moderne, die auch die feministische Theorie mitbestimmen und mit denen diese sich fortwährend auseinanderzusetzen hat.

Works Cited

Beauvoir, Simone de. *The Second Sex.* Trans. H. M. Parshley. New York: Vintage Books, 1974.

Göttner-Abendroth, Heide. *Die Göttin und ihr Heros: Die matriarchalen Religionen in Mythos, Märchen und Dichtung.* München: Verlag Frauenoffensive, 1980.

_______. "Hagia: Academy and Coven for Matriarchal Research and Experience." Trans. Lise Weil. *Trivia* 10 (Spring 1987): 91-98.

_______. *Die tanzende Göttin: Prinzipien einer matriarchalen Ästhetik.* 3rd ed. München: Verlag Frauenoffensive, 1985.

_______. "Urania, Time and Space of the Stars: The Matriarchal Cosmos through the Lens of Modern Physics." Trans. Lise Weil. *Trivia* 10 (Spring 1987): 77-90.

_______, and Rosmarie Schmid-Adam. *Hagia: Akademie und Coven für kritische matriarchale Forschung und Erfahrung.* Winzer: Edition Hagia, 1987.

Morgner, Irmtraud. *Amanda: Ein Hexenroman.* Darmstadt: Luchterhand, 1984.

_______. *Die Hexe im Landhaus: Gespräch in Solothurn.* 2nd ed. Zürich: Rauhreif, 1986.

_______. *Leben und Abenteuer der Trobadora Beatriz nach Zeugnissen ihrer Spielfrau Laura.* Darmstadt: Luchterhand, 1977.

Wesel, Uwe. *Der Mythos vom Matriarchat.* Frankfurt: Suhrkamp, 1980.

Eulalia Galvarriato: una sombra de la posguerra

Concha Alborg
Saint Joseph's University

La situación olvidada —"entre sombras"— de Eulalia Galvarriato es singular dentro de la escena literaria de la posguerra y se debe, sobre todo, a que su carrera no haya seguido las tendencias de la época y a que su producción no haya sido publicada asiduamente. Nacida en 1905 en Madrid, hizo estudios universitarios, y estuvo casada con el insigne académico Dámaso Alonso con quien colaboró en obras sobre Góngora y San Juan de la Cruz.[1] Además ha hecho traducciones del inglés (los ensayos de Stevenson, entre otros) y se ha dedicado extensamente a la investigación de la obra de Lope de Vega, en particular sobre la figura de la mujer en su teatro. Aparte de su trabajo crítico, Galvarriato fue conocida durante los primeros años de la posguerra como "una cuentista importante" y sus cuentos, entre los que se destacan "Raíces bajo el agua" y "Final de jornada," aparecieron en revistas y antologías.[2] Recientemente ha publicado su provocativo libro, *Raíces bajo el tiempo*, demostrando, que a pesar de su aparente silencio, Galvarriato había continuado escribiendo por más de cuarenta años.[3]

Cinco sombras, la única novela de Eulalia Galvarriato, quedó finalista con dos votos para el premio Nadal de 1946 (que ganó José María Gironella por *Un hombre*). Uno de los miembros del jurado, Néstor Luján, la consideró "como auténtica narración artística, de una humanidad infinita, y como una obra a la vez delicada, trascendente. Es un libro acabado y exquisito; una novela inolvidable" (citado en Martínez Cachero 115). *Cinco sombras* recibió una crítica excelente con comentarios similares de figuras tan destacadas como Ricardo Gullón, José Luis Cano y Vicente Aleixandre entre otros; Eugenio G. de Nora la considera una novela "excepcional" que se acerca a "la perfección irreprochable."[4] Los críticos también están de acuerdo al comentar que, pese su calidad artística, esta novela no tuvo la aceptación del público ni de las historias literarias porque era marcadamente diferente, por su estilo poético, de las novelas tremendistas y neorrealistas que caracterizaron las tendencias literarias de esa época.[5]

Cinco sombras es una novela única no sólo cuando se la considera dentro de las tendencias de la posguerra —y dentro de la misma creación de Eulalia Galvarriato— sino al examinarla con respecto a la caracterización de sus figuras femeninas. Las otras novelistas españolas: Carmen Laforet, Ana María Matute, Carmen Martín Gaite, por mencionar sólo a unas pocas, retratan preferentemente a una mujer en estado de cambio que se enfrenta con un mundo contemporáneo, mientras que Eulalia Galvarriato capta, como en un daguerrotipo, una situación que pertenece más al siglo XIX que al nuestro.[6] Es de particular interés, por lo tanto, el aplicar algunas teorías de la crítica feminista para darle a la obra una perspectiva contemporánea.

De forma tradicional, *Cinco sombras* consta de treinta y tres capítulos sin numerar, narrados, salvo las cartas de Julia y el diario de Rosario, en primera persona por Diego. Es éste un hombre ya mayor que recuerda su vida con las cinco hermanas que titulan el libro. La novela comienza en la casa, precisamente en el cuarto, donde se encuentra el costurero de los cinco lados alrededor del cual cosían, y vivían, estas mujeres. Diego les cuenta su historia a Julia y Elvira, con su novio Juan, que van a tomar posesión de la antigua casa. Huérfanas de madre, las cinco hermanas vivieron, casi sin salir a la calle, con su padre hasta que el joven Diego llegó como amigo y tutor introduciendo algo más de libertad en sus rutinas diarias. La narración se va interrumpiendo conforme se presentan cada una de las tristes historias de las hermanas, creando la tensión narrativa y el suspense que forman la dinámica estructural.

El padre fue un hombre despótico con sus hijas, incapaz de comunicarse con ellas ni de demostrarles el más mínimo afecto; su actitud patriarcal y opresiva es la mayor causa de la tragedia de sus hijas. Cuando Diego entró en la casa por primera vez casi ni se las presentó, mientras que le mostró su pajarera como su "orgullo" (11), "lo mejor de mi casa" (12), "su tesoro" (17) y a pesar de la presencia de las cinco jovencitas consideraba a su familia como "una pobre casa sin mujer" (12). La caracterización del padre por Diego es negativa; le tacha de "extraño", "contradictorio" (17), "indiferente" (18), "obstinado y duro" (77), "terco", "caprichoso", "déspota" (87) o "adusto, serio, callado" (102). Diego le disculpa por el dolor que le causó la muerte de su amada esposa y, en efecto, el padre acabó en un estado de locura que le hizo culpar a las hijas por la muerte de la madre.

El comportamiento de las hijas frente a la autoridad del padre, al que temían y respetaban, fue el de acatar sus órdenes y someterse "como flores ante el huracán" (27). Solamente en lo que se refiere a la elección de esposo para sus hijas se puede ver el detrimento de sus acciones. Cuando María, la mayor, se enamoró de un hombre al que conoció en la iglesia, el padre prohibió las relaciones. Como consecuencia, María, amargada y triste, pasó el resto de su vida cuidando al padre, las hermanas e inclusive al narrador. El recuerdo de su enlace frustrado la marcó para siempre y por esta razón les dejó la casa a Julia y Elvira, las hijas de aquél, su único amor. Isabel, una de las mellizas menores, sospechando la oposición del padre, se fuga con su enamorado causando el castigo del resto de las hermanas que por un tiempo no pueden salir ni de sus propias habitaciones. Mientras tanto Rosario, enamorada de Diego, se niega a casarse con el hombre que su padre propone, a quien Laura acepta sacrificada sólo para morir en un accidente el mismo día de su boda. De manera que por falta de libertad, de cinco mujeres, ninguna consigue felicidad en el amor.

Rosario, en su diario, cuestiona la actitud del padre atribuyéndole la responsabilidad por la fuga de Isabel, aunque también llega a culparse a sí misma por la falta de cariño que han recibido: "¡Papá es más bueno! Somos nosotras las injustas con él. Nosotras tenemos la culpa de todo, porque somos muy poco cariñosas... ¡Si nos atreviéramos a entrar en el despacho y darle un beso! Es nuestra la culpa. El nos quiere, lo sé" (214). Ante esta situación de "mansedumbre y resignación," Carmen Martín Gaite concluye sobre *Cinco sombras [de mujer en torno a un costurero]* que "aunque la autora no haga ningún comentario explícito acerca de esta asunción del papel de víctima por parte de las chicas encerradas, está sin duda proponiéndola como espejo negativo de conducta, y toda la novela es como un grito de protesta, aunque amordazado, contra el personaje de su padre."[7] Sin haber consultado con Eulalia Galvarriato, mi interpretación hubiera sido la misma; pero en una entrevista que le hice en 1988, la autora indica que no tuvo intención de censurar la educación patriarcal, sino que considera que está retratando a una familia parecida a la suya propia.[8]

No cabe duda que Galvarriato es ella misma un producto del patriarcado y que esto se ve reflejado en su novela. Lo mismo se puede afirmar de sus opiniones sobre el feminismo, pese su excelente formación intelectual, cuando afirma que "la mejor realización de la mujer es casarse y cuidar de sus hijos." Galvarriato escribe una novela que no refleja las inquietudes de la mujer española de la posguerra y que por su temática, no por su fecha de publicación, es muy anterior al tipo de novela que podría considerarse "neo-feminista" bajo la definición de críticas como Ellen Morgan.[9] En esta novela de posible desarrollo o *Bildungsroman*, la mujer se establece "contra la cultura patriarcal y sus instituciones," pero las figuras femeninas sufren unas vidas frustradas sin llegar a su autenticidad. En otras palabras, "they grow down" en lugar de "growing up"; lo que la heroína aprende es que se paga cuando se va en contra de las normas de la sociedad.[10] Isabel, Laura y Rosario en *Cinco sombras* toman decisiones contra el padre, pero su destino en la novela es la soledad y la muerte. Lo más sorprendente es que Eulalia Galvarriato no considere sus vidas como trágicas, sino que vea natural que hubiera sido así.

Las imágenes de encerramiento abundan en la novela, sobre todo al relacionar a los queridos pájaros del padre con las hijas. La primera tarde que el narrador conoce a las hermanas, las describe con bellos símiles poéticos y su movimiento se asemeja al de los pájaros: "Cincuenta, cien pájaros de todos los colores, saltaban, volaban, pirueteaban, piaban de un lado para otro confundiéndose y barajándose ante mis ojos asombrados" (11). La reacción de Diego ante ambos, las jóvenes y los pájaros, es de admiración:

> Yo era hombre de ciudad. Mis pájaros habían sido, entre los libres, el gorrión, el tordo, el mirlo, la golondrina. . . . Y enjaulados, atormentados, perdida su primera esencia, canarios y jilgueros. Esto era distinto. Esto eran las flores hechas pájaro, o el pájaro flor... Mas la sorpresa de este nuevo encuentro no me hizo olvidar la maravilla del primero. (11-12)

Es irónico que Gabriela, una de las dos pequeñas y la de espíritu más libre, sea la que muere primero sin haber conocido el amor (ni frustrado siquiera). Ella es de las cinco, continuando la ironía, la que cuida de arreglar la pajarera: "Los pájaros la conocían y la acosaban por todas partes, y ella, después de terminada la limpieza, todas las tardes se estaba allí un ratito encerrada con ellos" (26). A menudo, Gabriela sacaba a un pajarillo de la jaula que jugaba por unos momentos felizmente en la habitación del costurero, aunque "después se dejaba conducir dócilmente otra vez a la jaula" (27).

Las demás hermanas también se caracterizan con imágenes de los pájaros; recuerda el narrador una ocasión en que baila con Laura: "sentí un instante contra mi pecho el agitado latir del corazón de Laura, y el mío se conmovió de angustia y ternura, como cuando se siente en la mano el asustado palpitar de un pájaro" (43). Y sobre la malograda relación entre la mayor y su novio afirma: "María era en sus manos, sin remedio, el pobre pajarillo fascinado" (59). Hasta en la muerte se identifican las hermanas con los pájaros; cuando fallece la última, aparece muerto también el único pajarillo que quedaba: "Así acabaron nuestros pájaros y así ellas, mis cinco amigas" (177).[11]
Hay otras imágenes de encierro que ayudan a crear el ambiente

asfixiante en que viven las hermanas: "Ellas nunca salían de casa, nunca salían más lejos de lo que está la iglesia donde asistían a misa" (41).[12] El narrador se siente lejos de las jóvenes porque "estaba aquella pared que me cortaba, casi dolorosamente, el extenderse de mis ojos" (33) y a la vez confirma: "Me dolía aquel encerramiento casi constante, roto únicamente por la salida a la iglesia" (45). También sufre por María porque conocía "las angustias de su corazón que se debatía impotente, como esos insectos atenazados por los extremos de sus cuerpos que hacen esfuerzos desesperados por escapar" (60). Rosario, enamorada de Diego y él de ella, aunque no se lo declaren, es un "pomo cerrado" (76), y como "un muro de hierro" (159), la gente son "cajas cerradas, mudas y ciegas" (121), y el padre es como "una estatua ciega" (169).

Contrastan estas imágenes con otras muchas sutilmente poéticas y de gran originalidad que se juntan creando el tono lírico de la novela —el elemento que la crítica tanto ha admirado. Las hermanas de niñas fueron "cinco larvitas de mujer" (99) con los pies "como polluelos recién nacidos" (80) que se convirtieron en un "palpitante ramillete" (18) de "flores perfectas" (76), o son "como notas diversas de una perfecta sinfonía" (99), o "lo mismo que un río sobre un lecho de yerba" (19). Mientras que su risa es "como una lluvia más, más brillante y más pura" (49) o "como cuentas de un collar roto" (80). Rosario, la favorita del narrador, está representada con imágenes de la naturaleza: "lo mismo que la tarde", "lo mismo que un campo bellísimo iluminado por el sol, recién lavado por la lluvia" (49), y "como un alma ... en una frágil concha" (167). Sus ojos son "como tímidos cervatillos, o como niños que recelan" o "como el sol entre niebla" (35).

También se utilizan las figuras visuales para describir a la madre que falleció cuando las niñas eran pequeñas. En una imagen que se repite —la de la madre bailando con el padre en el salón— sus faldas están "infladas como farolillos" (38, 102). Se ha destacado la ausencia de la figura materna en la novelística de la posguerra —en esto *Cinco sombras* sí sería típica de esa época—, como sucede en las obras de Carmen Laforet y Ana María Matute, por ejemplo.[13] La crítica feminista tiene interés en estudiar las relaciones madre-hija en la literatura; Cathy Davidson y E. M. Broner en su capítulo "Daughters of the Patriarchy" analizan a George Eliot y Jane Austen en cuyas novelas las protagonistas son huérfanas y no son madres tampoco y concluyen que se debe a que la sociedad patriarcal, donde la madre sigue las normas sociales, no provee modelos maternales positivos. La madre ausente, por otro lado se relaciona mitológicamente con la tradición patriarcal que separa a la madre de la hija en el mito de

Deméter y Perséfone que representa a la hija en la eterna búsqueda de la figura materna.

En *Cinco sombras*, en el diario de Rosario, con un punto de vista femenino, se puede observar la reacción de la hija frente la ausencia de la madre. Rosario, ya de niña, tuvo un presentimiento de su muerte "y sentía que vivir sin mamá sería morir; sería como ahogarse de pronto; como sentir en torno y para siempre la más profunda y negra oscuridad. Ya para siempre" (219). Y de mayor, aunque la vida continúa, se entristece de existir sin su madre. Los recuerdos alegres de su madre contrastan con la seriedad de su padre. La madre reía siempre alegremente, cantaba o tocaba el piano, invitaba a amigos para cenar, salía al jardín con sus hijas sentándose en el tronco de un roble "donde quedaba para siempre nuestra infancia..." (216). Rosario cuenta detalladamente en su diario el incidente de un miruello que se cayó del nido y de cómo su madre le encontró para cuidarle, pero ella, al revés del pájaro, echa de menos a su madre y de aquí que se pregunte: "¿Quién me daría consuelo? Nadie puede. Lo sé" (225).

También las otras hermanas recuerdan a la madre. Isabel se complace en recordar el atuendo del cabello de su madre, o la anécdota del anillo perdido en la playa o su favorita de los padres bailando que Catalina, la criada que también conoció a su señora, les contaba a las niñas (38). María en particular, es la que más se parecía a la madre; por ser la mayor (aunque sólo tenía trece años cuando murió), trató de hacer su papel con las más pequeñas e igual que ella había hecho les enseñaba a tocar el piano.

El costurero, regalo de la madre que las quería ver unidas y cosiendo, se convierte en un símbolo materno y aunque la madre no llegó a verlas de mayores, su deseo y sus valores pasaron a las hijas. La continuidad en el tiempo es un mensaje implícito en la novela puesto que el costurero perdura; el narrador le dice a Julia: "... las dos vidas, la de entonces, cuando las cinco se movían aquí, y la de ahora, cuando usted me escucha y las comprende, me parecen la misma" (145). Julia inclusive, un personaje enigmático que merece ser estudiado, es semejante en varios aspectos a las cinco hermanas.

La caracterización de Julia pertenece a uno de esos silencios en el texto o lo que Elaine Showalter ha llamado una historia "muda."[14] Su función de receptor del discurso de Diego pasa casi desapercibido (por eso los críticos no lo han destacado), pero a través de las cartas que escribe a su amiga Carmen, hermana de Juan (capítulos 11, 18 y 20), se pueden deducir rasgos de su carácter. Mayor que Elvira, con quien ha heredado la casa que fue de las hermanas, hace el papel de dueña.[15] Julia es una mujer solitaria que prefiere la soledad sobre la amistad de Pedro (un posible pretendiente) o salir con Elvira y Juan. Ella misma se considera una "solterona inútil" (66) y se sacrifica por los demás. Totalmente capturada por la historia de las cinco hermanas, se siente identificada con ellas y como ellas se contenta bordando frente al balcón en el cuarto del costurero.

De la historia que le cuenta Diego ella percibe "una tristeza apacible y dulce" (122) y se pregunta quién la recordará a ella de la misma manera (125). Cabe deducir que como María, Julia, aunque ya esté en pleno siglo XX, será la protectora del costurero y los valores tradicionales, patriarcales que representa. Su historia no sería menos triste, a pesar de su dulzura, por la estrechez de sus horizontes y lo limitado de sus posibilidades.

Notas

1 *Para la biografía de Góngora: documentos desconocidos* (Madrid: Gredos, 1962) y *La poesía de San Juan de la Cruz* (Madrid: Aguilar, 1946). Además de estas admitidas colaboraciones ha ayudado asiduamente a su esposo corrigiendo las pruebas de todas sus obras. En un trabajo extenso, en proceso, exploro la posibilidad de que la creación literaria de Galvarriato haya quedado relegada en parte por la evidente trascendencia de la obra de Dámaso Alonso.

2 Así la califica Andrew Debicki en su libro *Dámaso Alonso* (New York: Twayne, 1970), 22. "Raíces bajo el agua" apareció en *Clavileño* 21 (1953): 53-64; "Final de jornada" está incluído en *Antología de cuentistas españoles contemporáneos (1939-1958)* (Madrid: Gredos, 1959), 22-36. Ambos de estos cuentos, en especial este último, han sido corregidos extensamente, lo cual indica que su supuesto estilo tan espontáneo no deja de ser igualmente trabajado. Nótese que en los estudios más contemporáneos sobre el cuento no se incluye a Eulalia Galvarriato; por ejemplo Erna Brandenberger, *Estudios sobre el cuento español contemporáneo* (Madrid: Editora Nacional, 1973) y Merardo Fraile, ed., *Cuento español de posguerra* (Madrid: Cátedra, 1980).

3 (Barcelona: Destino, 1985). El libro consta de cinco partes: "Cuentos," "Momentos vividos," "Poemillas en prosa," "Sueños," y

"Recuerdos de viaje." Apartes de las reseñas en periódicos, la crítica más extensa de este libro ha sido la de Clara Janés, "*Raíces bajo el tiempo*, de Eulalia Galvarriato," *Insula* 472 (1986): 8. Véase además mi artículo "Eulalia Galvarriato cuentista," *Monographic Review/Revista Monográfica* 4 (1988): 278-86.

[4] Los comentarios de José Luis Cano y Vicente Aleixandre están recogidos junto al de Eugenio García de Nora en *La novela española contemporánea*, vol. III (1939-1967) (Madrid: Gredos, 1979), 206-08. El de Ricardo Gullón pertenece a la obra de Martínez Cachero.

[5] Estelle Irizarry en el estudio más reciente que existe de esta obra afirma: "... es probable que esa misma singularidad, que hizo que se destacara en su momento, fuera responsable también de su olvido, pues, con el tiempo, ciertos autores adquieren relieve con su producción sostenida, y las obras suelen clasificarse en promociones y tendencias. Hoy como entonces, *Cinco sombras* subsiste como algo 'distinto' y ciertamente notable" (48). In "*Cinco sombras* de Eulalia Galvarriato: una novela singular de la postguerra." *Novelistas Femeninas de la Postguerra*, editado por Janet W. Pérez (Madrid: José Porrúa, 1983): 47-56.

[6] Rosalina R. Rovira en su artículo "La función de la mujer en la literatura contemporánea española," *Explicación de Textos Literarios* 3.1 (1974): 21-24, desarrolla un tema parecido y, aunque no menciona a *Cinco sombras*, cita *La esfinge maragata* de Concha Espina como otro ejemplo donde la figura de la mujer sigue las tradiciones fielmente (21).

[7] Carmen Martín Gaite afirmó esto en una conferencia de tema feminista, "La chica rara," recogida con otras del mismo tema en su provocativo libro *Desde la ventana* (Madrid: Espasa Calpe, 1987), 103. Janet Pérez ha publicado "Portraits of the 'Femme Seule' by Laforet, Matute, Soriano, Martín Gaite, Galvarriato, Quiroga and Medio" en *Feminine Concern in Contemporary Spanish Fiction by Women*, eds. Roberto C. Manteiga, Carolyn Galerstein and Kathleen McNerney (Potomac, Maryland: Scripta Humanistica, 1988), 54-77, donde desarrolla el mismo tema de la figura patriarcal en esta obra.

[8] El 7 de enero 1988, entrevisté a Eulalia Galvarriato en Madrid. En esta entrevista habló explícitamente de su padre, que aunque no fuera tan estricto como el de la novela, fue un hombre tradicional y protector. En casa de Eulalia también había cinco hermanas, de las cuales ella es la tercera.

[9] En su artículo "Humanbecoming: Form and Focus in the Neo-Feminist Novel" en *Feminist Criticism: Essays on Theory, Poetry and Prose,* editado por Cheryl L. Brown y Karen Olson (Metuchen, New Jersey: The Scarecrow Press, 1978), 272-78.

[10] En las palabras de Ellen Morgan, "She is pitting herself against her patriarchal culture and its institutions," 272-3. Annis Pratt también usa la terminología de "growing down" frente a "growing up" en el capítulo 2 de su libro *Archetypal Patterns in Women's Fiction* (Bloomington: Indiana UP, 1981).

[11] Es de destacar además el simbolismo de la escena donde el padre, ya trastornado, cuando sólo vivía María, da la libertad a los pájaros que escapan atolondradamente "con ansia de vuelo, con avidez de espacio..." (173) y de todos sólo vuelve uno que permanece en la jaula. También el narrador se identifica con un pájaro cuando dice: "... mi paso era más lento y más pesado, como si hubiera perdido las alas" (166).

[12] El significado de este tipo de imágenes en la obra literaria femenina es muy significativo de acuerdo con el estudio de Sandra M. Gilbert y Susan Gubar, *The Madwoman in the Attic (The Writer and the Nineteenth-Century Literary Imagination)* (New Haven: Yale, 1984).

[13] Véase la página 127 del artículo de Margaret E. W. Jones, "Del compromiso al egoísmo: la metamorfosis de la protagonista en la novelística femenina de postguerra", en *Novelistas femeninas de la postguerra,* editado por Janet W. Pérez (Madrid: José Porrúa, 1983), 125-34. Eulalia Galvarriato dedica *Cinco sombras* a su madre y a su padre muerto, justo lo opuesto de la situación en la novela. Se debe notar que, por lo menos durante la entrevista, Galvarriato no mencionó a su madre, mientras que habló extensamente de su padre. Entonces, al no saber todavía la dirección que iba a tomar este estudio, no le hice preguntas directas ni sobre su padre ni sobre su madre. En sus "Momentos vividos" tampoco se la nombra; "Mi querida Petra" es la madre de Dámaso Alonso, o sea su suegra por quien sentía un gran cariño.

[14] Elaine Showalter destaca un "double-voiced discourse" que contiene un relato "dominante" y otro "mudo" o lo que Gilbert y Gubar llaman un palimpsesto en "Feminist Criticism in the Wilderness" en *The New Feminist Criticism* (New York: Pantheon, 1985): 266.

[15] Hasta cierto punto esta herencia es algo inexplicable, puesto que Isabel tuvo una hijita, llamada Gabriela también por la

otra melliza, que no vuelve a ser mencionada en la novela y que hubiera sido la legítima heredera.

Obras citadas

Alonso, Dámaso y Eulalia Galvarriato de Alonso. *Para la biografía de Góngora: documentos desconocidos.* Madrid: Gredos, 1962.

______. *La poesía de San Juan de la Cruz.* Madrid: Aguilar, 1946.

Brandenberger, Erna. *Estudios sobre el cuento español contemporáneo.* Madrid: Editora Nacional, 1973.

Debicki, Andrew. *Dámaso Alonso.* New York: Twayne, 1970.

Fraile, Medardo. *Cuento español de posguerra.* Madrid: Cátedra, 1986.

Galvarriato, Eulalia. *Cinco sombras.* Barcelona: Destino, 1967.

______. "Raíces bajo el agua." *Clavileño* 21 (1953): 53-64.

______. *Raíces bajo el tiempo.* Barcelona: Destino, 1985.

García Pavón, Francisco. *Antología de cuentistas españoles contemporáneos (1939-1958).* Madrid: Gredos, 1959.

Gilbert, Sandra, y Susan Gubar. *The Madwoman in the Attic (The Woman Writer and the Nineteenth-Century Literary Imagination).* New Haven: Yale UP, 1984.

Irizarry, Estelle. "*Cinco sombras* de Eulalia Galvarriato: una novela singular de la postguerra." *Novelistas femeninas de la postguerra española.* Ed. Janet W. Pérez. Madrid: José Porrúa, 1983. 47-56.

Janés, Clara. "*Raíces bajo el tiempo*, de Eulalia Galvarriato." *Insula* 472 (1986): 8.

Jones, Margaret E. W. "Del compromiso al egoísmo: la metamorfosis de la protagonista en la novelística femenina de postguerra." *Novelistas femeninas de la postguerra española.* Ed. Janet W. Pérez. Madrid: José Porrúa, 1983. 125-34.

The Lost Tradition: Mothers and Daughters in Literature. Eds. Cathy N. Davidson y E. M. Broner. New York: Frederick Ungar, 1980.

Martín Gaite, Carmen. *Desde la ventana.* Madrid: Espasa Calpe, 1987.

Martínez Cachero, José María. *Historia de la novela española entre 1936 y 1975.* Madrid: Castalia, 1979.

Morgan, Ellen. "Humanbecoming: Form and Focus in the Neo-Feminist Novel." *Feminist Criticism: Essays on Theory, Poetry and Prose.* Eds. Cheryl Brown y Karen Olson. Metuchen, New Jersey: Scarecrow Press, 1978. 273-78.

Nora, Eugenio García de. *La novela española contemporánea (1939-1967).* Madrid: Gredos, 1979.

Novelistas españolas de la postguerra española. Ed. Janet W. Pérez. Madrid: José Porrua, 1983.

Pérez, Janet. "Portraits of the 'Femme Seule' by Laforet, Matute, Soriano, Martín Gaite, Galvarriato, Quiroga and Medio." *Feminine Concerns in Contemporary Spanish Fiction by Women.* Eds. Roberto C. Manteiga, Carolyn Galerstein and Kathleen McNerney. Potomac, Maryland: Scripta Humanistica, 1988. 54-77.

______. "Spanish Women Writers and the Essay." *Siglo XX / 20th Century* 4.1-2 (winter 1987): 43-54.

Pratt, Annis. *Archetypal Patterns in Women's Fiction.* Bloomington: Indiana UP, 1981.

Rovira, Rosalina R. "La función de la mujer en la literatura contemporánea española." *Explicación de textos literarios* 3 (1974): 21-24.

Showalter, Elaine. "Feminist Criticism in the Wilderness." *The New Feminist Criticism.* New York: Pantheon, 1985, 243-70.

Los Cuentos de Colombine (novelas cortas)

Herlinda Charpentier Saitz
University of Massachusetts, Lowell

A pesar de que durante su vida Carmen de Burgos fue una escritora reconocida, sorprende la escasa atención que ha merecido entre los estudios de la literatura feminista contemporánea.[1] Un breve vistazo a los pocos juicios valorativos dedicados a su obra concuerdan en ponderar su preocupación por los problemas sociales y la causa del feminismo. Se destaca, entre ellos, el libro *Carmen de Burgos, defensora de la mujer*, de Elizabeth Starcevic (1976), que estudia la visión de la mujer española en cuatro de los cuentos de Carmen, subrayando el valor informativo y socialmente útil de su cuentística, sobre todo porque "ofrece la posibilidad de contemplar la condición de la mujer con sus problemas, frustaciones y anhelos, victorias o derrotas" (70, 72).

Al tratar de determinar el mérito de su creación desde el punto de vista literario, las opiniones son pocas y revelan pareceres contradictorios. Por ejemplo, aunque Carmen pertenece a la promoción de "El cuento semanal" (1907-1917)[2] y Sainz de Robles la reconoce dentro de ese grupo como "maestra de la técnica novelesca y cultivadora de un crudo realismo" (*Novela española*, 173),[3] según Nora sus narraciones ni por su forma ni por su contenido logran ser novelas consumadas. Nora documenta esta opinión señalando que en ellas es notable un esquematismo narrativo y la subordinación de los personajes, los problemas de la vida y el relato, a una ideología previa con una misión admonitoria y pedagógica frente al lector (2: 53). Suárez-Galbán Guerra, al referirse a sus novelas cortas "El hombre negro" y "Villa María," señala el esquematismo narrativo y la poca objetividad. Además, observa una tendencia a la estereotipación de los personajes sin lograr que éstos tengan una función de valor representativo, y la carencia de conclusiones convincentes. Sin embargo, para él, al leer a Carmen de Burgos se experimenta un encanto y una "inconfundible sensación de 'descubrimiento'" inexplicable que merecen ser escrutinizados más a fondo (7).

Estos juicios, aparentemente contradictorios, son significativos, ya que dentro de un contexto que tome en cuenta el ambiente literario en que se mueven los miembros de la promoción de "El cuento semanal," permiten ver que la narrativa de Carmen participa del espíritu de experimentación y las actitudes de libertad e independencia en materia de técnica y temática narrativas que le sirven de eje al grupo.[4] Es importante tener presente que por lo menos la narrativa de otro miembro de esta promoción, Ramón Gómez de la Serna, ha merecido crítica semejante a la de Carmen al punto que ha desorientado hasta a sus admiradores. Pero en su caso, sometidas sus narraciones breves a un estudio que se desvincula de las pautas convencionales, éstas han revelado de manera consistente una armonía entre forma y significado hasta entonces no sospechada.[5] Por consiguiente, con el fin de iniciar una reevaluación de la narrativa de Carmen de Burgos, intentamos un estudio exploratorio de los *Cuentos de Colombine (novelas cortas)* (1908).

Lo primero que llama la atención en este libro es el título. Al yuxtaponer "cuentos" y "novelas cortas" Carmen sugiere que las selecciones pueden ser tomadas indistintamente como cuentos o novelas cortas.[6] Dicho gesto denota la actitud antiacadémica de nuestra escritora. Además, corrobora su participación activa en un clima de experimentación y deseos de innovación literarias en que los creadores del momento adoptan como una de sus tácticas el empleo de los términos "cuento" y "novela" de modo intercambiable, para liberarse de las vallas que una definición restringida de los mismos les impondría (Saitz 19-26).

También en el título, al incluir el pseudónimo "Colombine," Carmen tácitamente sugiere el tenor de las narraciones en materia temática como uno en que la preocupación principal será la vida. Esta temática está a tono con la divisa de la promoción de "El cuento semanal" de hablar "en nombre de la Vida" y buscar en "la Vida" lo que ella "puede ofrecer no sólo de rigurosamente vital sino también de apasionamiento y ensoñación" (Sainz de Robles, *Novela española* 109). Dicho fin se deduce cuando en las palabras preliminares a la colección, quien firma Pierrot[7] describe a Carmen como una "Colombine" melancólica "que sabe de sufrir y de soñar" y "también de los disfraternos horizontes" que "ha puesto palabras a la pantomima de la vida" (v, vi). Carmen misma explica que en ella el pseudónimo implica el ser que tras vivir en el teatro del mundo una comedia cada vez más dramática, con la sensatez derivada del sufrimiento, se torna vidente y soñadora, y al escribir cuentos, canta sobre la vida, sacudiéndose a veces las desilusiones con el gesto aparentemente frívolo del encogimiento de hombros (*Al balcón* 95-99).[8]

Además de esta primera impresión, un estudio global de las dieciséis selecciones permite afirmar que las narraciones están regidas por un patrón temático constante. Este patrón pone en evidencia, como problema central de todas las piezas, la preocupación humana por la búsqueda de la felicidad con distintas alternativas, que en última instancia revelan una visión trágica y resignada de la vida. En dicho patrón, un personaje, hombre en cinco, mujer en nueve, y una pareja en dos,[9] aparecen alejados de su rutina y bajo la influencia de un ambiente que les permite liberarse de la norma que por lo general rige sus vidas. En ese ambiente, vive una experiencia y vivida ésta, vuelve al mundo de su vida diaria. El personaje se caracteriza por ser ambicioso, un ser que antepone la razón al sentimiento y el análisis a la credulidad. Con frecuencia, se trata de un artista o de un ser con alma de artista, a la vez egocéntrico, altruista, celoso de su amor propio, vanidoso y soñador.[10] En el transcurso de la experiencia el personaje entra en interdependencia con otro u otros, en la mayoría de los casos del sexo opuesto, un objeto (un ídolo), una idea (la búsqueda de un tesoro) o la muerte, que se convierten en agentes representativos de ideas o actitudes tocantes al mundo de lo afectivo. Se hace evidente que para lograr la felicidad el personaje o la pareja toma tres caminos: uno, el del éxito personal y el bienestar material, sometiendo a segundo plano la felicidad que promete el amor natural o "verdadero" ("Los que no vivieron"). Otro, el de la realización del amor, dejando que triunfe el sentimiento por diferentes caminos. Por ejemplo, acomodándose a una moral acomodaticia ("Por las ánimas"), o ateniéndose a una moral no codificada que une gracias a la "fuerza misteriosa" del amor "verdadero" y legítimo. O sea, aquél sancionado por la "Naturaleza" ("El último deseo" 140). Y el tercero, escapando al mundo de las ilusiones.

Con excepción de dos cuentos en que una pareja parece lograr la felicidad subyugándose a los designios de la naturaleza ("El tesoro," "Madre por hija"), la conclusión de los otros se reduce a una: la felicidad es inalcanzable. En el primer caso, si el pensamiento y la razón triunfan sobre los sentidos "la Naturaleza lanza su anatema contra los que resisten sus leyes" (123) y "el triunfo llega con la vejez y la impotencia" (158). Esta solución ocurre claramente en "Los que no vivieron," donde el personaje, después de muchos años, se da cuenta de cómo al haber querido asegurarse el éxito personal antes de casarse, pierde la oportunidad de ser feliz con la única mujer que había amado. Si el personaje escoge el segundo camino y obedece los mandatos de la naturaleza, ya sea siguiendo la convención o no, el veredicto no es más favorable. Si se sujeta a las normas establecidas, la moral acomodaticia acaba por destruir la fe necesaria para alimentar el amor, aun de maneras insospechadas. Por ejemplo, en un caso, los trucos empleados por una mujer, de decir que va a misa cuando se escapa para visitar al amante, hacen que el amante sospeche, y el lector también, de si las acciones paralelas practicadas por la esposa, sean una estratagema de la esposa para un amor ilícito o no ("Por las ánimas"). Si el personaje ama libre de prejuicios, sin someterse a la norma, el problema es de conciencia o revela la inexorabilidad de la vida frente a la fatalidad. El problema de conciencia lo ilustra un personaje femenino que representa a la mujer liberada, cuando llega a la conclusión de que a pesar de rechazar la idea de "la legalidad en el amor," "el deber, no a la luz de las leyes estúpidas, sino al resplandor de su conciencia," se impone ("El último deseo" 140). La inexorabilidad frente a la fatalidad esencial a la vida se expresa cuando la felicidad de una pareja se desvanece tras la muerte del hijo que los hacía feliz a los dos ("¡Ay del solo!"). En el tercer caso, si el personaje ama una ilusión, al tratar de convertir ésta en realidad, se da cuenta de que el ensueño es irrealizable y por lo tanto, la felicidad, imposible. Por ejemplo, en la narración "En pos del ensueño" un artista, enamorado por correspondencia, tras mucho debatir, decide conocer en persona a la amada y al descorrer "el velo de la quimera" (190), comprueba su imposibilidad de convivir con ella, ya que si por cartas le parece la mujer ideal—una mujer plena, en cuerpo y alma, a su vez afectuosa y culta,—la realidad no concuerda con lo que se había figurado.

Una vez revelada esta verdad de lo imposible de dar con la felicidad real o soñada, ya sea por medio de la razón o de los sentimientos afectivos, el personaje reacciona de distintas maneras. En unos casos muere, sobrecogido por un sentimiento de soledad ("¡Ay del solo!") o por voluntad propia, declarándose cobarde y vanidoso ante el sufrimiento de la vida y el efecto del paso del tiempo en el ser humano ("El último deseo"). Pero en la mayoría, se resigna a su suerte, recordando con nostalgia el pasado, amoldándose a vivir en un mundo que hace necesaria la práctica de una moral acomodaticia ("Aroma de pecado"), o revistiéndose de una actitud frívola en que la ligereza y la sonrisa son la careta puesta que oculta el dolor. Así, María, en "En la sima," al oscilar entre subyugar su integridad por amor o no, decide que se imponga la razón al amor y escoge "restañar con carcajadas la sangre de su corazón" y adoptar "el gesto supremo que condensaba ya toda su vida: el encogimiento de hombros" (307, 310) .

Con este patrón es evidente que Carmen ofrece su visión sobre el problema de la búsqueda de la felicidad en un plano inmediato—el del ser humano frente a las presiones sociales y morales y ante la soledad personal que acarrea la muerte o el abandono de seres queridos—tratando de buscar un equilibrio entre razón y mundo afectivo.

Pero otro aspecto que merece ser abordado es el desempeñado por la naturaleza como parte integral en este patrón, y que permite vislumbrar en las narraciones el germen de un planteamiento al problema de la búsqueda de la felicidad de un modo más trascendental. Si bien a veces el ambiente en que ocurre la experiencia es el de otra ciudad ("Aroma de pecado" o "El último deseo"), la parada del tranvía ("¡Ay del solo!"), el piso donde se ve a la amante a escondidas ("Por las ánimas") o el Real de Madrid, ("Historia de carnaval"), lo dominante de ese ambiente es que representa, para el personaje, un mundo que lo induce a sentirse liberado de las presiones de su diario vivir. En él, el personaje actúa de manera que deja aflorar sentimientos pocas veces exteriorizados por él. Con mucha insistencia, Carmen expresa que esto es posible gracias a la influencia liberadora de la "Naturaleza" (57, 76). Al tener que escoger entre sentimientos afectivos y razón, a pesar de que en última instancia el personaje se decide en catorce de los dieciséis casos por la razón en el momento clave que revela su descontento, se observa que su anhelo es por optar hacia el dejarse llevar por los sentimientos afectivos y esto ocurre, por ejemplo, cuando cae en éxtasis bajo la influencia liberadora ejercida por "verdes colinas, árboles gigantes meciendo su ramaje a la orilla del río" (85), la luz de la luna (44), el aroma agudo de hierbas aromáticas y flores (104), o un ambiente de carnaval (111).

Una vez superado ese momento, la narración se convierte en un caso ilustrativo para formular una verdad que se deriva de la experiencia vivida por el personaje. Y las alusiones hacia la naturaleza, que son claves para dar con esa verdad, son directas y la definen como elemento equilibrador y revelador "sin límites . . . donde plantas, insectos, animales u hombres" se confunden "con las piedras mismas, para demostrar que no hay nada inanimado en la creación, cuando todo se suma y se une al gran himno armónico del alma universal" (147; también, 278). Vista la naturaleza bajo este tenor, es evidente que para Carmen, la búsqueda de la felicidad adquiere también una dimensión más trascendental. Específicamente, la que tiene que ver con el problema innato al ser, del anhelo a la perfección, de por sí irrealizable, que trae como consecuencia la consciencia del ser dividido y la lucha por compensar dicho sentir (el de saberse dividido), tras el amor, a falta de la imposibilidad de volver a la unidad cósmica.[11] Dicho por Sor Angeles, una monja cuya sensatez "no está en los libros" sino que es "ciencia de vida adquirida"[12]:

> Cada amor satisfecho engendra el deseo de un nuevo amor ... en toda alma de hombre o de mujer existe siempre el vacío de una aspiración y el anhelo de algo entrevisto que no se realizará jamás... forma perfecta...

> visión indefinida... lo imposible... La concepción del amor es demasiado grande para llegar a materializarse... en todos los seres existe el germen de un amor imposible... de un sueño que no se realizó... que no se realizará jamás. ("Como flor de almendro" 169)

Si bien se puede afirmar que las narraciones presentan, de manera constante y dentro del patrón expuesto, como motivo central el problema humano de la búsqueda de la felicidad, también es posible afirmar que dicho patrón es paralelo al que sirve de base al creado por Ramón Gómez de la Serna para elaborar sus *novelle*. En ambos autores, el personaje presenta características similares; el personaje aparece en situaciones que lo alejan de su rutina y lo enfrentan a personajes del sexo opuesto u objetos que adquieren un valor representativo. En ambos casos, el papel desempeñado por la naturaleza en esos ambientes es de una importancia fundamental dentro del desenvolvimiento significativo de la narración. Y en ambos, también, el autor plantea el problema como uno que radica en la pugna por tener que escoger entre sentimientos afectivos y razón o sea, entre esferas que por naturaleza no se excluyen sino que son complementarias.

Esta ha sido una exploración del primer libro de "Colombine." Ahora es necesario continuar leyendo el resto de su obra para determinar si su narrativa puede verse como precursora o complementaria a la de Ramón Gómez de la Serna. Creemos conveniente seguir explorando, no sólo la relación de la obra de Carmen de Burgos con la de Ramón, sino también la de ella y la de Ramón con la de otros miembros de la promoción de "El cuento semanal," para ver hasta qué punto estos autores coinciden en técnica y tratamiento entre sí y con los demás miembros de la promoción de "El cuento semanal." Ante todo, para ver en qué consiste el sello propio de Carmen, y cuál es la fórmula estructural que sirve de pilar a su patrón temático. En fin, para considerar su obra dentro del marco total del panorama literario en que le tocó vivir.

Notas

[1] Hasta 1986 sólo se le encuentra en la bio-bibliografía dedicada al estudio de la literatura social creada por escritoras españolas de Carolyn Galerstein (52-54), a pesar de que Carmen le dedicó un ensayo a Gertrudis Gómez de Avellaneda, quien ha gozado de una atención prominente a raíz de la inquietud feminista. Después de presentada esta ponencia han aparecido: un

estudio de su más distinguida investigadora, Elizabeth Starcevic (*Spanish Women Writers*, 148-57); uno de quien escribe (*La escritora hispánica*, 169-79) y una valiosa introducción de Conceptión Núñez Rey (*La flor de la playa*, 9-78).

[2] Esta promoción, formada por alrededor de cincuenta y dos escritores jóvenes entre los cuales figuran autores tales como Ramón Pérez de Ayala, Gabriel Miró y Ramón Gómez de la Serna, todos mucho más jóvenes que Carmen, inicia un período de vitalidad literaria extraordinaria, da vigencia a la novela breve en España y hace que el pueblo español vuelva a leer literatura. De acuerdo con Benito Pérez Galdós, logra "el milagro de que el pueblo [español] se apasione por las novelas literarias" (Sáinz de Robles, *Antología* 1: 13-14).

[3] Sainz de Robles considera a Carmen, junto con Sofía Casanova, Concha Espina, Blanca de los Ríos y Emilia Pardo Bazán, como una de las cinco mujeres que alcanzan una justa y honorable categoría literaria entre 1875 y 1939 (*Novela española* 132).

[4] Carmen, por su espíritu progresista, como traductora hace accesible en España a los escritores innovadores franceses e ingleses, y nutre, a la par que participa, del espíritu de renovación propio de los escritores asociados con la promoción de "El cuento semanal."

[5] En el caso de Ramón, un estudio de sus novelas cortas, tomando como base un patrón común a la *novella* moderna, ha permitido explicar las características mencionadas como partes integrantes de un modo deliberado de narrar con fines estéticos y narrativos que se resumen así: el fin estético es el de crear un efecto de amplitud temática a partir de una forma de expresión compacta y breve. El fin temático es de una preocupación humana, e intenta estimular el despertar de la consciencia del ser humano hacia su propia fatalidad, para avivar la noción de lo que significa la vida en el lector (Saitz 47-78).

[6] Carmen sustenta esta interpretación del empleo intercambiable entre "cuento" y "novela" al yuxtaponer los dos términos en el título *Mis mejores cuentos (novelas breves)* (1923). Además, al emplear en el "Prólogo autógrafo" al libro, el término "novelas" para referirse a lo que el lector encontrará en el mismo dice: "Nunca pensé que me sería tan difícil elegir entre mis novelas. Existe un sentimiento casi maternal que nos hace amar las novelas como se ama a los hijos, aun conociendo sus defectos. Prefiero las obras

que forman este tomo porque son las que he sentido más íntimamente . . . " (5-6).

[7] Quien firma "Pierrot" ha sido identificado como José Francés (Núñez Rey, 23).

[8] Carmen dice que en su confidencia "Colombine" le ha revelado "toda la ingenuidad de su alma, toda su infelicidad y todo su gran deseo de grandeza dentro del desarreglo aparente de su vida" (*Al balcón* 99).

[9] El personaje es un hombre en "La muerte del recuerdo," "Por las ánimas," "El viejo ídolo," "Los que no vivieron," y "En pos del ensueño." Mujer en "Alma de artista," "¡Ay del solo!," "La incomprensible," "¡Triunfante!," "Historia de carnaval," "El último deseo," "Como flor de almendro," "Aroma de pecado," "En la sima." Una pareja en "Madre por hija" y "El tesoro."

[10] Según declara Carmen, ella misma, desengañada de la vida, es la escritora que "sueña, piensa y analiza" (*Al balcón* 96) y "En la sima," el eco autobiográfico se refleja en un personaje que encarna estas mismas características (*Cuentos* 276-77).

[11] Es preciso notar que la búsqueda de la felicidad, ausente a causa del sentimiento de soledad creado por la consciencia del ser dividido, es central en las *novelle* de Ramón Gómez de la Serna (Saitz 65, 66, 82, 101, 110).

[12] Aquí también hay un germen de lo que más tarde aparece en las *novelle* de Ramón como elemento esencial. En todas ellas, partiendo de un andamiaje simbólico que toma como base el rito a Dionisos, un agente narrativo, que es clave para vislumbrar verdades últimas, se caracteriza como dotado de la sensatez o experiencia adquirida, no en los libros, sino en la vida (Saitz 86-94; 149, 152). Es necesario añadir que aparte de las coincidencias expuestas en este estudio, Carmen emplea, esporádicamente, imágenes menádicas similares a las que aparecen en las narraciones de Ramón como punto de partida para sus imágenes simbólicas. Aunque mucho se ha escrito sobre la relación personal de estos dos escritores, es necesario explorar más hasta qué punto ella influyó en la formación creativa de Ramón.

Obras citadas

Burgos, Carmen de. *Al balcón.* Valencia: Sempere, [1911].

_____. *Cuentos de Colombine (novelas cortas).* Valencia: Sempere, 1908.

_____. *Mis mejores cuentos (novelas breves).* Madrid: Prensa popular, 1923.

Galerstein, Carolyn L., ed. *Women Writers of Spain. An Annotated Bio-Biographical Guide.* New York: Greenwood Press, 1986.

Nora, Eugenio de. *La novela española contemporánea (1927-1939).* 2a ed. 2 vols. Madrid: Gredos, 1968.

Núñez Rey, Conceptión. "Introducción." *La flor de la playa y otras novelas cortas.* Madrid: Castalia, 1989. 9-78.

Sainz de Robles, Federico Carlos. *La novela española en el siglo XX.* Madrid: Pegaso, 1957.

_____. *Antología de la novela corta.* 2 vols. Barcelona: Andorra, 1972.

Saitz, Herlinda Charpentier. *Las novelle de Ramón Gómez de la Serna.* London: Tamesis Books, 1990.

_____. "Carmen de Burgos-Seguí (Colombine), escritora española digna de ser recordada." *La escritora hispánica.* Actas del XIII Congreso de Literaturas Hispánicas. IUP, 1987. Florida: Eds. Universal, 1990. 169-79.

Stacevic, Elizabeth. *Carmen de Burgos. Defensora de la mujer.* Almería: Cajal, 1976.

_____. "Carmen de Burgos (Colombine) (1867-1932)." Eds. L. Gould Levine, E. Engelson Marson, G. Feiman Waldman. *Spanish Women Writers. A Bio-Bibliography Sourcebook.* Westford, Connecticut: Greenwood Press, 1993. 148-57.

Suárez-Galbán Guerra, Eugenio. "Nota de lectura. Sobre dos novelas cortas recuperadas de Carmen de Burgos." *Insula* 37.430 (septiembre 1982): 7.

El cuarto de atrás and the Role of Writing

Catherine G. Bellver
University of Nevada, Las Vegas

Why do writers write? Octavio Paz once said this is the only valid question. However, when asked why they write, writers are often elusive, incomplete, or flippant in their answers. For example, Samuel Johnson once said, "No man but a blockhead ever wrote except for money" (19). While most professional writers do not disparage financial gain, they usually point to other less material reasons for writing. María Zambrano, for one, maintains that "escribir es defender la soledad en que se está" (54). More recently a Spanish novelist stated that "he contestado a esta cuestión con una afirmación que sostenía Saroyan cuando le hacían esta pregunta: 'Mire usted, lo único que sé es que todo escritor ha sido un niño mentiroso'" (Sánchez Arnosi 10). Loneliness and the child's urge to tell stories also impel Carmen Martín Gaite to write; but when asked in an interview why she wrote, she avoided giving a complete answer, saying instead that writing for her was as natural as eating or breathing (Gautier 10). Despite her contention that writing for her is a spontaneous, unexplainable activity, in *El cuarto de atrás* she discloses the important reasons she took up the pen (Levine).

A multifaceted novel combining many narrative genres and modes, this critically acclaimed work is an excellent example of the metafiction that emerged in Spain in the seventies. The novel incorporates intertextual references to other literary genres—to the fantastic mode defined by Todorov and to sentimental romance novels. As it turns outward to other genres, this novel also turns inward to consider its own coming into being and to reflect upon the meaning of literature. In fact, Linda Gould Levine has seen *El cuarto de atrás* as "a portrait of the artist as woman," as an enumeration of the process of creation and a telling biography (162). In this "remarkable hybrid," as Joan Lipman Brown calls it (13), literature, the writer, and the act of writing converge.

As a child in Salamanca the narrator/protagonist of *El cuarto de atrás* enjoyed privacy and freedom in the spare room at the back of her home. In this large, cluttered, neglected room, the strictures of the adult world were superseded by the innocent pleasures of childhood; it was "un reino donde nada estaba prohibido . . . aquella holgura no nos la había discutido nadie, ni estaba sometida a unas leyes determinadas de aprovechamiento: el cuarto era nuestro y se acabó" (*El cuarto* 187). But this childhood oasis was destroyed during the Civil War when her parents converted it into a supply pantry to cope with wartime scarcities. Once expelled from her childhood paradise, the protagonist was obliged to confront the deprivation, destruction, and terror that define war and shape society. Too young to understand fully the implications of war or to deal with them as an adult, she resorted to the ways of a child to surmount these horrors. With the help of a school friend, she invented a fictitious island named Bergai where they took refuge from the fearful and limiting adult world. The urgency of war stimulated in her the ability to fantasize that would be channeled a little later toward literary creation. This connection between her island and literature and between them and evasion can be inferred from the author's combination, in an interview, of references to her "isla de Bergai" and her "primer esbozo literario" with a mention of her "deseo de aislarme, de evadirme de la realidad" (Gautier 10).

At an early age, the narrator/protagonist of *El cuarto de atrás* received an important exposure to literature from popular romance novels. The freedom, the emotion, and the adventure portrayed in these "novelas rosa" provided, in the words of Debra A. Castillo, "a safe transgression," a welcome escape from the submissiveness, self-sacrifice, and stoicism promoted by the Sección Femenina of Franco's Falangist party (820). At present, her feelings toward these romantic fantasies are mixed. As a mature writer, she rejects their stereotypes, stock solutions, and melodrama. Yet her attitude toward this traditional female literary form, as Elizabeth J. Ordóñez has shown, is "lovingly selective"; she subverts some of its more restrictive features while preserving its attractive aspects (176). As part of her most vivid recollections of the past, this feature of her youth cannot be completely eschewed nor denigrated. The sentimental fiction she read as a girl nurtured her adolescent need to dream and taught her to equate literature with escape.

First the need to escape the trauma of war and then the example of the "novela rosa" nurtured the inventive spirit that the child exercised in her original "cuarto de atrás." Her definition of evasion through daydreaming as "esa capacidad de invención que nos hace sentirnos a salvo de la muerte" (195) shows that what at first sight might seem to be a simple escape mechanism was actually a tool for self-preservation. The maturing young girl continually reforms her childhood hideaway in an unending search for a personal space, for "a room of her own," in which to work, grow, and dream. The line of evolution from "el cuarto de atrás" to the island of

Bergai and from there to literature follows the protagonist's development from child to adult and her aspirations from playful escape through creative evasion to self-affirmation. Literature, then, emerges as a sublimated version of the protaganist's "cuarto de atrás" with its comparable attributes of freedom, disorder, and joy.

Within the context of her personal experience, her first writing attempts were a natural consequence of the oral tales she and her school friend had invented earlier. Building on Derrida's theories, Castillo views Martín Gaite's effort to write memoirs as part of the fall into thought represented by the transition from the spoken to the written word and from creative to mechanical memory (817). Within this scheme Martín Gaite's evolution from spinner of childish yarns to the architect of adult tales would mark her fall into the sterile repetition Derrida equates with the written word. We nevertheless observe that there usually exists a line of succession between the two forms of communication. The gradual evolution from oral discourse to conscious, mediated writing in the life of the protagonist of *El cuarto de atrás* parallels on an individual level the literary development typical of social groups as they seek to affirm, interpret, and perpetuate themselves. This drive toward conscious self-realization becomes a particularly significant rebellious stance for a writer who, as a woman, was reared to embrace self-renunciation, subordination, and inactivity. Carmen Martín Gaite withdraws into the written word, her new "cuarto de atrás," but in her withdrawal, she assumes the active posture of creator and critic.

Despite the changes her creative work undergoes, Martín Gaite never loses the child's joyful talent to evade reality. The narrator of *El cuarto de atrás* makes clear her definition of literature as escape when she responds to her nocturnal visitor's question as to when she began to write by asking, "¿Quiere decir que a qué edad empecé a refugiarme?" (58). The child began to write to evade distressing, immediate circumstances while the adult would use writing as a vehicle for more comprehensive liberation. Early in life her exuberant, independent spirit fostered in her a lingering desire to run away; "me gustan mucho las fugas," she confesses to the gentleman in black. In her youth, "running off" carried with it an aura of adventure because transgression of social rules was an appealing rebellion in an era when even laughter was programmed by the state. As the narrator reasoned, if Don Quixote, Christ, and Santa Teresa could run away, "Yo pensaba que también podía ser heroico escaparse por gusto, sin más, por amor a la libertad y a la alegría . . . no a la alegría impuesta oficial y mesurada" (125). Her adult longings for freedom translate into a desire to dismantle through literature the very logic that supports human existence; "La literatura es un desafío a la lógica" (55), she says. Sharing more with dreams than with logical reality, literature tolerates the ambiguous, the ambivalent, and the incongruous. Not satisfied in *El cuarto de atrás* merely to take refuge from reality, Martín Gaite also attempts to distance herself from literature itself, or at least from its mimetic forms of historical account, realistic portrayal, and autobiography.

Much has already been written on Martín Gaite's flight to fantasy in *El cuarto de atrás.* For example, Robert C. Spires demonstrates that the fantastic mode resolves the conflict in the novel between orderly, historical narrative and the subjective essence of memories (142); and Brown shows that the fantastic makes easier the retrieval of perturbing, forgotten memories (19). Carmen Martín Gaite's early works coincided with the prevailing social novel of the "generación de medio siglo," but with her 1978 novel she eludes any vestiges of that outmoded approach to fiction. Reality and dream, past and present, fact and fiction unite; biography, theory, and social history coalesce; and the identities of character, narrator, and objects shift. As one critic states, she does not merely substitute reality with another system of a different content, she chooses to flee "toda determinación racional del mundo" (Navajas 18).

Literature for Martín Gaite is "un castillo de paredes de papel" (56) and to write, then, is to retreat into this make-believe refuge filled with surprises, pleasures, and endless possibilites for game playing and happy transformations. The ludic element, to be sure, permeates *El cuarto de atrás*, as Kathleen M. Glenn maintains, but in her retreat Martín Gaite does not remain idle, trapped, or oblivious of the outside world. On the contrary, from the vantage point of her magical castle she hurls her arrows at the world below, exposing and confronting social ills. Her gentleman caller tells her she must choose "entre perderse o defenderse"; she has chosen to defend herself. Long before she wrote *El cuarto de atrás*, in an article first published in 1966, Martín Gaite expressed her firm belief in the capacity of narration to transform "las vivencias demasiado efímeras." Narration, she says, makes them "durar en otro terreno y de otra manera . . . los episodios vividos, antes de ser guardados en el arca de la memoria . . . son sometidos . . . a un proceso de elaboración y recreación particular, donde, junto a lo ocurrido, raras veces se dejará de tener presente lo que estuvo a punto de ocurrir o lo que se había deseado que ocurriera" (*La búsqueda* 22-23). Therefore by writing, an author both prolongs the past and transforms experience.

In addition to wielding the transformative power of literature to retrieve and retell personal memories, by writing Martín Gaite also becomes an active, creating subject whose stance subverts the demands for silence and submission imposed on women by the Franco regime. Despite all her efforts to envelop her historical portrait of the thirties and forties and the particulars of her personal story in a veil of fantasy, she still writes a telling testimony of the spirit and times of her youth. The Franco years were a period of stagnation in which time itself seemed to cease to exist in "un mundo de anestesia," where the dictator was felt as "unigénito, indiscutible y omnipresente" (132). The crushing weight of the regime's oppression was particularly great for women, who had to endure not only the restrictions of an authoritarian government but also those of traditional womanhood. With the aid of the church, the schools, and the Sección Femenina, the government fabricated a distorted view of history, a patronizing vision of the state, and a rigid concept of womanhood based on a list of sanctioned virtues.

As recounted by Martín Gaite in *El cuarto de atrás*, women's sense of self was defined by banal, inane tasks: "hacer la señal de la cruz sobre la frente de nuestros hijos, ventilar un cuarto, aprovechar los recortes de cartulina y de carne, quitar manchas, tejer bufandas y lavar visillos" (96). Intellectual growth in women was condemned; as one of her mother's friends told her, "Mujer que sabe latín no puede tener buen fin" (93). Her travel was restricted; her activities were monitored; and her destiny was prescribed. The personal story told in the novel provides a case study of the restrictions, stagnation, and emptiness that plagued a whole generation of Spanish women. Franco kept his stronghold on the national consciousness, but women did not forfeit all their imagination. According to Martín Gaite, romance novels and the songs of Conchita Piquer were available to them as possible avenues of release. Nevertheless, the fact that Martín Gaite resumed writing the day of Franco's funeral attests to her sense of renewal upon his disappearance. The instructions in "proper" behavior she received in her youth engendered in her a distrust for the resolute and a longing for disorder. As she says, "Bajo el machaconeo de aquella propaganda ñoña y optimista de los años cuarenta, se perfiló mi desconfianza hacia los seres decididos y seguros, crecieron mis ansias de libertad y se afianzó la alianza con el desorden" (96). Franco's death allows her longings for freedom to be brought to fruition. The cluttered, disorganized apartment that serves as the setting for her novel stands as a symbolic revolt against domestic order. But her reaction against order in *El cuarto de atrás* goes beyond this private gesture of protest and the exposure of Francoist authoritarian tactics to include a formal ambivalence that dismantles the conventions separating literary genres and reducing innovation. Above all, she undermines, through personal example, the very foundations of the literary and the social establishment that fixes women's role as subordinate. Asserting herself as a creative being, Carmen Martín Gaite challenges the concept of women perpetuated not only by the Franco regime but by all patriarchal cultures. Through the act of writing she subverts and reshapes reality; she exposes the oppression of women and she expropriates the male prerogative to fashion his ideal Other and to place himself at the center of the universe.

Julia Kristeva tells us that the writer is both actor and author, the active speaking participant in a text and the ultimate owner of a literary product (44-45). This activity and authority, over the centuries, have endowed the author with a sense of power, mastery, and superiority, characteristics deemed inappropriate or unattainable for women. As Sandra M. Gilbert and Susan Gubar have stated, because the pen represents autonomy, writing implies subjectivity and announces assertion, qualities that defy the archetypical male portrait of submissive woman enshrined in domesticity (19). Thus by writing her memoirs, Carmen Martín Gaite in *El cuarto de atrás* challenges the traditional concept of women, transcends the silence to which they have been condemned, and establishes herself as the center of her created universe. Literature, the haven where she took refuge from the world, becomes a workroom where she metaphorically erects her own literary edifice, she openly probes the crevices of her psyche, and she literally reshapes her social world.

By committing to paper her protest against the Franco regime, she enters that arena of public debate long considered masculine domain and inserts herself into the core of her contemporary literary world. The partition of the world along sexual lines, with the home designated as woman's proper "place" and "outer" space reserved for men, is so old and so ingrained on the collective consciousness that, as Elizabeth Janeway states, it continues to produce an "illusion of inevitability and revealed truth" (7). Martín Gaite disregards these rules of exclusion from male, outer space, perhaps because of her own attitude or because the circumstances of her university years allowed her to be an active participant in the group of writers who would shape Spanish literature in the 1960s. At any rate, she dares to intrude in a territory unfamiliar to most of her gender. It is this element of intrusion, of invasion into someone else's private space, that makes writing an act of aggression.

El cuarto de atrás definitively established Martín Gaite's literary presence in Spain and in the sphere of Hispanic letters elsewhere. The novel won the Premio Nacional de Literatura, beginning for its author a period of national recognition that has continued through her acquisition of the Príncipe de Asturias prize in 1988. Published in 1983 by Columbia University Press under the title *The Back Room*, the novel is one of the relatively few works of contemporary Spanish literature available in translation. The intriguing complexities of *El cuarto de atrás* have made it a subject of numerous articles as evidenced by its predominance among the essays included in *From Fiction to Metafiction: Essays in Honor of Carmen Martín-Gaite*. Following the success of *El cuarto de atrás*, Martín Gaite has been invited more than ever before by American hispanists to speak at conventions and lecture at universities. The secrecy with which she composed her first writing attempts has been left far behind. What is more, she has inscribed within the repertoire of the cultured public the experiences and the popular romance fiction that have shaped reality for many women.[1]

Because the associations of the pen with masterly execution, creativity, and generative literary power have led men to consider writing a male prerogative, women who write have been forced to redefine themselves. Gilbert and Gubar maintain that the anxiety caused by their difference profoundly marks women's writing with a sense of self-doubt, inadequacy, and expressed or feigned inferiority (Ch. 2). Linda Huf observes that when portrayed as an artist, the female hero is a divided self torn not only, as are male artists, between life and art, but also between her role as woman, demanding selfless devotion to others, and her aspirations as an artist, requiring exclusive commitment to work (5). Martín Gaite, however, both rejects feminism and disavows any notion of limit imposed by gender on her right to create, confidently affirming that "Para escribir basta con un cuaderno y un bolígrafo" (Villán 23) or "A mí personalmente nunca me ha parecido un desdoro ni ser una mujer ni haber recibido la mayor parte de mi instrucción de los discursos y estudios elaborados por los hombres" (*Desde* 16).[2] Nevertheless the issue she makes of her need to evade reality suggests a subconscious participation in the alienation generally felt by women in the "outside," male world. Unlike the nineteenth-century writers Gilbert and Gubar studied, Martín Gaite has no doubt she is entitled to freedom; but she still exercises her right in seclusion. In her childhood, it was in a literal room, not unlike the physical space removed from demands of household work and financial responsibility that Virginia Woolf recommended. Later it was in literature, her ultimate "room of her own," where haven was slowly substituted by transcendence, transcendence of reality and the self.

The duality of escape and self-affirmation, of evasion and transcendence announced in the novel's title converge in her third reason for writing: to find the perfect interlocutor. Withdrawing from reality and transcending the capacities of literature merely to chronicle reality, Martín Gaite takes advantage of the freedom available to the writer to restructure the world and to invent her ideal, attentive listener. Openly expressing her perennial desire, in one article appropriately entitled "La búsqueda de interlocutor," she affirms that "se escribe y siempre se ha escrito desde una experimentada incomunicación y al encuentro de un oyente utópico" (28). Many of her narratives contain moments of intense, meaningful conversation. Her novel *Retahílas* prefigures *El cuarto de atrás* in having its narrative scheme follow the nightlong conversation between a forty-five-year-old woman and her twenty-year-old nephew as they await the death of her grandmother in an adjacent room. In *El cuarto de atrás* the narrator reveals that she and her childhood friend invented handsome storybook men to assuage their adolescent romantic cravings and to quell their war-induced fears. In that magical "castillo de paredes de papel" she identifies with literature, Martín Gaite finds a tall, dark, and mysterious companion willing to accommodate her need for conversation and self-exploration. The adult woman's invention transcends the implications of the child's game-playing to include a comprehensive reversal of the patriarchal conception of the Other.[3] The male-generated Other is a subordinate, docile and passive being disposed to dominion. And the magical castle, traditionally serving to imprison a beautiful princess, symbolizes male desire to dominate. Martín Gaite, however, imprisons no one; her night visitor comes and goes freely. Although displaying some of the traits of the Jungian *animus*, his strength is not particularly evident and his protectiveness is transitory.

He resembles more closely the figure and relationship Evelyne Sullerot discovered female storytellers have evolved over centuries of writings as a counterimage to male rape fantasies. She singles out particularly the female-authored "Bluebird" story, in which a young prince transforms himself into a bird in order to visit his beloved at the window of her dungeon cell (5). Martín Gaite removes the element of romance from her fantasy, but she conjures up basically the same accommodating listener Sullerot found.[4] Martín Gaite's gentleman in black does not return on successive nights, but his visit is nocturnal; his present form is the result most likely of a mysterious metamorphosis; and she, though not trapped, is enclosed within her home and perhaps within a dream.

Her visitor is no more autonomous than a male-generated Other. Although his subordination to his creating subject is not demanded as a moral obligation nor justified as a "natural" fulfillment of destiny, his very existence depends on the narrator—her past experiences, her fears, and her present desires. His definite identity is never established, but all the possibilities are projections of the protagonist herself: he is a character from a *novela rosa* she invented; he is the incarnation of her ideal interlocutor; or perhaps he is only a manifestation of the fear provoked by the cockroach that startles her at the beginning of the novel.[5] Whoever he is, he is only a product of her imagination, a creation designed by the strokes of her pen.

Just as her initial intention to escape reality through literature unwittingly evolves into a direct confrontation with that reality, so her desire to create an ideal listener is only partially realized. The very temporal limits of literature Martín Gaite attempts to transcend through flashback and fusion terminate her conversation with the mysterious man in black; all good conversations, like all good novels, must unfortunately come to an end. Only through repetition of the writing act can she resume the cycle that begins with evasion and communication and ends in reality and silence. The close of the novel hints at a possible return to the dream state of literature as she slowly falls asleep again after having awakened to find beside her the stack of pages produced in her previous ambiguous level of consciousness.

Carmen Martín Gaite wrings out the fatalistic element from the notion "life is a dream," leaving instead "to dream is to live." For her, dreaming is synonymous with the evasion only storytelling provides. As a child she had already discerned in the act of reading a pleasurable, secret retreat, as she documents in *El cuento de nunca acabar* (197-202), but it would be as an adult writer that she would elaborate upon these early experiences. "Un desafío a la lógica," "un castillo de paredes de papel," "un refugio"—all definitions of literature proposed in *El cuarto de atrás* —attest to her enduring faith in its liberating magical powers. However, as shown earlier, evasion does not mean idle retreat. On the contrary, exploiting the qualities of challenge ("desafío"), difference ("castillo"), and distance ("refugio") available in literature, she actively confronts, reshapes, and transcends reality. As Martín Gaite explains, narration is alluring because it is an act of creation: "Cuando vivimos, las cosas nos pasan; pero cuando contamos, las hacemos pasar; y es precisamente en ese llevar las riendas el propio sujeto donde radica la esencia de toda narración, su atractivo y también su naturaleza heterogénea de los acontecimientos o emociones a que alude" (*Búsqueda* 22). Because narration is communicated to the listener through the linguistic medium, language is the bridge in the equation dream=life. Continuing the syllogism, she equates living and the use of language: "vivir es disponer de la palabra, recuperarla, cuando se detiene su curso se interrumpe la vida y se instala la muerte" (*Retahílas* 87). Her conclusion coincides with that of one of her preferred authors: Todorov, who identifies narration with life and the absence of narration with death (74). Todorov goes on to observe that "man is only a narration"; but Martín Gaite suppresses restricting adverbs, celebrating instead existential affirmation. Carmen Martín Gaite writes for three reasons: to evade reality, to criticize society, and to find companionship; but in the last analysis she writes to live.

Notes

[1] The prevailing tendency to equate male experience with universals and to consider the female perspective as a deviation from the norm has made even female readers hesitate to accept the female experience as valid fictional material. One might speculate that the process of familiarization undertaken by Martín Gaite, along with a growing number of other female novelists, can, in part, account for the discrepancy between Olga Prjevalinsky Ferrer's 1962 derisive description of *Entre visillos* and John W. Kronik's 1983 more generous appraisal of the same book.

[2] A contradiction exists between Carmen Martín Gaite's open rejection of feminism as a social movement or as a source of personal significance, on the one hand, and her implicit practice of feminist discourse and criticism, on the other, not only in her novels but also in *Desde la ventana*, her collection of reflections on several Spanish women authors. Here she says of feminist criticism, "no me convence mucho," but then engages in it in her discussions from a feminine perspective.

[3] Julian Paley suggested earlier that one might interpret the narrator/protagonist's night caller as Other or alter ego.

[4] Ruth El Saffar maintains that Carmen Martín Gaite excludes romance from *El cuarto de atrás* because she perceives courtship and marriage as tending to destroy communication (189). It must be noted in addition that because of its focus on childhood, the novel excludes other significant aspects of the author's life including motherhood and her university years.

[5] Debra A. Castillo (819) offers a comprehensive list of the

numerous interpretations that have been given to the mysterious man in black by critics including Kathleen M. Glenn, Linda Gould Levine, Elizabeth J. Ordóñez, Julian Palley, Ruth El Saffar, Mirella d'Ambrosio Servodidio, Aleida Anselma Rodríguez, and Jean Alsina.

Works Cited

Boswell's Life of Johnson. Ed. G. B. Hill. Revised by L. F. Powell. Oxford: Clarendon Press, 1934. Vol. 3. April 5, 1776.

Brown, Joan Lipman. "A Fantastic Memoir: Technique and History in *El cuarto de atrás*." *Anales de la Literatura Española Contemporánea* 6 (1981): 13-20.

Castillo, Debra A. "Never-Ending Story: Carmen Martín Gaite's *The Back Room*." *PMLA* 102 (1987): 814-28.

El Saffar, Ruth. "Liberation and the Labyrinth: A Study of the Works of Carmen Martín Gaite." *From Fiction to Metafiction: Essays in Honor of Carmen Martín-Gaite*. Ed. Mirella Servodidio and Marcia L. Welles. Lincoln, Nebraska: Society of Spanish and Spanish-American Studies, 1983. 185-96.

Ferrer, Olga Prjevalinsky. "Las novelistas españolas de hoy." *Cuadernos Americanos* 20.118 (1962): 211-23.

Gautier, Marie-Lise Gazarian. "Conversación con Carmen Martín Gaite en Nueva York." *Insula* 36.411 (febrero 1981): 1, 10-11.

Gilbert, Sandra M. and Susan Gubar. *The Madwoman in the Attic*. New Haven: Yale UP, 1979.

Glenn, Kathleen M. "*El cuarto de atrás*: Literature as *juego* and the Self-Reflexive Text." *From Fiction to Metafiction: Essays in Honor of Carmen Martín-Gaite*. Ed. Mirella Servodidio and Marcia L. Welles. Lincoln, Nebraska: Society of Spanish and Spanish-American Studies, 1983. 149-59.

Huf, Linda. *A Portrait of the Artist as a Young Woman. The Writer as Heroine in American Fiction*. New York: Frederick Ungar, 1983.

Janeway, Elizabeth. *Man's World, Woman's Place: A Study in Social*

Mythology. New York: William Morrow, 1971.

Kristeva, Julia. *Desire in Language. A Semiotic Approach to Literature and Art.* Ed. Leon S. Roudiez. Trans. Thomas Gora, Alice Jardine, and Leon S. Roudiez. New York: Columbia UP, 1980.

Kronik, John W. "A Splice of Life: Carmen Martín Gaite's *Entre visillos.*" *From Fiction to Metafiction: Essays in Honor of Carmen Martín-Gaite.* Eds. Mirella Servodidio and Marcia L. Welles. Lincoln, Nebraska: Society of Spanish and Spanish-American Studies, 1983. 49-60.

Levine, Linda Gould. "Carmen Martín Gaite's *El cuarto de atrás*: A Portrait of the Artist as Woman." *From Fiction to Metafiction: Essays in Honor of Carmen Martín-Gaite.* Ed. Mirella Servodidio and Marcia L. Welles. Lincoln, Nebraska: Society of Spanish and Spanish-American Studies, 1983. 161-72.

Martín Gaite, Carmen. *La búsqueda de interlocutor y otras búsquedas.* Barcelona: Destino, 1982.

______. *El cuento de nunca acabar.* Madrid: Trieste, 1983.

______. *El cuarto de atrás.* Barcelona: Destino, 1978.

______. *Desde la ventana.* Madrid: Espasa-Calpe, 1987.

______. *Retahílas.* Barcelona: Destino, 1974.

Navajas, Gonzalo. "Retórica de la novela a través del vehículo de la imaginación postmodernista española." *Siglo XX/20th Century* 4 (1986-87): 16-26.

Ordóñez, Elizabeth J. "Reading, Telling and the Text of Carmen Martín Gaite's *El cuarto de atrás.*" *From Fiction to Metafiction: Essays in Honor of Carmen Martín-Gaite.* Ed. Mirella Servodidio and Marcia L. Welles. Lincoln, Nebraska: Society of Spanish and Spanish-American Studies, 1983. 173-84.

Palley, Julian. "El interlocutor soñado de *El cuarto de atrás* de Carmen Martín Gaite." *Insula* 25.404-405 (julio-agosto 1980): 22.

Sánchez Arnosi, Milagros. "Juan García Hortelano, entre la realidad y el deseo." *Insula* 42.491 (octubre 1987): 10-11.

Spires, Robert C. "Intertextuality in *El cuarto de atrás.*" *From Fiction to Metafiction: Essays in Honor of Carmen Martín-Gaite.* Ed. Mirella Servodidio and Marcia L. Welles. Lincoln, Nebraska: Society of Spanish and Spanish-American Studies, 1983. 139-48.

Sullerot, Evelyne. *Women on Love. Eight Centuries of Feminine Writing.* Trans. Helen R. Lane. Garden City, NY: Doubleday, 1979.

Todorov, Tzvetan. *The Poetics of Prose.* Trans. Richard Howard. Ithaca, NY: Cornell UP, 1977.

Villán, Javier. "Carmen Martín Gaite, habitando el tiempo." *La Estafeta Literaria* 549 (1 octubre 1974): 21-23.

Zambrano, María. "Por qué se escribe." *Revista de Occidente,* No. 32 (junio 1934). Rpt. in *Anthropos*, Suplemento, 70-71.2 (marzo-abril 1987): 54-57.

An Ecofeminist Reading of Cristina Lacasa's *Ramas de la esperanza*

Barbara Dale May
University of Oregon

Several years ago, when I began shifting the focus of my teaching away from the male canon, I became accustomed to my students' amazement that, yes, there *are* women writers in Spain and, yes, they *are* writing about women's lives, women's issues. Recently, when I used Cristina Lacasa's *Ramas de la esperanza: poemas ecológicos* in a course on modern poetry it was not so much the writer's gender or her female perspective that startled my students, but, rather, the fact that here was a Spaniard writing about ecology. More disturbing than the attitude of superiority that sparked this reaction was the tendency to label Lacasa's work "more universal"—because of its subject matter—than other, more openly feminist works studied in the same course.

Why did Lacasa's *poemas ecológicos* seem to reveal, at least to me, a feminist, not just a female or feminine perspective regarding nature and civilization's relationship to it? I would find the answer to this question in the poems themselves and with the aid of an invaluable work outside of Spanish letters.

At the same time that I find myself working to expand the literary horizon for my students I am engaged as well in a personal struggle to free myself of that terrible tunnel vision that seems to afflict the majority of Hispanists. Since so many of our professors were men and since nearly all of the literature *they* taught *us* was, after all, Peninsular (with the emphasis on insular) male literature, it isn't surprising that some of us are only now catching up on that core reading list familiar to our conscious colleagues in English departments and Women's Studies programs around the country.

One item on that list which surely will be a necessary piece of equipment for those of us who plan to teach literature of the 21st century is Susan Griffin's wonderful book *Woman and Nature: the Roaring Inside Her* which enriched my re-reading of Lacasa, now as an eco-feminist, and inspired the writing of this paper. Asked to deliver a lecture on women and ecology, Griffin began to think through some of the ideas that would eventually lead her to write *Woman and Nature.* She was concerned that the ecological movement had often placed the burden for solving its problems on women, and in her lecture she noted that women are, traditionally, always being asked to clean up. To this she added the observation that men consider women to be more material than themselves, or more a part of nature. "The fact that man does not consider himself a part of nature, but indeed considers himself superior to matter," writes Griffin, "seemed to me to gain significance when placed against man's attitude that woman is both inferior to him and closer to nature" (xv).

Noting that patriarchal thought, also referred to as the thought of civilized man, claims to be objective and separated from emotion, detached, bodiless, Griffin examines the effect of that logic on material beings, drawing a dramatic analogy between man's relationship to the earth and his relationship to woman. Using familiar male metaphors, she writes: "He has pierced the veiling mountains, ridden the rivers, spanned the valley, measured the gorge: he has discovered" (48). And, further:

> He clears the land of trees, brush, weed. The land is brought under his control; he has turned waste into a garden. Into her soil he places his plow. He labors, he plants, he sows. By the sweat of his brow, he makes her yield.... Whatever she brings forth he calls his own. (53)

Griffin's imitation of the "objective," patriarchal voice is impersonal, disembodied, a parody, but not a distortion of male judgments about the nature of matter and the nature of woman.

Although it is unlikely that Lacasa is familiar with Griffin's work, she is well aware of the male objectification of nature and the female in her poetry. In a number of poems the persona of the poet is aligned with nature in a defensive position against an aggressive and male-identified civilization. In the first poem of the collection, Lacasa underscores the urgency of nature's plight:

> Una ballena perseguida, un bosque en llamas,
> la secuencia de un ala y un disparo,
> el persistente embargo de las olas
> por buques que supuran negros códigos...
> (Lacasa 9),

and states her position as a committed writer:

> Presto todos mis índices sonoros,
> mis documentaciones de desarme,
> mis materiales de dulzura y huesos.

Recurro a mi minúscula parcela cultivable,
a mis zumos de letras combinadas,
a los derrames de la luz que absorbo.
Tomo mi corazón, su sangre alerta,
y los suelto a racimos por los aires.
Es todo lo que tengo
para intentar vencer comandos de sarcomas.
(Lacasa 9)

Like Griffin, Lacasa exposes the consequences of a patriarchal system of exploration and exploitation and its dubious underpinning of "objectivity." In "Explosión nuclear" she mocks the same Freudian assertions parodied by Griffin in *Woman and Nature*. Far from the grand and tragic struggle between and powerful (and masculine) forces of Love/Eros and Death/ Thanatos, nuclear war is exposed as the last hand in an absurd, man-made game.

No es un magma-equilibrio, Eros y Tánatos,
rescatando provincias de su imperio.
Es un fin sin retorno;
atroz juego del hombre apostando
en el odio. (Lacasa 25)

At stake in this game is nature, life itself, which, not infrequently in Lacasa's poems, is described as pleading for mercy or fleeing from the violence of civilization:

La perdiz pide treguas de tomillo
en patético acorde con la voz del coral;
el aire prisonero se desangra
en la demanda de amnistía
y, en forzoso holocasto, la espiga cae, clamando
por un régimen luz de justicia ecológica.
Todo un bosque de adioses concentra su amargura
en la noche de gas y de cemento. (21)

In many of the poems collected in *Ramas de la esperanza*, the aggressor is male; the victim/sacrifice, female. Although most of the poems were written in the late 1970s and early 1980s, one striking expression of Lacasa's early concern for the destruction of nature and a dramatic example of this "atroz juego del hombre" is a poem written in 1960, entitled "Los árboles talados" and dedicated to a stand of plantains cleared for a roadway in Lérida. While the trees are indeed trees, they are at the same time, mother, martyr, home, holocaust:

> Os han hecho a pedazos, a rodajas
> (¿y con destino a qué entremés
> gigantesco?) Y estabais preparando
> maternalmente vuestros tiernos vástagos
> para la primavera, cuando todo
> se dispone a vivir y por los cauces
> transitan nuevas aguas, otros peces
> y las cuerdas del sol desata el día.
> Mártires del ensanche, habéis caído
> como los inocentes caen siempre
> en las tupidas trampas, con los brazos
> desnudos de defensa...
> La civilización os sacrifica.
> Y se han quedado sin hogar los pájaros. (18-19)

Both writers, Griffin and Lacasa, each in her own way, express horror at the separations demanded by patriarchal logic: of mind from emotion; body from soul; civilization from nature. Each rejects the male dream to map, chart, conquer, exploit. Each questions the fundamental purpose of patriarchal knowledge: to name, to tame, to possess. In *Woman and Nature*, Griffin sketches, from the ornithologist's own journal, an image of John James Audubon stalking an eagle to its nest in a magnolia, patiently observing its behavior, then shooting it, piercing its body with wires, stuffing the dead bird, propping it up in a lifelike position, creating, writes Griffin with bitter irony:

> an effect whose grace and naturalness were later said to have rivaled life. . . Finally he would capture the eagle on paper. . . He was meticulous and painted with great accuracy even every barb on every feather, so great was his love for his subject. And, in this way, he preserved the birds of America. (113-14)

Lacasa, in the same way, is well aware of the irony of destroying nature, ostensibly in order to preserve it. Her birds, nature's dispossessed, now encased in museums, are presented as non-images, in that living birds, themselves never described, are recorded only as an absence. In "Pájaros sólo en los museos" they are

> Alas fósiles, trinos disecados
> en Museos de Ciencias Naturales,
> los pájaros son tema prehistórico,

vuelos y melodías inmolados. (30)

Lacasa consistently represents her landscapes as female forms, vital and vulnerable spaces connected with the natural elements. Rivers are curious, playful children, unseparated from the earth that both gives them shape and is shaped by them. To the river Segre, she writes:

Francia, útero fértil, te alumbra
entre montañas,
te abriga su placenta cuando trémulo y tierno
buscas cauces vitales.
Y los hallas, intrépido alpinista.... (84)

Cityscapes, on the other hand, are represented as the deformed issue of civilization and its builders. In a brief, biting series of verses entitled "El aire aherrojado," the air is

Pálido espectro... [que]
no consigue dar vida a las ventanas.
Y es un monstruo ciego la ciudad,
sin un remoto aroma de tomillo. (49)

And in "Explotación del suelo urbano" Lacasa again points an accusatory finger at those responsible, the men who have designed the destruction around her:

Pérfidos arquitectos de lo oscuro,
decapitando olivos, siembran muros.
Prostituido el suelo alumbra monstruos. (47)

Ramas de la esperanza is a brilliant collection of poems of rage and despair in which the writer examines man's tradition of exploiting nature and brutalizing its inhabitants. Like Griffin, she sees nuclear madness as the end result of his "atroz juego del hombre." But both women, as they view with horror the chaotic consequences of male-defined "objectivity," speak of revolution and hope. Each demands rejection of the patriarchal vision of separation, hierarchy, black/white, top/bottom, splittings.

"Even if over our bodies they have transformed this earth, we say, the truth is, to this day, women still dream," writes Griffin (175). The dream in *Woman and Nature* takes woman down through a labyrinth, through a room of dressing—filled with male-designed images of woman—through another room of undressing, into darkness, into

> the shape of a cave, the bud, the chrysalis, the shell, what new form we seek in this darkness, our hands feeling these walls, here wet, here damp, here crumbling away; our hands searching for signs in this rock, certain now in this darkness, what we seek is here . . . what we have drawn here gleams back at us from the walls of the cave, telling us what is, now, and who we have become. This round cavern, motion turned back on itself, the follower becomes the followed, moon in the sky, the edge becoming the center, what is buried emerges, light dying over the water, what is unearthed is stunning, the one we were seeking, turning with the ways of this earth, is ourselves. (160)

Griffin's inner space becomes an internal landscape,

> where we go into darkness. Where we embrace darkness. Where we lie close to darkness, breathe when darkness breathes and find darkness inside ourselves. The room of the darkness of women. Where we are not afraid. Where joy is just under the surface. Where we laugh . . . where revelation fills us with glee. (157)

Lacasa's inward journey, unlike Griffin's, is not expressed as movement through the cave, but rather as a flowing movement through a river. In a number of poems the image of returning, going back, in order to move forward, is expressed through a liquid rather than linear movement. In "Alcanadre," a poem dedicated to her cousin Cristina Campo Lacasa, she floats through time and memory, carried along by the river Alcanadre:

> Tú llegas con esquilas
> a la provincia más oriental de mi alma.
> Tu casta biografía de anacoreta y nube
> es una fiel paloma mensajera
> transportando el legado del recuerdo....
> Me muestras tu cintura en el congosto,
> tu sinuosa cadera circundada
> de hipótesis de trigos,
> y aprendo de tu voz canción y risa...
> la ausencia de cautela, la pauta del almendro. (80)

The poet's movement through/with/in the water becomes, much like Griffin's journey through the cave, a freeing and at the same time, bonding experience with nature:

tú eres el verano sin borrones,
la muralla abatida, el sol sin grietas
escapando de jaulas, grises dientes
que abarrotan espacios en invierno.
El tomillo tenaz, el baño más radiante,
el olvido de aristas y de ácidos desplomes;
la estrella de agua que me habló del mar
antes de que la ola se acercara
a mi oído en clamor de caracolas. (80)

Lacasa's book is not without its occasional disappointment for the radical reader aligned with Griffin's re-vision of the world through re-discovery of the nature of woman, our nature, and the nature of nature. Reading Griffin is much like reading the essays of other radical activists like Mary Daly or Sonia Johnson, and one is always reminded of the old saying that "only those who risk going too far can possibly find how far they can go." At times Lacasa holds back when she should let go in these poems, give flight instead of perch. But one poem stands out among those collected in *Ramas*, and that is "Campo de espliego" in which the central image is of a woman absorbed in a field of lavender.

Nunca vi ese transporte de carretas jardín
y hoy, que acerqué mi vida a este cáliz agreste,
me encontré con mi alma.
Recuperé el sentido, reposté en la amplitud
y me llamé a mí misma
hasta obtener respuesta. (107)

The experience of the woman takes on a sacred, spiritual meaning with Lacasa's use of language. "Espliego," is, after all, the "alhucema" used as incense in religious celebration for fragrance and purification. The "cáliz" likewise refers to the calyx of the flower, its association with the female gender and, of course, the sacred chalice. Linking woman's inner space, both physical and spiritual, to a holy celebration of the earth, here seen in the asylum and renewal represented by the field of lavender, Lacasa identifies the rebirth of the female identity with a healing of the split between self and the natural world.

. . . En espiral
las sílabas brotaban, señalándome.
Era mi nombre, dulcemente amargo,
quien me asumía, íntegra.

Se me había olvidado en los naufragios
de tanta burocracia y armamentos.
Reíntegrada a mi nombre, a sus cristales vivos,
identidad si herida no negada,
en virtud del espliego y sus señales. (107)

To posit that Lacasa envisions precisely the same return to the female that Griffin articulates so lyrically would be absurd. But there is a common thread here, very conscious and politicized in Griffin, less clear in Lacasa. Each requires a restoration of the female self as a necessary rehabilitation of nature, an erasure of the wounding separations imposed by patriarchy and healing of the inner space.

In a cryptic little poem entitled "La luna" Lacasa envisions the moon as a kind of warrior woman:

Legendaria amazona de la noche
la luna se declara en rebeldía
ante el acoso de banderas; pide
libertad de expresión y de sufragio. (111)

And what does the moon, this legendary Amazon, demand? A voice. A vote. A new way.

What Griffin and Lacasa are urging is that we rethink the contours of our inner space and the external ecology that, like us, reflects the deforming consequences of patriarchal exploitation, that we survey the cancerous construction around us that separates us from this earth. That we act to redirect the path of humanity.

Works Cited

Griffin, Susan. *Woman and Nature: the Roaring Inside Her.* New York: Pantheon, 1978.

Lacasa, Cristina. *Ramas de la esperanza: poemas ecológicos.* Lérida: Dilagro, 1984.

Metafiction as a Subversive Device in Rosa Montero's *Te trataré como a una reina*

Mary C. Harges
Southwest Missouri State University

Metafiction has been defined as a type of narrative that consciously and systematically focuses on certain aspects of its own creation by examining the relationship between reality and fantasy (Waugh 3). This tendency emerges particularly during periods of social and cultural exploration and reform (Spires 128). The metanovel written by several post-Civil-War Spanish women writers exposes the patriarchal myths perpetuated by the conventions of mass culture and attempts to provide an alternate discourse from a female perspective. More than a mere reflection of reality, these novels often intend to change reality by employing subversive strategies to deconstruct male paradigms.

Rosa Montero's use of the metafictional mode as a subversive device is characteristic of many of her contemporaries' conscious rebellion against male-dominated fiction. The metafictional nature of Montero's writing is perhaps best seen in her third novel, *Te trataré como a una reina* (1983), where she combines the literary with a number of modes of discourse which represent various versions of reality. At issue here is *which* reality is being constructed, by *whom*, and *how* these representations are structured so as to produce a particular reading of the text.

Te trataré como a una reina differs from Montero's other novels in that the characters are not middle-class professionals but working-class outcasts living on the margin of society. A grotesque parody of the images of male-dominated society, the third person extended flashback deals with alienation, power arrangements, and the limitations on and the devastation of women's lives in a phallocentric culture.

Bella, Vanessa, and Antonia have constructed romantic fantasies in order to escape their miserable realities. They are exploited, abused, and virtually destroyed by the men they trust. The principal male characters, Antonio, Poco, and Damián, are dominated by their insecurities and egotism. Involved in a perpetual struggle to gain power, they manipulate and deceive the women in their lives. In spite of the violence they experience, the female protagonists are unable to extract themselves from their debilitating situations.

The novel is framed by a magazine article from *El criminal* and the transcriptions of interviews regarding the attempted murder of Antonio, Antonia's older brother who is a government clerk, by Bella, a singer at a rundown nightclub in the red-light district of Madrid. In contrast to the male point of view revealed by the opening document and interviews, the main body of the narrative provides a collective female perspective on the same events during the months preceding the crime.

A review of the novel suggests that the documents inserted throughout the text would better serve the novel had their "objective" accounts been incorporated directly into the main body of the text (Suñén 5). The documents assert a male value system and underscore traditional male authority to create, read, and interpret. I propose that it is precisely the juxtaposition of the masculine and feminine discourse that exposes the distortions of mass culture and subverts the stereotypes generated by patriarchal society.

The opening article written by Paco Mancebo offers a detailed account of a violent attack on Don Antonio Ortiz, beaten and thrown out of the fourth story window of his home at 17 Reina Street, by Isabel López. The appellative irony is clear from the journalist's one-sided story. Mancebo does not draw the line which customarily separates a journalist's personal opinions from his professional responsibility to accurately report the facts. Instead he seizes the opportunity to exercise male authority to determine who is the victim and who is the criminal. He describes Bella as "la bestial homicida", "la mujerona" "sin principios morales" (10), "la asesina fumadora" and "la sanguinaria mujerzuela" (11). Portraying her as a monster overtaken by "un rapto de locura" (10), Mancebo makes no attempt to disguise his own verdict.

In contrast, Mancebo describes Antonio as "la víctima" and "el desdichado" (11). It gradually becomes obvious that none of Mancebo's characterizations is accurate. Through his account of the attack, which represents the struggle as a role reversal, Montero ironically subverts the myth of the female as the weaker sex: "La susodicha era más alta y mucho más corpulenta que el infortunado, de modo que le podía, lo que demuestra que no siempre el sexo débil es el débil" (10).

Mancebo is further discredited by his admission that he has been unsuccessful in locating Vanessa, Antonio's fiance who is in the hospital, and his failure to contact Bella or Antonia. Mancebo's interviews with Menéndez, Benigno, and Antonio are interspersed throughout the text, each one corroborating his opinions. The fact that his questions are not included in the transcriptions, but must be surmised from the responses, undermines Mancebo's authority to interpret the reality of the crime.

Vicente Menéndez, the owner of El Desiré and Bella's boss, is a selfish, unambitious man. He spends his time devouring pornographic magazines that he hides beneath the cover of *Los tres mosqueteros*, which he has been "reading" for seven years. With the bar on the verge of financial ruin, Menéndez lives in a constant state of anxiety. In order to distance himself from the potential problems of being associated with Bella he denies any friendship: "Nunca me gustó la acusada, nunca me gustó" (94), explaining: "Manteníamos una simple relación profesional. Bella era una mujer ... grosera. Esa es la palabra. Poco educada. Muy respondona. Una verdulera" (94). By denigrating Bella, using adjectives that might more appropriately describe himself, Menéndez is able to bolster his own ailing ego.

Speculating about the motive behind the attack: "a mí me parece que si hizo lo que hizo debió ser por una cuestión ... de cama, a ver si usted me entiende" (95), Menéndez assumes a complicity between himself and Mancebo. He adds self-righteously: "ésas son cosas que pasan cuando... Cuando no llevas una vida muy decente, usted ya me entiende. Por celos, lo hizo por celos, estoy seguro" (95). The double standard evident in Menéndez' discourse exemplifies the male point of view about promiscuity revealed throughout the novel.

The interview with Antonio takes place in the hospital four months after the attack and begins with his pleas for pity: "Se me saltan las lágrimas. ¿Se da cuenta? Déjeme en paz. No quiero hablar de esto. Me hace daño. Tengo los nervios hechos cisco" (237). He pretends to protest the invasion of his privacy when, in fact, attention is precisely what he wants: "Me ha destrozado, y todos ustedes aquí, hurgando en la herida, como buitres" (239). Echoing Mancebo's description of Bella: "bestia," "monstruo," "energúmena" (238) and underscoring Menéndez' assessment of her motives, Antonio surmises that she simply could not tolerate the idea of his impending marriage to Vanessa. He accepts no responsibility for what he calls her "ilusiones injustificadas" (238), adding in his customary pejorative tone: "Las mujeres siempre son así, muy posesivas, irracionales" (238). He maintains that while she is certainly irrational, she is definitely not crazy.

Robbed of his precious sense of smell, Antonio is forced abruptly into the role of a dependent woman: "Es una mutilación. ¿entiende? Es una castración... Mi olfato era mi don, mi arte, mi razón de ser, mi vida... Sin mi nariz no soy nada, no soy nadie" (239). The destruction of his nose, an obvious phallic symbol, results in the total loss of his masculinity.

The interview with Benigno, a lonely thirty-six-year-old bachelor and Antonio's secretary, is another example of the misrepresentation of those involved in the crime. He exaggerates both the importance of his position and his relationship with Antonio: "yo era su más íntimo colaborador" (201). The falsity of Benigno's statement reduces the credibility of his testimony since the reader is keenly aware of Antonio's bitter hatred for Benigno. The subversive potential of his name is rather obvious. Although he is not a vindictive man, Benigno's negligent distortions of Antonio's character are potentially harmful to Bella's case and in the end only serve to perpetuate a value system which ultimately benefits those in positions of power.

Perhaps the most dynamic example of fiction within this fiction is the boleros the protagonist sings. Their incorporation into the main level of the narrative provides a structural framework for the novel which implies an ironic reading of the entire text. Like the traditional bolero dance, the novel revolves around the tension maintained by the constant alternation of partners (Alborg 71).

Bella, in her forties, appears to be a streetwise, independent woman. However, she rather quickly becomes enthralled with Poco, a downtrodden bar dweller, and falls victim to the romantic illusions of the boleros she sings. The cardboard palm trees and the faded neon signs which provide the atmosphere of the bar enhance the romanticized image of Havana already embedded in her by the Hollywood movies. Her dreams, revealed through interior monologues and reflected in the words of the boleros, clash with the harsh realities of her daily existence at El Desiré: "claro de luna, en La Habana, sobre tus playas quiero, quiero yo soñar, playas de verdad, de azúcar, de arena calentita entre los dedos" (87).

When Poco promises to take Bella to Cuba where he assures her his friend, Trompeta, will secure her a position as an entertainer at the Tropicana Club, she is caught in the trap set for her by the illusions of mass culture. Her heartfelt interpretation of the bolero she assumes Poco has written for her expresses her deepest desires: "No sé cómo contarte, la profunda finura de mi amor, que quisiera rodearte, de un cariño que te libre del dolorrrrr... Envolver tu cuerpo con mis besosss, inventar un mundo para ti, comprender el más profundo de tus sueños, casi me da miedo el querertea-siiiiii... Por eeeeeso, por eeeeeso, por eso en mi locura, sólo sé jurar, que te trataré como a una reinaaaaaa..." (178). The type of relationship idealized in this bolero is the source of disillusionment for all the characters in the novel since their realities cannot possibly live up to their fantasies.

While Bella succumbs to her dreams of an exciting life in Cuba with Poco, he constructs his own escape from reality around Juana, alias Vanessa, for whom he has truly written the bolero which gives the novel its title. Juana is a voluptuous eighteen-year-old small-town girl who aspires to be a singer. A cleaning lady by day, by night she assumes an identity entirely different from the plain-Jane image her given name implies. Searching for a surrogate father rather than a man who seeks only immediate physical satisfaction, she accepts Antonio's marriage proposal, thereby, ironically, commiting herself to precisely the type of life she intends to avoid. Learning of Antonio's intention to marry Vanessa, Poco is overcome with jealousy to the point of severely beating her, clearly demonstrating the ultimate subversion of his promise to her.

It is only after Poco's death that Bella finds and rereads the letter from Trompeta. She is angry when she finally realizes that the light blue ink and the coffee-colored paper she had once thought so romantic are merely the faded pages of a thirty-year-old letter written in 1954. Soon after, Antonia's announcement that her brother has forbidden her young lover, Damián, from seeing her again forces a violent reaction from Bella. In a complete upheaval of all her senses, she is overcome by a strange serenity where past and present mix. Demanding Antonio's address, her voice seems to be just another detached fragment of her life, a part of "ese organizado caos de sensaciones" (235). Her sudden act of revenge results in the intense release of years of suppression and represents the total subversion of traditional masculine authority.

Juxtaposed with the numerous male-authored documents are Antonia's letters to her mother. As evidence of her self-perception as a powerless victim, she routinely reports on her brother's activities, clearly regarding his life as more significant than her own. Incapable of making her own decisions, she constantly seeks her mother's approval of her friends: "estoy segura de que a usted le gustaría" (64). However, an interesting transformation begins to take place in her last letter. Although still plagued by guilt, Antonia shows signs of a growing self-awareness: "a ratos estoy feliz y a ratos me entra como una angustia muy grande por dentro, pero los ratos de felicidad son más largos" (149). As evidence of her coming to consciousness, she mentions Antonio only in a brief postscript: "Antonio está bien y manda besos" (150).

Kathleen Glenn states that "the idea that there is no way out for any of the women is forcefully conveyed in the final pages of the novel" (Glenn 200). Since the use of the metafictional mode in the novel offers alternative accounts of reality and primarily serves a critical function rather than an utopian one, one might conclude, as does Glenn, that Montero suggests there is no exit for women living in a world which restricts their freedom and limits their self-expression.

While I agree that these women appear to be confined by their circumstances, when Antonia courageously decides to leave Madrid, her exiting train ride is a conscious choice to free herself of her illusions rather than, as Glenn suggests, "the same old train... back to her mother's house" (Glenn 200). Boarding the train, Antonia is elated by her decision: "Lo había hecho. Había sido capaz, lo había logrado" (245).

Although Bella's and Vanessa's dreams of love and fame have turned into nightmares, the novel hints at a different future for Antonia. Her survival of the loss of Damián and Antonio's financial support is evidence of a new-found perspective on her life. Watching the countryside unfold as "un destino insospechado, hacia la novedad" (245), her vision of a potentially autonomous existence seems to take hold.

Antonia's undefined future reflects a pattern found in many contemporary Spanish women's novels. Although these writers may not yet be able to envision fully the alternatives available to women, they are actively involved in the demythification of a value system which has denied female creativity. Through the use of the metafictional mode, Montero subverts male-defined history of feminine passivity and transforms phallocentric narrative into a new paradigm of female subjectivity.

Works Cited

Alborg, Concha. "Metaficción y feminismo en Rosa Montero." *Revista de estudios hispánicos* 23 (1988): 67-76.

Glenn, Kathleen. "Victimized by Misreading: Rosa Montero's *Te trataré como a una reina.*" *Anales de la literatura española contemporánea* 12.1-2 (1987): 191-202.

Montero, Rosa. *Te trataré como a una reina.* Barcelona: Seix Barral, 1983.

Spires, Robert. *Beyond the Metafictional Mode. Directions in the Modern Spanish Novel.* Lexington: UP of Kentucky, 1984.

Suñén, Luis. "La realidad y sus sombras: Rosa Montero y Cristina Fernández Cubas." *Insula* 446 (enero 1984): 5.

Waugh, Patricia. *Metafiction. The Theory and Practice as Self-Conscious Fiction.* London: Methuen, 1984.

Techniques narratives d'ouverture et de clôture dans *Kamouraska*, *Héloïse* et *Les fous de Bassan* d'Anne Hébert

Frédérique Chevillot
University of Denver

Les toutes premières pages d'un roman, comme les toutes dernières, sont des moments stratégiques de narration; mais plutôt que de conventionnels débuts ou fins romanesques—termes qui me paraissent imposer une diégèse au roman—, je parlerai de mouvements d'ouverture et de clôture. Le terme de "mouvement" me semble plus apte à évoquer le déplacement mental de la lectrice et la progressive aspiration de son attention par le texte. L'étude des techniques narratives d'ouverture devra certes s'intéresser au "comment ça commence," elle devra également s'interroger sur le pourquoi d'un tel commencement. Il en sera de même pour les techniques de clôture. Cependant, si parce qu'il stimule le désir, le mouvement d'ouverture est un moment euphorique de découverte pour la lectrice, un minutieux travail d'information et de séduction pour l'écrivaine, qu'en est-il du mouvement de clôture? La lectrice comme l'écrivaine, ne sont-elles pas condamnées à rester sur leur faim? Angoissante fin de non-recevoir: faim de lire pour l'une, faim d'écrire pour l'autre qui ne pourront se satisfaire que dans une nouvelle ouverture. En butte à un impossible point final, le mouvement de clôture n'est-il pas toujours à la recherche d'une nouvelle ouverture?

Jusqu'à présent, la critique s'est surtout intéressée, d'une part au travail de l'*incipit* ou phrase-seuil—Victor Brombert, Claude Duchet, Raymond Jean, Steven Kellman se sont penchés sur la question, d'autre part et de façon privilégiée, au phénomène de la clôture—Barbara Herrnstein Smith, Frank Kermode, Armine Mortimer, Marianna Torgovnick, entre autres. Avec *Beginnings: Intention and Method* (1975), Edward Said paraît être le seul à avoir destiné tout un ouvrage au problème de l'ouverture. Peu d'études ont enfin été consacrées à la dialectique circulaire qui anime les mouvements d'ouverture et de clôture, ainsi qu'au phénomène de réouverture narrative qui y est lié.

Les techniques narratives d'Anne Hébert sont "fascinantes": elles charment au sens le plus fort du terme, elles envoûtent. Dès l'ouverture, la lectrice est comme happée par le texte hébertien qui n'a de cesse de l'inquiéter, de la choquer, de lui dire que cette lecture est folie; elle continue pourtant de lire, et même de relire. J'ai toujours lu les romans d'Anne Hébert d'une traite; j'en ai toujours relu les premières pages après en avoir lu plusieurs fois les dernières. Je voudrais ici montrer comment et pourquoi à l'aide de trois textes: *Kamouraska* (1970), *Héloïse* (1980) et *Les fous de Bassan* (1982).

Anne Hébert attache énormément d'importance au premier mouvement de ses romans. Au cours d'une entrevue, Donald Smith demandait à l'écrivaine à propos de la technique narrative de *Kamouraska*, si elle avait "beaucoup réfléchi sur les différents points de vue," ou si c'était chez elle "une technique toute naturelle." Anne Hébert répondait ainsi:

> J'ai commencé plusieurs fois *Kamouraska*. Une première fois, je le racontais tout à la troisième personne, comme un fait divers. C'était très plat, exactement comme un fait divers qu'on lit dans le journal. Alors, il a fallu que j'essaie de comprendre Elizabeth de l'intérieur, de la faire parler de l'intérieur, pour que ça s'anime un petit peu, pour que ça devienne plus vrai. (Smith 51)

Hébert n'envisage ni l'une ni l'autre des possibilités que lui propose son interlocuteur. Elle répond en fait entre les deux: pour redonner son naturel à la voix d'Elizabeth d'Aulnières, elle n'a fait qu'écrire et réécrire. Comme une diva se fait la voix pour trouver la parfaite inflexion, l'écrivaine se fait la plume pour laisser se dire son seul personnage. Il ne pouvait s'agir de simplement réviser les différentes versions d'un texte, mais bien de "commencer plusieurs fois *Kamouraska*" (51) comme si cela avait été, à chaque fois, la première et dernière ouverture possible: la primultième.

Je placerai les techniques narratives hébertiennes sous le signe du mystère de la folie ordinaire: une "inquiétante étrangeté" annoncée par touches en ouverture et qui a pour corollaire, en clôture, son angoissant rappel. J'étudierai dans chacun des trois romans la dialectique circulaire qui régit les mouvements d'ouverture et de clôture; j'analyserai ensuite l'impact d'un tel mécanisme sur le processus de lecture.

L'ouverture de *Kamouraska* est rendue étrange par la triple mise en abyme du processus de narration; elle annonce du même coup trois récits. Le récit premier—celui d'une narratrice anonyme, extradiégétique, sorte de conteuse mythique—, est présent dans les deux premiers paragraphes racontés au passé et à la troisième personne. Le récit second est celui d'un personnage hybride qui n'est qu'apparences sociales et sens de l'honneur: Mme Rolland est une Elizabeth innocentée, mais prisonnière de cette innocence. Enfin, le récit troisième est une voix qui vient de l'intérieur: dans un demi-sommeil, le délire du passé remonte à la conscience d'Elizabeth d'Aulnières-Tassy, celle qui a trompé son mari et comploté sa mort: femme passionnée et coupable, elle jouissait alors de la liberté.

A chaque récit correspondent un temps et un espace de narration définis, mais en ouverture du roman, les trois niveaux narratifs sont si intimement mêlés les uns aux autres que la lectrice s'y perd. Le récit premier a pour lieux extra- (ou méta-) diégétiques ceux de l'ouverture et de la clôture du roman; il réapparaît également dans le corps du texte à chaque fois que Mme Rolland, ou Elizabeth, perdent le fil de leur propre récit. N'appartenant pas à la diégèse, le récit premier donne voix à une narratrice omnisciente qui "saurait tout," mais qui par complicité avec l'héroïne, ne révélerait rien. Dans le temps, ce récit est ultérieur aux deux autres: "L'été passa en entier" (7).

L'incipit de *Kamouraska* laisse ainsi entendre que tout aurait commencé à la fin de l'été. Or, deux paragraphes plus loin, laissant apparaître le "je" pour la première fois, Mme Rolland introduit ainsi le récit second:

> Il aurait fallu quitter Québec. Ne pas rester ici. Seule dans le désert du mois de juillet. Il n'y a plus personne que je connaisse en ville. (7)

Pour celle qui veille Jérôme Rolland, c'est encore l'été. Pour la conteuse du récit premier, ça ne l'est déjà plus. Le récit second a en effet pour lieu de narration la maison de la rue du Parloir (et surtout la chambre des époux Rolland) quarante-huit heures avant la mort de Jérôme Rolland. Il commence au milieu de la nuit, se poursuit dans la journée jusqu'en fin d'après-midi. C'est l'été à Québec.

Du troisième paragraphe à la fin du chapitre d'ouverture, le récit troisième commence d'envahir par touches progressives le récit second: la vie intérieure d'Elizabeth d'Aulnières va s'imposer au personnage extérieur de Mme Rolland. La coupure définitive n'aura lieu qu'à la page 40, marquée par le changement du lieu de remémoration: lors d'une deuxième tentative, Elizabeth finit par trouver le sommeil dans la chambre de l'institutrice, où "ça sent l'encre et la vieille fille" (30). A travers le lent cauchemar du récit troisième, Mme Rolland redevient Elizabeth d'Aulnières-Tassy: c'était alors l'hiver à *Kamouraska.*

Le mouvement d'ouverture de *Kamouraska* aura été très lent. Mélangeant les lieux et temps de narration, les temps et lieux des histoires racontées, les débuts de *Kamouraska* auront été étrangement compliqués. Car la lectrice n'a de cesse de se poser la question: qui parle en cette triple ouverture et d'où viennent ces voix? Le premier chapitre n'est en fait que l'amorce du long processus de familiarisation de la lectrice avec les voix de *Kamouraska*: celui-ci ne prendra fin que vers la quarantième page du roman, lorsque le récit troisième se sera figé au coeur de l'hiver, la saison du grand pays.

Le retour à la réalité se fait toujours trop brusquement; la remontée d'Elizabeth à la surface du présent de Mme Rolland donne lieu à un mouvement de clôture rapide et violent. Il est marqué par un nouveau déplacement: Mme Rolland retourne dans la chambre conjugale, suivant le mouvement inverse de celui de l'ouverture. Pour mieux signifier son changement de personnage, Elizabeth change également de costume: "Il faudrait me préparer une autre robe," dit-elle à sa fille au tout début du chapitre de clôture (246). Reprenant la place et le récit de Mme Rolland là où elle les avait laissés, Elizabeth continue de mélanger, par condensation, les derniers événements du récit troisième avec ceux du récit second. Cependant, au bas de l'avant-dernière page du roman, la conteuse mythique reprend son récit en voix off:

> Jérôme Rolland, calme et doux, trône, appuyé à une pile d'oreillers frais. Dans la chambre, aux volets à demi fermés, flotte une odeur de cierge. Florida plie une nappe blanche, avec des airs de sacristine. Mme Rolland a les yeux bouffis. (249)

Jérôme Rolland vient de recevoir les derniers sacrements. Mais pour Mme Rolland, cette vie qui s'achève marque aussi la fin d'une respectabilité dûment payée. Davantage que la mort de son mari, Elizabeth d'Aulnières-Rolland pleure le recommencement de son cauchemar. C'est ce que révèle la conteuse anonyme dans la violence d'une fantasmagorique image de clôture:

> Brusquement le cauchemar déferle à nouveau, secoue Elizabeth d'Aulnières dans une tempête. Sans que rien n'y paraisse à l'extérieur. L'épouse modèle tient la main de son mari, posée sur le drap. Et pourtant... Dans un champ aride, sous les pierres, on a déterré une femme noire, vivante, datant d'une époque reculée et sauvage. Etrangement conservée. (250)

Pour la lectrice, le récit se clôt sur son obsédante réécriture dans l'inconscient d'Elizabeth. Au moment où elle croyait mettre de l'ordre dans toutes ces voix étranges et disparates, la figure fantasmatique de la femme noire remet la narration en question: le récit n'aurait-il en fait jamais cessé d'être fantas(ma)tique? Le malaise initial ne se trouvant pas résorbé en clôture, la lectrice cherche une autre clé, dans une nouvelle (re)lecture.

C'est sur l'attente que s'ouvre *Héloïse*: l'appartement dont la minutieuse description fait l'objet du chapitre d'ouverture, attend, comme dans les romans balzaciens, les protagonistes. Ici cependant, deux mondes s'affrontent: le monde des Morts et celui des Vivants. Au cours de cette même entrevue avec Donald Smith, Anne Hébert faisait les remarques suivantes à propos d'*Héloïse*:

> En exergue au livre, il y a un extrait d'un poème—"Le monde est en ordre / Les morts dessous / Les vivants dessus"—qui veut dire que le monde paraît en ordre, mais qu'un petit événement peut tout bouleverser. Le monde paraît exceptionnellement en ordre pour Christine et Bernard. Ce sont deux jeunes gens. Ils sont beaux. Ils sont gentils. Ils ont des parents gentils. Ils ont une vie toute tracée. Il suffit d'une rencontre pour que tout soit bouleversé. Le monde n'est jamais en ordre. (Smith 56)

Tout paraît même anormalement ordonné dans ce petit roman: l'ouverture semble annoncer le monde des Vivants et la clôture, en effet, celui des Morts; mais l'échelle des valeurs est inversée: l'ouverture d'*Héloïse* est aussi annonciatrice de mort que la clôture se veut grouillante de vie. De ce contraste naît le malaise de la lectrice: s'agirait-il d'une représentation poétique de la mort? Est-il vraiment question d'un réel étrange et morbide? Que faudrait-il ne pas croire? Par son hésitation entre l'étrangeté du quotidien et le merveilleux de l'imaginaire, l'ouverture d'*Héloïse* est, en termes de Todorov, fantastique: "Le fantastique, c'est l'hésitation éprouvée par un être qui ne connaît que les lois naturelles, face à un événement en apparence surnaturel" (Todorov 29).

On entre dans le récit d'*Héloïse* comme on entre dans un appartement; on en découvre progressivement chaque pièce; comme toute future propriétaire qui se respecte, on en inspecte avec minutie chaque recoin. Le texte fait passer sa lectrice dans des zones d'acclimatation, des sas de réduction spatiale: de la ville à "l'enclave oubliée"; de l'immeuble à la villa; du hall qui rappelle une "gare désaffectée" (préfigurant la station de clôture) à l'ascenseur; de l'entrée au petit salon; de la chambre à la salle de bain; de l'armoire à linge au réservoir d'eau; du fourneau à charbon à l'évier de pierre (9-12). L'espace de visite se réduit progressivement, de plus en plus fermé, de moins en moins respirable. L'élan narratif s'intensifie avant de se laisser mourir sur l'évier en pierre de la cuisine—pierre tombale de l'ouverture:

> Dans son ensemble l'appartement produisait une sorte de malaise, pareil à une demeure déjà quittée et cependant hantée.
> Tel qu'il était dans son ambiguïté, l'appartement attendait Christine et Bernard. Mais Christine et Bernard ne s'en souciaient guère, ayant déjà visité quantité de studios et d'appartements, pour finalement se fixer rue du Commandeur, dans un immeuble neuf. (12)

L'inquiétant appartement paraît donc en attente de personnages qui n'en ont que faire, puisqu'ils "se sont fixés" (est-ce un hasard?) "rue du Commandeur," dans un immeuble aussi neuf que celui-ci est ancien. A quoi servirait alors de poser en ouverture un espace qui n'a rien à voir avec la suite des événements (puisque Bernard et Christine ne semblent pas s'en soucier), sinon pour suggérer le pouvoir maléfique du lieu clos qu'est l'ouverture du roman? Qu'ils le veuillent ou non, l'appartement attirera, fascinera Bernard et Christine et les entraînera dans la mort. Comme pour en faire discrètement frémir la lectrice, tout le chapitre d'ouverture (représentation symbolique du monde des Vivants, au-dessus) se conjuguait à l'imparfait alors que le chapitre de clôture (représentation symbolique du monde des Morts, au-dessous) est écrit au présent. Rien n'annonce donc en ouverture que le personnage-titre du roman est une vampire, mais son atmosphère fantastique inquiète et fascine la lectrice, la pousse à lire dans l'espoir de mettre un terme à son hésitation: ou ce monde relève de l'étrange, ou il relève du merveilleux. Au niveau de l'écriture, il n'a de cesse de relever des deux.

Au dernier chapitre, Bernard "dégringole l'escalier du métro" (119) après avoir découvert dans l'appartement hanté "le corps de Christine à moitié caché sous la table. Ses vêtements sont déchirés. A son cou trop blanc une blessure fraîche" (118). Tel Orphée (dont la présence était annoncée en ouverture par le bronze de la cheminée) (10-11), Bernard se rue dans le métro à la recherche de son Eurydice. A l'heure de la fermeture, le métro redevient le royaume des Morts, ses passagers sont des revenants: Terminus, Père-Lachaise, tout le monde descend aux enfers. Bernard a en poche le revolver qu'il vient d'acheter dans l'intention de tuer Héloïse; la lectrice le suit dans son désir de vengeance humaine. Car malgré les indices disséminés dans le texte (un daneau a été "saigné à blanc" au jardin des plantes (76); une tâche de sang apparaît sur la manche d'Héloïse (83); au cou "trop blanc" de Christine s'inscrit une blessure fraîche (118)—indices auxquels la lectrice voudrait ne pas s'arrêter) Bernard réagit comme s'il était dans le réel. Or, au moment de tirer sur le fantôme qu'est Héloïse "[e]n dehors de toute volonté déjà brisée, la main seule, dans un dernier réflexe, vise cette cible inattaquable, laisse tomber son arme et se rend" (123). Comme la lectrice l'est de l'écriture hébertienne, Bernard est sous le charme d'Héloïse. Le texte reste volontairement évasif: on ne sait pas si Bernard n'ose tuer Héloïse parce qu'il l'aime avec fascination, ou s'il ne peut la tuer parce qu'elle est une vampire, morte et vivante à la fois. Le doute persiste alors que Christine vient d'être égorgée et que Bottereau apparaît: "Il se faufile au premier rang, sa petite trousse d'une main, de l'autre il tient le bras de Christine, dépenaillée et complètement indifférente" (124). La "petite trousse" pourrait-elle être celle d'un médecin? Et si Christine était vivante? Et si toute cette histoire n'avait été qu'un cauchemar? Peut-être aurait-on mal lu? Peut-être la lectrice n'aurait-elle pas désiré voir ce que le texte voulait lui faire lire? Pour mettre un terme à ces hésitations, une seule voie s'offre alors: celle de la relecture.

Par sa structure narrative même, *Les fous de Bassan* pose la question de l'ouverture et de la clôture: les cinq narrations qui forment le récit constituent autant d'ouvertures que de clôtures secondaires. Il s'agit à chaque fois d'entrer dans une narration pour en sortir quelques pages plus loin, avant de s'aventurer dans une autre, et ainsi de suite. "Le livre du révérend Nicolas Jones" et la "dernière lettre de Stevens Brown à Michael Hotchkiss" ne font qu'encadrer le récit sans le borner. On sait dès la première page, l'histoire que narratrices et narrateurs n'ont cessé de raconter. On retrouve, en ouverture de ce roman, l'atmosphère de folie anormalement ordinaire d'*Héloïse*. Je citerai ici le commentaire vitriolé de Karen Gould:

> Hébert begins and ends her novel with the obsessive delirium of two old men, Nicolas Jones and Stevens Brown, both of whom interpret the events leading up to 31 August 1936 from a great distance, as if the act of writing in the autumn of 1982 might somehow finally put an end to the undying presence of Nora and Olivia Atkins. Structurally speaking, their texts provide a gender-marked symmetry of male delusion, insanity, and impotence. (Gould 930)

Au moment où elle croit reconnaître le quotidien, la lectrice perçoit comme un vent de folie qui jette le doute sur l'ensemble: le texte balance comme un pendule. Le début du "livre du révérend Nicolas Jones" hésite entre un réel quotidien inquiétant et un merveilleux mystique. La phrase-seuil des *Fous de Bassan* illustre ce malaise initial: elle n'a ni sujet ni verbe. Le sens de mots pourtant familiers échappe à la lectrice; en demeure une étrange poésie: "La barre étale de la mer, blanche, à perte de vue, sur le ciel gris, la masse noire des arbres, en ligne parallèle derrière nous" (13). Une phrase sans verbe, c'est un peu comme une suite de mots qui n'arriverait pas à prendre son envol: fous de Bassan. Car c'est de folie dont il s'agit dans ce début d'histoire qui n'en finit pas de commencer, de retracer ses origines, de montrer du doigt son point de départ, de chercher son coupable. "Nous," rejeté à la fin de l'incipit, en l'absence de tout sujet grammatical ou actant, est inclusif d'une narrataire. L'insidieux pronom entraîne la lectrice (par narrataire interposée) à participer malgré elle à la folle hantise du souvenir qu'est le récit du révérend Jones. Tout commence en effet par un retour en arrière: le nouveau village de Griffin Creek, qui s'oppose en tout à l'ancien, célèbre le bicentenaire du pays. Mais il y a imposture: ce ne sont pas eux "les fondateurs, les bâtisseurs, les premiers dans la forêt, les premiers sur la mer, les premiers ouvrant la terre vierge sous le soc" (13). Selon le révérend, les "premiers fondateurs" étaient ces "robustes générations de loyalistes prolifiques" (14) dont lui, Nicolas Jones, père sans fils et pasteur sans troupeau, est le dernier représentant. La célébration du bicentenaire du pays en automne 1982—temps de narration du révérend Jones—renvoie à l'époque de la première colonisation de Griffin Creek en 1782:

> Jetés sur la route, depuis la Nouvelle-Angleterre, hommes, femmes et enfants, fidèles à un roi fou, refusant l'indépendance américaine, ont reçu du gouvernement canadien concession de la terre et droit de chasse et de pêche. Les Jones, les Brown, les Atkins, les Macdonald. (14)

Car ce peuple fidèle à un roi fou, était aussi un peuple élu, choisi de Dieu. La terre qui lui était destinée, était également à la hauteur de ses mérites: c'était un paradis terrestre. Unissant dans une même mystique Genèse et Exode, Nicolas Jones raconte la terre d'avant la venue du peuple élu:

> Au commencement, il n'y eut que cette terre de taïga, au bord de la mer, entre cap Sec et cap Sauvagine. Toutes les bêtes à fourrure et à plumes, à chair brune ou blanche, les oiseaux et les poissons dans l'eau se multipliaient à l'infini. (14)

Or, comme déjà Adam et Eve dans le Jardin d'Eden, le peuple élu ne saura pas honorer la confiance du Très-Haut; il sera déchu : "Il a suffi d'un seul été pour que se disperse le peuple élu de Griffin Creek" (13). D'élu, ce peuple est devenu damné, condamné à ne jamais pouvoir oublier sa faute, à en demeurer obsédé.

Le mouvement d'ouverture des *fous de Bassan* prend fin au moment où le cycle de remémoration a rejoint son point de départ: 1) célébration du bicentenaire du pays en automne 1982, 2) qui renvoie à la venue à Griffin Creek des loyalistes en 1782, 3) qui renvoie aux Commencements bibliques de la Genèse et de l'Exode, 4) qui renvoie à la chute, le 31 août 1936: "Dernier jour de l'été. Dernier jour du monde peut-être" (162); 5) qui renvoie au lendemain de la chute: l'automne. Le cycle de remémoration prend fin au moment où le révérend Jones reconnaît dans son récit la présence de l'automne: "C'est l'automne. Chaque fois qu'on ouvre la porte, l'odeur des feuilles croupies entre dans la cuisine avec des paquets d'obscurité froide" (18). Nicolas Jones est revenu à son point de départ. Au moment où le récit se fait auto-référentiel, l'ouverture prend fin.

Pour clore cet étrange récit pluriel, Hébert redonnera la parole à Stevens, l'assassin, qui dans sa dernière lettre avoue enfin ses crimes. Mais, serait-il le seul à être coupable? La "dernière lettre de Stevens Brown à Michael Hotchkiss" est également datée de l'automne 1982. Elle constitue à elle seule les vingt dernières pages du roman: j'y vois un lent mouvement de clôture; Griffin Creek se referme sur lui-même. Le coupable le plus vraisemblable prétend s'ouvrir, mais sa parole n'est pas celle d'un simple assassin: elle est celle de tout un peuple qui, à force de se chercher dans ses origines bibliques, en a oublié de vivre. Stevens est fou, rendu fou par le fanatisme puritain du peuple élu de Griffin Creek. Le roman se clôt sur le post-scriptum du délire: tout n'a pas été dit, tout n'a pas été écrit. Celui qui vient de reconnaître son crime après avoir tout fait pour le taire, annonce—odieux coup de théâtre—son acquittement:

> P.S. Tu seras peut-être étonné, Old Mic, si je te dis qu'aux assises de février 1937 j'ai été jugé et acquitté, mes aveux à McKenna ayant été rejetés par la cour et considérés comme extorqués et non conformes à la loi. (249)

Sauvage ironie du sort; le crime aurait-il pour autant payé? Alors que tout au long des cinq récits, la lectrice n'a pu décider si la culpabilité venait de l'esprit janséniste d'une certaine société, ou si elle venait des crimes passionnels qu'elle pousse ses victimes à commettre, rien, au moment de la clôture, ne peut l'aider à prendre parti. Entre la loi de Dieu, et celle des hommes, le récit n'a pas choisi. Alors que le temps de narration en clôture rejoint celui de l'ouverture, quarante-six ans après le drame, rien n'a changé. Et c'est également en automne 1982 que *Les fous de Bassan* paraît aux éditions du Seuil, faisant que le temps de la lecture, à travers celui de la fiction, croit rencontrer celui de l'écriture. Au moment où la relecture s'offre et s'impose, la proximité temporelle des dates de publication et de narration fait renaître l'angoisse: cette boucle est vicieuse.

Dans chacune des ouvertures des trois romans, la lectrice est dérangée par l'étrangeté de ce qui se présente faussement comme le familier, l'ordinaire. C'est d'ailleurs ce qui attire et retient son attention, ce qui stimule son désir: l'ouverture hébertienne est étrangement fascinante. Or, loin de la détourner d'une lecture angoissante, la clôture hébertienne confirme le malaise initial en le poussant à son paroxysme: l'étrangeté du texte ne sera pas démentie. Une seule issue se présente alors en clôture: une relecture qui tentera de dominer le malaise de la lecture initiale grâce à la connaissance préalable de l'histoire. A la deuxième lecture, ce n'est plus le conscient qui se défend, mais l'inconscient qui se libère. En invitant à la réouverture narrative, Anne Hébert, sorcière littéraire, exorcise les limites de son écriture: la clôture romanesque, ça n'existe pas.

Oeuvres citées

Brombert, Victor. "Opening Signals in Narrative." *New Literary History* 11.3 (Spring 1980): 489-502.

Duchet, Claude. "Pour une socio-critique, ou variations sur un incipit." *Littérature* 1 (1971): 5-14.

Freud, Sigmund. *Essais de psychanalyse appliquée.* Paris: Gallimard, 1971.

Genette, Gérard. *Figures III.* Paris: Seuil, 1972.

Gide, André. *Les faux-monnayeurs.* Paris: Gallimard, 1925.

Gould, Karen. "Absence and Meaning in Anne Hébert's *Les Fous de Bassan.*" *The French Review* 59.6 (May 1986): 921-30.

Hébert, Anne. *Les fous de Bassan.* Paris: Seuil, 1982.

______. *Héloïse.* Paris: Seuil, 1980.

______. *Kamouraska.* Paris: Seuil, 1970.

Herrnstein Smith, Barbara. *Poetic Closure: A Study on How Poems End.* Chicago: U of Chicago P, 1968.

Jean, Raymond. "Ouvertures, phrases-seuils." *Critique* 288 (Mai 1971): 421-31.

Kellman, Steven. "Grand Openings and Plain: the Poetics of First Lines." *Sub-Stance* 17 (1977): 139-47.

Kermode, Frank. *The Sense of an Ending.* New York: Oxford UP, 1967.

Martin, Terence. "Beginnings and Endings in the Leatherstocking Tales." *Nineteenth-Century Fiction* 33.1 (June 1978): 69-87.

Mortimer, Armine. *La clôture narrative.* Paris: Corti, 1985.

Pestre de Almeida, Lilian. "*Héloïse*: la mort dans cette chambre." *Voix & Images* 7.3 (Printemps 82): 471-81.

Prévost, L'abbé. *Histoire du chevalier des Grieux et de Manon Lescaut.* Paris: Flammarion, 1967.

Robbe-Grillet, Alain. *La jalousie.* Paris: Minuit, 1957.

Said, Edward. *Beginnings: Intention and Method.* New York: Basic Books, 1975.

Schwab, Gabriele. "The Dialectic of Opening and Closing in Samuel Beckett's *Endgame.*" *Yale French Studies* 67 (1984): 190-202.

Smith, Donald. "L'écrivain devant son oeuvre." (Entrevue avec Anne Hébert.) *Québec/Amérique* (1983): 37-58.

Todorov, Tzvetan. *Introduction à la littérature fantastique.* Paris: Seuil, 1970.

Torgovnick, Marianna. *Closure in the Novel.* Princeton: Princeton UP, 1981.

Welsh, Alexander. "Opening and Closing *Les misérables.*" *Nineteenth-Century Fiction* 33.1 (June 1978): 8-23.

"Poétice" affective de Marie-Claire Blais

Victor-Laurent Tremblay
Wilfrid Laurier University

Depuis la parution de son célèbre roman *Une saison dans la vie d'Emmanuel* en 1967, Marie-Claire Blais, reconnue comme l'un des plus importants écrivains du Québec, oeuvre patiemment, dénonçant l'oppression universelle sous toutes ses formes. Nul doute que cette constante romanesque a été renforcée par l'opprobre d'être [femme et] lesbienne, et aussi, jusqu'à récemment, par l'infériorité "congénitale" d'être québécoise.[1] Il est très probable que cette "différence" et la culpabilité qui en résulta, qui hantent ses écrits, dépendent en partie du catholicisme inflexible qui a laissé son empreinte chez nombre d'auteurs québécois.

Pour une fillette à caractère mystique comme Marie-Claire Blais, il fut impossible d'échapper à cet enseignement qui non seulement remplaçait les contes de fées par l'Histoire Sainte, mais truffait les manuels scolaires de bondieuseries. De plus, la misogynie religieuse qui unissait la destinée de la femme à celle d'Eve, la soumettant au mâle et la rendant seule responsable de la "faute originelle," a dû aussi laisser des traces. Cependant, au-delà de l'éducation traumatisante reçue, n'y aurait-il pas des circonstances plus personnelles qui aient contribué à influencer l'imaginaire de cette écrivaine? Ainsi, qu'en est-il de l'origine de la trilogie thématique de la hantise de la mère, du combat contre les jougs sociaux et de la joie artistique, qui tisse le contenu de ses livres?[2]

Selon nous, ces interrogations trouvent leur réponse dans la poésie de jeunesse de Marie-Claire Blais. Son analyse, en effet, permet de déceler un "noyau métaphorique" dont le pouvoir structurant est corroboré par l'étude des romans publiés par la suite. Découvrir le sens de ce "mythe personnel"--pour employer l'expression consacrée de Charles Mauron--importe, croyons-nous, afin de mieux apprécier non seulement l'importance de l'oeuvre blaisienne, mais la place qui lui revient dans la remise en question féministe de la "doxa patriarcale."

Au tout début de sa carrière, Marie-Claire Blais s'adonne avec passion à la poésie. Entre 1957 et 1959, elle publie quinze poèmes qui constituent un bloc à part des deux recueils publiés quelques années plus tard: *Pays voilés* (1963) et *Existences* (1964).[3] Une simple lecture de ces premiers poèmes nous assure de l'homogénéité de leur imagerie dégagée de l'intellectualisation plus prononcée de ceux qui suivront. Lorsque plus tard on l'interrogera sur l'origine de sa poésie, elle répondra: "la mémoire . . . choisit les mots et me conduit où elle veut. Il y a des poèmes qui naissent spontanément, dans un frémissement d'idées et d'émotions, mais il y en a d'autres dont la racine me demeure inconnue . . . Je les écris pour me reconnaître, je crois, et parce que tout en me libérant, ils m'éclairent."[4]

Les premiers écrits, plus encore s'il s'agit de poésie, sont chargés d'un bagage intime dont la psycho-critique reconnaît la valeur. La poésie, en effet, existe d'abord par les métaphores qui sont, d'après Serge Leclaire, des "traces mnésiques inconscientes" s'ordonnant selon la logique du désir: ce qui s'écrit, c'est le récit ineffaçable d'un événement libidinal.[5] Plus que la poésie des recueils qui formule déjà en images une "vision du monde," celle de l'adolescence s'offre donc révélatrice d'inconscient. Des fantasmes chargés d'émotion surgissent de l'enfance et sont saisis par les mots dans toute leur imminence et leur sensualité, sans être criblés ou tamisés encore par la conscience de l'auteure expérimentée qu'elle deviendra.

C'est un peu avec gêne qu'on relit ces poèmes et les analyse, car la répétition de mêmes symboles lancinants nous ouvre les portes de "l'interdit" des origines. Trois thèmes dominants s'y recoupent: une hantise d'oiseaux féroces et une obsession ambiguë de la mer à laquelle est relié un moment de répit procuré par l'art. Avant d'en tenter le déchiffrage métaphorique, soulignons l'unité thématique de ces constantes.

L'inventaire des images d'oiseaux de proie, souvent associés au ciel ou au soleil oppresseur, est représentatif: douze des quinze poèmes ressuscitent l'atmosphère brutale et sanglante où l'enfant-poète est déchiré ou brûlé. Persistantes au même degré, les allusions à la mer et à l'eau offrent cependant une dualité bien prononcée: "le" poète assoiffé d'amour chante souvent la mer ou bien demande son aide, mais celle-ci reste muette ou, ironique et dédaigneuse, le rejette. De même, l'activité artistique est évoquée dans presque tous les poèmes. Un survol de leurs titres nous renseigne là-dessus. On y retrouve les mots: saltimbanque, gammes, piano, symphonie, poético, ode, lever de rideau et cinéma. Toutes ces formes d'art, quand elles ne constituent pas un pacte de paix, cherchent à surseoir à la souffrance, et renferment parfois même une promesse d'amour et de liberté.

A partir de cette symbolique, il s'agit maintenant, comme le dit si bien Serge Leclaire de "démasquer le réel . . . faire apparaître la place inconcevable où se déploie l'angoisse . . . éclairer la faille où se dérobe la jouissance" (Leclaire 30). De prime abord, selon la psychanalyse classique,[6] les trois métaphores poétiques que nous avons précédemment déterminées se rapprocheraient de constantes qu'on retrouve chez la lesbienne: la peur du père et de l'homme, l'attachement exagéré à la mère qui est de plus désespérément crainte, et enfin une activité quelconque, ici artistique, afin d'atteindre l'égalité vis-à-vis du mâle, et même de le battre sur son propre terrain de puissance, la création (Siegel 9-12).

Attardons-nous premièrement à ce que l'on sait de l'enfance de l'auteure afin d'examiner son besoin exacerbé de la mère. Jusqu'à l'âge de presque six ans, Marie-Claire est fille unique. Le père travaillant chaque jour à l'"extérieur," il est naturel qu'entre mère et fille se développent des liens très forts. Aussi la présence du père déclenche-t-elle l'habituel conflit ou l'enfant, se croyant supplantée dans l'affection maternelle, développe une certaine anxiété. Mais c'est surtout la naissance d'un jeune frère, sans doute bien attendu par le jeune couple, qui psychologiquement marque la fillette jusqu'alors sans rival dans l'affection de sa mère. Comment ne pas s'être sentie de plus en plus rejetée quand ce frère, avec l'âge, a accès a des privilèges, comme tous les garçons qui l'entourent, pendant qu'elle-même, comme toutes ses compagnes, ne subit que des interdits? Son besoin d'affection est probablement alors dirigé vers de jeunes amies. Ces attachements, bien décrits dans *Les Manuscrits de Pauline Archange,* son autobiographie romancée,[7] laissent leurs traces dans l'émotivité infantile.

Seule la résultante de cette histoire familiale nous importe: l'amour passionné pour la mère est brisé. Solitaire, il ne reste à la fillette que le rêve d'antan à chérir. C'est ce rêve et ce drame amoureux qui resurgissent puissants et grandioses dans la première poésie de l'auteure. Ce schéma de comportement infantile correspond bien d'ailleurs à la symbolique maternelle ambivalente des poèmes ou mer et mère se confondent. Inutile d'insister sur les corrélations symboliques millénaires existant entre ces deux termes. Quant à l'ambiguïté affective envers la mère, voici un exemple de cette double contrainte amour/haine, que l'on trouve dans la dernière strophe d'un poème intitulé "Le Cinéma du Petit Poète":

> La Mer... j'ai voulu l'endormir dans le bruit du vent, et
> la descendre jusqu'au secret des roseaux.
> Je l'ai couverte de tous les remous des lits,
> De la gloire de ceux qui ne dorment pas,

Une étreinte... lui ai promis,
    de l'étreinte elle a bien ri... La Mer! La Mer!
Elle m'a tué à Midi.

Une autre proposition psychanalytique suggérée par les poèmes est celle d'une peur chronique du père, auquel réfère le mot Midi des vers que nous venons de citer, peur s'étendant à toute présence masculine. Pour Freud, le père est étranger à la fillette parce qu'il se différencie totalement d'elle-même et de sa mère. Cet inconnu représente une autorité parfois effrayante qui s'identifie à l'image du Dieu-père omniscient. Sans doute, devine-t-elle qu'en étant féminine comme sa mère elle pourrait enjôler celui-ci, mais elle ne peut aimer cet être réticent à l'amour: elle préfère la douceur maternelle. Peut-être même s'identifie-t-elle à celui-ci et à son jeune frère pour rivaliser contre eux dans l'affection de sa mère, selon la "dialectique triangulaire" du désir telle qu'explicitée par René Girard.[8] Plus tard, elle préférera la douce compagnie de ses jeunes compagnes à la rude impudeur des garçons à l'endroit de laquelle on l'a mise en garde. Dans le Québec d'alors, n'est-il pas coutumier, de mère en fille, de souffrir pour l'amour de Dieu le désir brutal du mari? Ainsi masculinité et sexe, honte et douleur deviennent synonymes non seulement dans le langage que l'enfant assimile, mais aussi dans son émotivité.

Ce rejet d'une masculinité considérée comme agressive et même brutale correspond bien aux images oppressives des oiseaux de proie, de la violence furieuse du ciel et du soleil, qui hantent les poèmes et auxquelles participe la mère par son rejet. Dans le poème "Gammes de la mer," le plus représentatif, le poète exhorte six fois la mer à éloigner ces oiseaux prêts à déchirer sa chair, mais sans succès. Quant au soleil, symbole masculin, l'on rêve de sa mort dans le poème "L'Enterrement du soleil," car les promesses de celui-ci sont "Eclatante[s] du rire de toutes les femmes qui ont pleuré." Ce roi-soleil attaque "le" poète et sa parole, l'emprisonne solitaire et meurtri. Enfin dans "Abstraction des souffrances," sous l'"Homme" qui "empoign[e] ses couteaux froids et lourds," se dessine l'idéologie patriarcale, responsable des guerres et de l'oppression.

Toujours selon la théorie freudienne, qu'en est-il de la troisième constante de l'homosexualité féminine: cette identification au mâle par désir d'égalité, d'être traitée en sujet et non en objet, dont nous considérons toute activité artistique comme significative? Cet aspect du lesbianisme repérable entre autres dans le mot masculin "poète," auquel s'identifie maintes fois l'écrivaine, s'avère problématique du fait que la fonction de l'art chez Marie-Claire

Blais n'est ni destructrice, ni dominatrice. Cette attitude créatrice ne divergerait-elle pas de la théorie freudienne même? Bien sûr, l'on peut discerner dans le désir de création un moyen de surmonter le complexe d'infériorité de "n'être que femme," afin de gagner l'affection de la mère qui, semble-t-il, lui préfère le père ou le frère. Ainsi dans le poème "Poétice," auquel réfère le titre de notre propos, "le" poète reconnaît le pouvoir des mots se transformant en soleils (s'opposant au "midi masculin"?) et rêve d'"Une musique démesurée, [d'] une vibration de parfums [...qui le] multiplient comme les nuages chassent les peuples d'aigles et de corbeaux. Vols de prismes Dans le lit glacé de l'univers."

Cependant, il est difficile de concilier l'opposition qui existe entre cette nouvelle puissance acquise, présumée "masculine," et le rôle de l'art sur lequel ces poèmes insistent. Selon l'auteure, par exemple, la "Musique, [qui est] Amour et Pardon" ("La Mer dans les Mains") s'affirme contre toute puissance, opposée à la guerre et au sang. Plutôt que d'être un apanage de force masculine, la musique et, par extension, tout art se transforment en l'opposé extrême, suggérant une certaine "essence" féminine et proposant un retour à l'enfance et à la mère que l'on adore, mais dont on continue à se méfier à cause de sa "trahison" avec le père, puis le frère.

La seule avenue psychanalytique qui reste vraiment ouverte est donc dans l'approfondissement de la relation de l'enfant à la mère.[9] Aussi, plutôt que de continuer au stade oedipien faut-il remonter à un stade antérieur, celui de la première enfance de l'auteure. Le temps préoedipien, celui où la mère et l'enfant vivent en symbiose, correspond au stade oral: période narcissique et non sociale où seule la présence maternelle, non encore partagée, peut satisfaire le désir et le combler.

Soulignons que cet attachement inconditionné à la "mère primitive" se fait indépendamment du sexe. En effet, la première libido est globale, c'est-à-dire non différenciée et essentiellement bisexuelle. N'étant pas encore déterminée génitalement, la sexualité est alors répartie dans tout le corps. Cette période correspond au mythe paradisiaque d'avant la séparation du premier être humain en mâle et femelle. L'enfant, n'ayant pas encore été soumis à la dualité des rôles sexuels, est androgyne et ne forme qu'une entité avec la mère. Nouveau au monde et entièrement érotisé, son langage s'il pouvait s'exprimer correspondrait à celui des mystiques par sa sensualité: seul l'idiome érotique pourrait décrire maladroitement cette osmose "divine" où identité et fonction sexuelle n'ont plus leur raison d'être.

D'après nous, la poésie de Marie-Claire Blais, comme d'ailleurs toute sa production littéraire, repose sur la nostalgie de cet état de jouissance paradisiaque, l'androgynie adamique. Son lesbianisme, désir sexualisé de retour à la mère, ne fait qu'amplifier le souvenir de ces instants paradisiaques d'union de tout enfant à sa mère. L'imaginaire de l'écrivaine, croyons-nous, doublement motivé par ce "besoin maternel," cherche à reproduire avec art l'intense passion de ce premier souvenir universel, espérant le recréer partout et maintenant, en dénonçant toutes les répressions et toutes les violences. Son rêve: révolutionner la société entière pour créer un monde fraternel où, tous, nous pourrions nous materner l'un l'autre et ainsi revivre le temps primordial du bonheur de l'enfance.

En terminant, ajoutons à ce souffle d'espoir si rare dans l'oeuvre blaisienne celui de Rimbaud rêvant des poètes futurs dont nous croyons Marie-Claire Blais être l'annonciatrice. "Ces poètes seront, disait-il, quand sera brisé l'infini servage de la femme, quand elle vivra pour elle et par elle . . . Alors la femme trouvera de l'inconnu. Elle trouvera des choses étranges, insondables, repoussantes, délicieuses; nous les prendrons, nous les comprendrons."[10]

Peut-être. Pour le salut du monde, espérons-le.

Notes

[1] Le retour de Marie-Claire Blais au Québec vers la fin des années 70, après qu'elle eut vécu de nombreuses années aux Etats-Unis et en France, correspond à la parution des *Nuits de l'underground*, son premier roman traitant de l'amour entre femmes. Il faut voir entre ces deux événements, non pas une coïncidence mais une relation exprimant un engagement personnel de la part de l'écrivaine, une libération: elle se reconnaissait Québécoise, [femme] et lesbienne. A propos de la pudeur des critiques vis-à-vis de son homosexualité, Marie-Claire Blais répond dans une interview: "J'ai l'impression que la vérité les gêne." *Books in Canada* (February 1979): 8, notre traduction.

[2] Voir notre thèse de maîtrise, "La Révolte contre le patriarcat dans l'oeuvre de Marie-Claire Blais," Diss. of British Columbia, 1980.

[3] Voici la liste de leur publication: "Roman vacances," "Luigi (ou l'histoire d'un saltimbanque)," "Abstractions des souffrances," *Emourie* 5 (1957): 49-54; "La Mort d'un Seigneur," *Revue*

Dominicaine, (sept. 1959): 65-66; "Poèmes," *Ecrits du Canada Français* 5 (1959): 173-91. Les poèmes de cette dernière série, qui ont une date de composition, sont ordonnés ainsi: "La Mer dans les mains," janv. 58; "L'Enfant d'Espagne," nov. 58; "Gammes de la mer," juil. 59; "Le Piano ouvert sur les flots (Symphonie en rire d'enfants)," oct. 58; "Poétice," nov. 57; "Le Soulier pourpre," 1959; "L'Enterrement du soleil (Ode à la Mort)," nov. 58; "Lever de rideau," 9 oct. 58; "La Route enchantée," janv. 58; "Le Cinéma du petit poète," 1957; "Les Noces mystiques." Pour une analyse textuelle plus serrée de ces poèmes et de leur thématique commune, voir notre thèse de maîtrise, pp. 14-40.

[4] "Témoignages des poètes canadiens-français" dans *Archives des lettres canadiennes*, Tome IV (Ottawa: Fides, 1969) 529.

[5] Serge Leclaire, "Le Réel dans le texte," *Littérature* 3 (1971): 30.

[6] Voir le résumé de Elaine V. Siegel dans *Female Homosexuality: Choice Without Volition* (Hove and London: The Analytic Press, 1988) 9-12.

[7] *Les Manuscrits de Pauline Archange,* dit l'auteure, sont . . . plus près de la réalité que de la fiction . . . J'ai emprunté mon entourage des personnages, des situations, tout en évitant d'être tout-à-fait Pauline Archange. Néanmoins, je crois être partout présente dans la majorité des dialogues. Cette situation me permet d'entretenir un échange toujours fructueux avec mon intériorité." "Libre conversation avec Marie-Claire Blais" de Gabrielle Frémont dans *Québec français* (octobre 1981): 40.

[8] Voir entre autres *Mensonge romantique et vérité romanesque* (Paris: Grasset, 1961) et *Des choses cachées depuis la fondation du monde* (Paris: Grasset, 1978).

[9] Dans son analyse du lesbianisme, *Female Homosexuality* (1988), Elaine V. Siegel se distancie de la théorie freudienne sur l'oedipe pour privilégier le stade pré-oedipien de la dyade mère-enfant (et de ses conflits).

[10] *Lettres du voyant* (Paris: Minard, 1975) 141.

Growing Up in Winnipeg: Gabrielle Roy's Manitoba Heritage

Roseanna Lewis Dufault
Ohio Northern University

In her article, "Mon héritage du Manitoba," Gabrielle Roy describes the fervor of French culture in Saint-Boniface, Winnipeg's francophone suburb, as she experienced it as a child. She observes that Saint-Boniface was one of several "répliques presque exactes du Québec" (1970, 76) established by homesteaders like her grandparents on the Manitoba plains. Roy recalls that, during her childhood, Saint-Boniface "respirait, priait, espérait, chantait, souffrait, on pourrait dire, en français, gagnant cependant son pain en anglais, dans les bureaux, les magasins et les usines de Winnipeg" (1970, 75). She emphasizes a contrast between "la douce rusticité" of Saint-Boniface and the "flot multiple, bizarre, torrentiel, nostalgique" (1970, 76) of immigrants inhabiting the anglophone city center. When crossing the Provencher Bridge, she affirms, "nous entrions dans un autre monde" (1970, 76).

Although Roy tends to play down the French-speaking ethnicity of her Saint-Boniface setting in *Rue Deschambault* (1955), a semi-autobiographical novel, Québécois critic Pierre de Grandpré acknowledges her ability to "traduire avec fidélité l'âme secrète de notre pays" (91).

Contemporary English-Canadian author Alice Munro has similarly received recognition for her ability to capture "the myriad details of mundane existence" (Perrakis 61), as she offers "fragile insights into the complexity of personal relationships" (Conron 109). Munro's semi-autobiographical novel, *Lives of Girls and Women* (1971), is set in Jubilee, a fictional town inspired by Wingham, her own early home in rural southwestern Ontario.

Lives of Girls and Women has been classified as a feminist Bildungsroman (Gros-Louis 8). Recent studies maintain that Munro was seeking "an alternative" to the typically male genre (Ricou 23), noting that "the traditional Bildungsroman takes on different forms and emphases when its subject is female" (Hutcheon 133). Many observations made in studies of Munro's novel could also be applied to *Rue Deschambault*. Both Roy's novel and Munro's consist of a collection of self-contained short stories arranged roughly in chronological order. Each of the novels is narrated by a young woman who, having become a writer, attempts to record accurately the people, places and experiences that shaped her childhood and adolescence.

Although Munro and Roy differ somewhat in their treatment of childhood, Munro being rather cynical (Ricou 21) while Roy establishes "an atmosphere of purity, innocence, and simplicity" (Lewis 27), both authors emphasize strong mother-daughter relationships. Ricou observes that, in Munro's work, "the girl's search for a relationship with her mother" constitutes "an important narrative element" (24), while Lewis comments on the powerful influence of mothers in Roy's fiction, remarking that intimate mother-daughter relationships "are always realistically described" (35).

While fathers play only a minor role in both novels, mothers set an example of relative independence by testing the limits of their traditional roles, undertaking ambitious projects that set them apart from their peers. On one hand, Christine's mother traverses Canada by train, at a time when respectable women did not travel alone, to visit relatives in Québec. With gentle humor and a note of irony, Christine expresses admiration for her mother's determination to satisfy her "goût de la liberté," undiminished by years of domestic captivity (99). Christine also admires her mother's insight into human character; she instinctively strikes the right chord to calm her husband's protests and overcome his relatives' disapproval. On the other hand, Del's mother earns the reputation of a "wild woman" (54) by learning to drive and by selling encyclopedias. Del feels embarrassed by her mother's provocative letters to the local newspaper, although she understands her need to be "remarkable." Del represents her child-self as wiser than her parent: "I myself was not so different from my mother, but concealed it, knowing what dangers there were" (68). Del and Christine observe their mothers' lives sympathetically and critically, and as a result, aspire to a freer existence.

Both mothers expect their daughters to marry eventually and have children, but they encourage them to experience freedom and mobility first through educational opportunities and careers. Del's mother urges her to "use her brains" (217) to compete for a university scholarship. When a boyfriend threatens to impede Del's academic success, her mother scolds, "Do you want to be the wife of a lumberyard worker? Do you want to join the Baptist Ladies Aid?" (217) Such admonitions irritate Del: "Her concern about my life, which I needed and took for granted, I could not bear to have expressed" (173). Del fails to qualify for the scholarship, but she leaves Jubilee nonetheless and manages to earn a living on her own by writing.

In *Rue Deschambault*, Christine's mother instills in her daughter an appreciation for literature: “Elle m'avait enseigné le pouvoir des images, la merveille d'une chose révélée par un mot juste et tout l'amour que peut contenir une simple et belle phrase” (246), yet she seems surprised when Christine confides her decision to become a writer. Tactfully alluding to some potential hazards inherent in the profession, she suggests that Christine also prepare to teach. Recognizing the value of a steady income, Christine complies. She also pleases her mother by rejecting her well-intentioned but inept first suitor, along with several subsequent Sunday callers, thereby firmly establishing her identity and independence as a young woman.

Lives of Girls and Women resembles other novels by English Canadian women such as Margaret Laurence's *A Bird in the House* (1970), Fredelle Bruser Maynard's *Raisins and Almonds* (1972) and Audrey Thomas's *Songs My Mother Taught Me* (1973), in which daughters acknowledge the influence of their mothers, “whose limited, dependent lives offered negative models for them to react against, but whose encouragement led them to create more positive models” (Gros-Louis 13). Roy's novel stands out from a feminist perspective since it was published more than a decade before these English Canadian works. Further, Roy's treatment of the mother sets *Rue Deschambault* apart from novels published subsequently by women writers in Québec, such as Louise Maheux-Forcier's *L'Ile Joyeuse* (1964) and Marie-Claire Blais' *Manuscrits de Pauline Archange* (1968), in which daughters receive little, if any, encouragement to pursue a more independent life.[1]

Ronald Sutherland has declared that “when French-Canadian and English-Canadian novels are examined together, it becomes evident that . . . a good number of the accepted differences between the cultures of French Canada and English Canada do not in fact exist” (3). While strong parallels may be drawn between Roy's novel and Munro's, some accepted cultural differences, especially in the treatment of religious beliefs and in patterns of social interactions, are in fact reinforced in the two works.

In *Rue Deschambault*, Christine derives her concept of God from a pious picture portraying “Dieu le père . . . dans les nuages” (96), and from platitudes such as “Dieu punit toujours l'orgueil” (91). Christine's report of advice her mother received from Montréal's famous thaumaturge contains more than a hint of humor and skepticism: “Le Frère André n'entendit peut-être pas bien. Il se dépêcha de répondre à maman: 'Priez bien saint Joseph, ne buvez pas trop de café et ayez confiance'" (119). Christine never acknowledges deeply-held spiritual beliefs, nor does she openly challenge Québécois Catholicism's tenets. She intimates a fleeting doubt, perhaps, when she confides, "Partout, en nous, autour de nous, il m'a semblé que c'était plein de brume" (96).[2]

In contrast, Del approaches religious matters quite irreverently in her survey of Jubilee's churches. Raised by an avowed atheist in a protestant environment, Del seeks answers to metaphysical questions on her own. Initially elated by her effectual prayer to escape a dreaded sewing class, Del inevitably experiences doubts: "Suppose it was going to happen anyway?" (113) Del frankly abandons her quest for God when she perceives a fundamental incompatibility between religion and everyday life.

A second cultural difference appears in the way in which the two protagonists relate to their childhood friends and classmates. In *Lives of Girls and Women*, Del defines herself in terms of her relative social status at school. She remarks that certain students, by virtue of their parents' influence in the community, automatically succeed, while children of recent immigrants and unattractive "misfits" figure at the lower end of the classroom social scale. In between, Del joins the ranks of "the ambitious and unsure," who strive to improve their position by associating with successful friends (122).

Del's behavior matches a pattern observed by Richard Coe, who states, "The North American child (U.S. or English-Canadian) appears fascinated over and over again, not by its own past self, but rather that self's relation to the community" (Coe 279). Another critic, Pierre Spriet also draws attention to the importance of "conformisme social" in English Canadian literature (Spriet 308). Protagonists in other English Canadian novels of childhood and adolescence, including Sylvia Fraser's *Pandora* (1972) and Fredelle Bruser Maynard's *Raisins and Almonds*, which treats the attempts of a Russian-Jewish immigrant child to assimilate English Canadian culture, exhibit the same concern for social acceptance as Del.

In contrast, Christine, who bases her friendships on mutual interests and enjoyment, expresses little or no concern for her social status. Immersed in her own culture, Christine apparently experiences a sense of belonging which Del feels compelled to earn. Sociologists Alan Anderson and James Frideres maintain that the Québécois form "a very cohesive group" because "they claim a common heritage derived from French history" as well as "a longstanding variety of French culture developed during three and a half centuries of residence in Canada" (86). In Christine's case, the French-speaking community forms a firmly established, clearly defined minority. The stable boundaries of her cultural enclave apparently spare her the need to jostle for status. Further, Christine's only substantial allusion to the larger anglophone community, and hint of its economic superiority, occurs when her mother sews for Mrs. O'Neill to earn money for her journey. In this context, Christine's mother has the advantage; she judges Mrs. O'Neill's character and very subtly manipulates her. Christine treats Mrs. O'Neill sympathetically as an immigrant from Ireland: "A quelqu'un venu de ce pays-là, notre petite ville de maisons, de trottoirs en bois devait paraître bien sèche" (103). Throughout *Rue Deschambault,* and throughout her article, "Mon héritage du Manitoba," Roy conveys a strong appreciation for cultural diversity.

While Roy and Munro each treat aspects of their youthful experiences, especially their attitudes toward friendships, in ways that reflect the disparate cultural environments in which they grew up, it is important to note that both authors emphasize solitude and even feelings of alienation as crucial elements in their artistic development. Relatively indifferent to social matters, Christine continually retreats to her attic to meditate alone; she discusses with her mother the fact that writing well requires distance: "Ce don, c'est un peu comme une malchance qui éloigne les autres, qui nous sépare de presque tous" (246). In an interview, Munro confides, "I always realized that I had a different view of the world, and one that would bring me into great trouble and ridicule if it were exposed. I learned very early to disguise everything" (Gibson 246). In this light, Del's efforts to "fit in" could be seen as a means of artistic self-preservation.

Born and raised in the heart of Canada, descended from one of Québec's earliest families, Gabrielle Roy states, "je me sens Canadienne jusqu'à la moelle" (1970, 69). As one of Canada's most prominent novelists, she bridges two cultures. Her contribution to Canadian literature is valuable and unique as she communicates authentically the stability and strength of Canada's deep-rooted francophone culture within the context of her Manitoba heritage. Further, as Roy treats the growth and development of a young woman writer in *Rue Deschambault,* she distinguishes herself as a feminist foremother by portraying a strong mother-daughter relationship comparable to those developed in English-Canadian and in Québécois women's writing more than a decade later.

Notes

[1] Mary Jean Green discusses the tradition of strong mother-daughter relationships in Québécois literature and society in her article "Redefining the Maternal: Women's Relationships in the Fiction of Marie-Claire Blais," in *Traditionalism, Nationalism, and Feminism*, ed. Paula Gilbert Lewis (Westport: Greenwood Press, 1985). Social transformations apparently caused a disruption of this tradition during the 1960s; strong relationships between women have been reestablished in works published since the late 1970s.

[2] For a more in-depth analysis of Gabrielle Roy's treatment of religious faith see *The Literary Vision of Gabrielle Roy*, by Paula Gilbert Lewis, Birmingham: Summa Publications, 1984.

Works Cited

Anderson, Alan B. and James S. Frideres. *Ethnicity in Canada*. Toronto: Butterworths, 1981.

Blais, Marie-Claire. *Manuscrits de Pauline Archange*. Montréal: Editions du Jour, 1968.

Coe, Richard N. *When the Grass Was Taller*. New Haven: Yale University Press, 1984.

Conron, Brandon. "Munro's Wonderland." *Canadian Literature*. 78 (1978): 109+.

Fraser, Sylvia. *Pandora*. Toronto: McClelland and Stewart, 1972.

Gibson, Graeme. *Eleven Canadian Novelists*. Toronto: Anansi, 1973.

Grandpré, Pierre de. *Dix ans de vie littéraire au Canada français*. Montréal: Beauchemin, 1966.

Green, Mary Jean. "Redefining the Maternal: Women's Relationships in the Fiction of Marie-Claire Blais." In *Traditionalism, Nationalism, and Feminism*. Ed. Paula Gilbert Lewis. Westport: Greenwood Press, 1985.

Gros-Louis, Dolores. "Pens and Needles: Daughters and Mothers in Recent Canadian Literature." *Kate Chopin Newsletter* 2.3

(1976-77): 8-15.

Hutcheon, Linda. *The Canadian Postmodern.* Toronto: Oxford University Press, 1988.

Laurence, Margaret. *A Bird in the House.* Toronto: McClelland & Stewart, 1970.

Lewis, Paula Gilbert. *The Literary Vision of Gabrielle Roy.* Birmingham: Summa Publications, 1984.

Maheux-Forcier, Louise. *L'Ile joyeuse.* Ottawa: Cercle du Livre de France, 1964.

Maynard, Fredelle Bruser. *Raisins and Almonds.* Toronto: Doubleday, 1972.

Munro, Alice. *Lives of Girls and Women.* New York: McGraw-Hill, 1971.

Perrakis, Phyllis Sternberg. "Portrait of the Artist as a Young Girl: Alice Munro's Lives of Girls and Women." *Atlantis* 7.2 (1982): 61-67.

Ricou, Laurie. *Everyday Magic: Child Languages in Canadian Literature.* Vancouver: University of British Columbia Press, 1987.

Roy, Gabrielle. "Mon héritage du Manitoba." *Mosaic* 3.3 (1970): 69-79.

______. *Rue Deschambault.* 1955. Montréal: Stanké, 1980.

Spriet, Pierre. "Une littérature canadienne d'expression anglaise en gestation." *Canada et Canadiens.* Eds. Pierre Guillaume, Jean-Michel Lacroix and Pierre Spriet. Bordeaux: Presses Universitaires de Bordeaux, 1984. 287-342.

Sutherland, Ronald. *Second Image: Comparative Studies in Québec Canadian Literature.* Don Mills, Ontario: New Press, 1971.

Thomas, Audrey. *Songs My Mother Taught Me.* Vancouver: Talonbooks, 1973.

Annie Ernaux ou la double aliénation langagière

Claire-Lise Tondeur
Bradley University

De nombreuses critiques contemporaines[1] cherchent à voir dans le texte dont le scripteur est féminin, une étude du développement de l'identité chez la femme. Dans la tradition du "devenir" hégélien, elles ont recours à la notion de "subject in process" qu'Alison Light définit ainsi: "the acquisition of gendered subjectivity is a process, a movement towards a social 'self' fraught with conflicts and never fully achieved." Dans cette approche-là, tout texte féminin est donc un avatar mais en même temps une image négative du *Bildungsroman* masculin. Les textes écrits par Annie Ernaux se prêtent particulièrement bien à cette doxa critique. Dans l'élaboration de l'identité d'une femme française, la composante langagière prend une plus grande importance que dans le contexte anglo-saxon car la parfaite maîtrise de la langue, qu'elle soit orale ou écrite, est qualité sacro-sainte, qui n'est même pas remise en question par les féministes les plus radicales. D'autre part une aspiration à la plénitude anime le développement de l'identité. Chez Ernaux, les aspirations se trouvent frustrées, ses rêves s'avèrent irréalisables et par conséquent elle se sent flouée.

Annie Ernaux est née en 1940 à Lillebonne en Normandie dans un milieu très modeste, ses parents tenaient une petite épicerie-buvette de quartier. Son premier roman *Les armoires vides*, paru en 1974, est un ouvrage semi-autobiographique de la déchirure sociale. Il parle de l'abîme qui sépare la narratrice Denise Lesur, qui est maintenant étudiante, de ses parents qui appartiennent à un milieu ouvrier. Entre la fille qui est devenue une intellectuelle et la mère qui a été une ouvrière d'usine avant de devenir commerçante, la communication est pratiquement impossible. L'adolescente fait siens les jugements que son nouveau milieu social porte sur celui de ses parents. Elle se met à les mépriser, les trouve "minables" mais elle souffre car ils l'adorent et elle a honte de son attitude.

> Ça suffit d'être une vicieuse, une cachottière, une fille poisseuse et lourde vis-à-vis des copines de classe, légères, pures de leur existence. . . . Fallait encore que je me mette à les mépriser mes parents. Tous les péchés, tous les vices. Personne ne pense mal de son père ou de sa mère. Il n'y a que moi. (99)

Cette déchirure sociale est ressentie avant tout à travers la différence langagière, leurs langues respectives étant incompatibles. La langue des parents est jugée erronée. "La faute, c'est leur langage à eux" (115) alors que la langue de l'école, reflet de la langue de la culture, n'est pas simplement normative, elle est aussi idéale.

> Le bien, c'était confondu avec le propre, le joli, une facilité à être et à parler. Bref avec le 'beau' comme on dit en cours de français; le mal, c'était le laid, le poisseux, le manque d'éducation. Mais je l'ai su avant qu'on le dise à l'école, ça me crevait les yeux. (107)

La langue d'origine doit être évacuée en faveur de la langue de la classe dominante. Il s'agit d'un des phénomènes culturels dont parle Marina Yaguello dans son "essai d'approche socio-linguistique de la condition féminine" intitulé *Les mots et les femmes* avec "domination d'une langue et hiérarchisation sociale fondée sur la maîtrise de la langue dominante" (41).

Dans la vision de la narratrice Denise Lesur, ses parents, ce sont des gens qui sont toujours à "bafouiller devant les types importants" (97) alors que "les personnes bien ont une voiture, des porte-documents, un imper, les mains propres. Ils ont la parole facile, n'importe où, n'importe comment." Ils ont "continuellement la réplique" (96). "N'avoir rien à dire" (114), c'est le lot de sa classe, à laquelle elle va chercher à échapper par la voie de l'écriture. Posséder à fond le maniement de la langue est donc une échappatoire mais cette maîtrise renforce aussi l'aliénation, car en adoptant la langue d'une autre classe, elle se coupe de ses racines comme en témoignent les épisodes pénibles lorsqu'elle retourne occasionnellement chez ses parents.

Dans *La femme gelée* (1981), la narratrice (alter ego de Denise Lesur) retrace son enfance sans contrainte entre une mère ardente et un père affectueux. Elle a donc connu une enfance insouciante et heureuse auprès de parents qui ont fait de grands sacrifices pour l'envoyer dans une école tenue par des religieuses, ayant toujours peur qu'elle "tourne mal," hantise d'un atavisme de classe. Une fois à l'école elle découvre l'humiliation répétée de ne pas appartenir à la bourgeoisie comme ses camarades et elle prend sa revanche en devenant la meilleure élève. Pour "conserver [sa] supériorité, [sa] vengeance" elle entre de plus en plus dans le jeu scolaire, dans ce milieu qui la rejetait; et elle prend ainsi conscience de tout ce qui la sépare irrémédiablement de ses parents. Plus elle avance dans ses études et plus elle s'éloigne du monde parental. Par ses lectures elle a accès à un nouveau langage qu'elle ne pourra s'approprier que par l'écriture.

> Ce n'était plus pour fermer la gueule des filles que je racontais des histoires, c'était pour vivre dans un monde plus beau, plus pur, plus riche que le mien. Tout entier en mots. Je les aime les mots des livres, je les apprends tous. Ma mère m'offre le *Larousse* aux pages roses dans le milieu, elle confie fièrement à la maîtresse que je passe des heures le nez dedans. La grâce, toujours! Langage bizarre, délicat, sans épaisseur, bien rangé et qui prononcé, sonne faux chez moi. (77)

Le mécanisme qui pousse Annie Ernaux à écrire naît de l'attirance qu'elle éprouve envers les mots, "ces beaux objets fascinants mais vides," codes qui lui viennent d'un autre monde, ainsi que de son besoin impérieux de faire coïncider mots et choses.

Depuis son entrée à l'école, Annie Ernaux est déchirée entre deux langages: langue maternelle et langue d'adoption: "Je porte en moi deux langages, les petits points noirs des livres, les sauterelles folles et gracieuses, à côté des paroles grasses, grosses, bien appuyées, qui s'enfoncent dans le ventre, dans la tête" (77). La première langue que lui a transmise sa mère, langue de son milieu d'origine est extrêmement concrète, presque dépourvue de mots abstraits; elle possède sa propre syntaxe et a un rapport au réel plus direct, plus physique. La seconde langue, celle d'adoption, qu'Annie Ernaux considère comme un moyen de libération est le langage appris à l'école, qu'elle nomme elle-même "le français correct." C'est une langue qu'elle trouve beaucoup plus riche, plus nuancée, capable d'exprimer un éventail d'expériences infiniment plus large.[2]

Pour Annie Ernaux, l'écrivain a des "comptes à rendre" à son public. Aussi veut-elle témoigner dans son oeuvre de l'aliénation que représente pour elle sa situation sociale, cette appartenance au départ à une classe dominée. "Pour moi écrire est profondément lié à ma situation sociale en tant qu'individu" (Tenth Cincinnatti Conference). Ce qui domine, qu'on lise ses romans ou qu'on l'écoute parler de ses oeuvres, c'est ce sentiment aigu de sa différence, une différence qu'elle articule sur un plan beaucoup plus social que sexuel. La marginalité culturelle, économique, politique et sociale de sa famille est vécue comme une différence infériorisante. Or, si écrire pour elle, c'est témoigner dans son oeuvre de son expérience de vie, elle ne peut le faire qu'en utilisant la langue d'adoption mais sans pour autant "trahir le premier monde dont [elle] vien[t]." Elle y parvient en ayant recours à une écriture extrêmement dépouillée. Il y a chez elle une méfiance envers la métaphore, par exemple, qu'elle considère comme quelque chose de gratuit, de précieux dont elle ne désire pas se servir. Elle se contente d'énoncer les faits sans commentaires parce qu'elle se veut à la "jointure entre l'histoire et la sociologie." Sur un ton détaché, impersonnel, dans une langue sobre, drue et vive, elle dit avec un minimum de mots. Son style lapidaire, sa sécheresse apparente donnent à l'oeuvre une densité qui libère l'émotion latente. Elle voudrait "aller à l'abstraction à force de concret."

Une autre manière de témoigner du malaise profond qu'elle ressent est d'avoir recours à la transgression. Annie Ernaux désirait faire de son premier roman *Les armoires vides* un livre de la transgression. Elle voulait, d'une part, transgresser l'ordre social, échapper à son milieu qui n'écrit pas et d'autre part transgresser l'institution scolaire en ne respectant pas le "langage correct" enseigné à l'école.

Cette "exilée de l'intérieur" comme elle se nomme elle-même ne peut parvenir à remplir les "armoires vides" de la dépossession culturelle familiale que par l'écriture. Mais ces mots acquis à l'école ne couvrent pas l'expérience vécue, ce sont eux aussi des "armoires vides." Le divorce entre les deux langues subsiste et l'oralité ne peut être complètement maîtrisée.

> Flouée, flouée, que je suis, mais personne comprendrait chez moi ce que ça veut dire. . . . C'est pour ça que je n'employais mes nouveaux mots que pour écrire, je leur restituais leur seule forme possible pour moi. Dans la bouche, je n'y arrivais pas. Expression orale maladroite en dépit des bons résultats, elles écrivaient, les maîtresses sur le carnet de notes. (78)

Pour acquérir cette aisance dans la langue parlée qu'elle enviait à ses camarades de classe plus privilégiées, Annie Ernaux a dû renoncer au monde de son origine pour lequel elle garde de la nostalgie et subir les conséquences de cette déchirure sociale.

A l'aliénation d'origine sociale vient s'ajouter celle qui provient de la découverte de son identité sexuelle. Comme enfant de prolétaires, elle était libre. C'est le mariage dans un milieu bourgeois, la maternité et son activité professionnelle (elle était professeur de lycée) qui finalement lui ont fait prendre pleinement conscience de sa nouvelle identité. C'est alors la découverte du piège, sans échappatoire possible. "Toute mon histoire de femme est celle d'un escalier qu'on descend en renâclant" écrit Annie Ernaux dans *La Femme gelée* (181). La lente élaboration de son identité amène l'auteur à découvrir ce que cela représente d'aliénation pour elle. Elle se sent dupée. Son "ascension" socio-linguistique est un leurre. Ses aspirations à la plénitude de son identité se révèlent être des rêves piégés.

La seule échappatoire réside dans l'écriture, par exemple dans le roman *La Place* témoignage empreint de remords sur la vie de son père qu'elle s'accuse d'avoir renié socialement et linguistiquement. Dans cet ouvrage, elle continue à utiliser la veine autobiographique. Après la mort de son père, la narratrice veut témoigner de sa vie, sentant que par son propre métier de professeur et son mariage bourgeois, elle semble avoir désavoué ses parents, son père surtout, garçon de ferme, ouvrier d'usine puis épicier-cabaretier dans une petite ville de Normandie. Se fondant sur des faits, des photos, des souvenirs de scènes précises et de phrases souvent entendues, elle cherche à faire revivre son père et le monde qui l'entoure parce qu'ils "méritai[en]t de venir à l'écriture" (Tenth Cincinnati Conference). Mais ce roman est aussi le récit d'une éducation où l'héroïne est déchirée entre son milieu familial étroit, suffocant et l'aspiration à la connaissance qui est ressentie comme une promesse de liberté. Au fur et à mesure qu'elle "s'élève," elle s'éloigne de l'épicerie-buvette paternelle et prend son milieu social en horreur. En changeant de milieu, de classe sociale, elle change inévitablement de langage. Le père qu'elle adorait, enfant, lui est devenu étranger. Ils n'ont plus de langue commune. Symboliquement, celui-ci meurt au moment où sa fille accède au professorat et elle se reproche de l'avoir "trahi."

Avec *Une femme* (1988), Annie Ernaux veut faire pour sa mère ce qu'elle avait fait pour son père dans *La Place*. Sa mère venant de mourir après une longue maladie qui lui avait dérobé la mémoire et sa personnalité, l'auteur en écrivant sur elle veut la "mettre au monde"(43) et la comprendre comme elle n'a jamais pu le faire auparavant. C'est ainsi qu'elle revient à son thème principal: la déchirure de classe au sein même de la famille. Cette mère qui considérait parfois sa fille comme une "ennemie de classe,"(65) était aussi de son côté, prenant toujours le parti du corps enseignant, poussant sa fille à faire des études pour qu'elle puisse échapper à ce milieu, "désirant s'élever"(57) par sa fille, vivant à travers elle. Celle-ci se fait à son tour archiviste de sa mémoire, de sa langue et de son "savoir-faire." Avec minutie, elle met au jour les coutumes, les goûts, le vocabulaire, les valeurs du milieu maternel, tout un héritage culturel des dominés chez qui la religion par exemple est vécue comme une culture à leur mesure, la seule à laquelle ils aient accès, et qui leur donne une dignité que leur refuse la société.

La Femme gelée, parue en 1981, donne un inventaire désenchanté de la condition féminine. C'est le roman d'Annie Ernaux qui privilégie le plus ses sentiments d'attente trompée, d'aspirations déçues. "La Femme gelée ou trente ans après *Le Deuxième Sexe* une femme toujours piégée"; voilà comme l'auteur a présenté son roman. La narratrice a trente ans, elle est professeur, mariée à un cadre, mère de deux enfants. Elle habite un appartement agréable dans une petite ville de province mais pourtant c'est une femme gelée, prise dans l'engrenage des obligations domestiques qui lui ont ôté toute liberté d'esprit et de mouvement. Après avoir connu la curiosité, l'élan, le bonheur, la complicité d'un amour à deux, sa vie se fige au fil des jours entre les courses à faire, le dîner à préparer, les soins à donner à ses deux petits enfants et son travail d'enseignante; ce que l'on dit être la condition "normale" de la femme. La narratrice retrace son enfance sans contrainte entre ses parents qui se partageaient le plus naturellement du monde les tâches de la maison et du commerce. Elle raconte ses problèmes d'adolescente quand, pour être aimée, elle se conforme au modèle qu'"ils" préfèrent, s'efforçant de paraître mignonne, gentille et compréhensive. C'est ensuite l'oscillation entre les rêves romanesques et la volonté de rester indépendante, la poursuite sérieuse d'études et la recherche obstinée de l'amour. Elle rencontre enfin le frère d'élection avec qui elle pourra tout partager. Elle avait imaginé leur vie commune comme une aventure. Après le mariage et la venue des enfants, elle découvre la réalité, avec les rôles inégaux que la société et la tradition ont dévolu à l'homme et à la femme. Tous deux exercent un métier après des études d'un niveau égal, mais c'est à elle et à elle seule de s'occuper des enfants, du ménage, de la "nourriture corvée," simplement parce qu'elle est née femme. La narratrice ne gémit pas, elle ne s'apitoie pas sur son sort, elle consent par vanité à "tout concilier." Elle rit, crie, et constate:

> Elles ont fini sans que je m'en aperçoive, les années d'apprentissage. Après, c'est l'habitude. Une somme de petits bruits à l'intérieur, moulin à café, casseroles; prof discrète, femme de cadre vêtue de Cacharel ou Rodier dehors. Une femme gelée. (185)

Mais le ressentiment est là, on sent la révolte sourdre, on devine la rage qui va éclater. "Toutes les femmes à mari et à mômes font partie d'un univers mort" (113), pense-t-elle comme étudiante. Enfant, la narratrice était libre de devenir ce qu'elle voulait, "devenir quelqu'un ça n'avait pas de sexe pour mes parents" (39), et voilà qu'elle est maintenant piégée, elle ne voit pas d'issue possible. Elle avait pourtant imaginé sa vie d'adulte comme un moyen d'acquérir un équilibre qui lui manquait. "Je me persuade qu'en me mariant je serai libérée de ce moi qui tourne en rond, se pose des questions, un moi inutile. Que j'atteindrai l'équilibre" (127). Mais elle "s'enlise" dans l'activité ménagère et le maternage finit par l'incarcérer. Cette réclusion est devenue mentale, elle ne peut pas y échapper physiquement.

> Je sortais le Bicou [son fils] pour être une mère irréprochable. Sortir, appeler ça sortir, le même mot qu'avant. Il n'y avait plus de dehors pour moi, c'était le dedans qui continuait, avec les mêmes préoccupations, l'enfant, le beurre et les paquets de couches que j'achèterais au retour. Ni curiosité, ni découverte, rien que la nécessité. (160-61)

Avec le maternage, elle a dû renoncer à toutes ses activités favorites, telle la manipulation de symboles ou le recours à l'abstraction, ce qui comme intellectuelle la définissait, pour régresser à un niveau qui soit compatible avec celui de ses petits enfants. "La vie, la beauté du monde. Tout était hors de moi. Il n'y avait plus rien à découvrir" (162). Sa conviction qu'elle est en train de perdre son identité, de "couler" ne va pas sans culpabilisation. "Dire le coinçage, l'étouffement, tout de suite le soupçon, encore une qui ne pense qu'à elle" (162). Elle ne rejette pas la responsabilité de son sort sur ses deux fils, en tout cas pas explicitement mais indirectement, c'est une conclusion inéluctable. La narratrice dans *La Femme gelée* prend pleinement conscience qu'elle ne peut pas échapper à l'aliénation due à son identité de femme, qui l'oblige à endosser le rôle traditionnellement réservé aux femmes et qui dans son cas menace de la détruire.

Dans *Une vie pour deux*, Marie Cardinal laisse clairement entendre que le maternage représente pour la femme une perte d'identité, une sorte de mort. C'est une vision du maternage comme une des sources du servage féminin. Le travail ménager et le maternage, c'est-à-dire les travaux domestiques et l'élevage des enfants sont, dans nos sociétés, des responsabilités exclusives des femmes et non rémunérées. On peut donc en tirer la conclusion, comme le font les féministes radicales du M.L.F., que les femmes ont "un rapport spécifique à la production, qui est assimilable au servage" (Albitur & Armogathe 2:676).

Sur la marginalisation due à son identité sexuelle--les femmes dans la société patriarcale n'ayant jamais vraiment eu voix au chapitre--vient se greffer, chez Annie Ernaux, une seconde marginalisation: l'acquisition d'une langue qui n'est pas la sienne mais qui se révèle être libératrice. Les mots appris à l'école ne couvrent pas l'expérience vécue dans son milieu prolétaire mais ce sont pourtant ceux qu'elle doit utiliser pour pouvoir porter un témoignage sur son parcours socio-linguistique. Dans la double aliénation langagière dont souffre Annie Ernaux, la composante sociale est beaucoup plus importante que celle qui tient à son identité sexuelle. Annie Ernaux se perçoit d'abord comme issue du prolétariat, classe qui n'a jamais vraiment eu droit à la parole, et ensuite, beaucoup plus accessoirement comme handicapée parce qu'elle est née femme.

A travers la lecture, elle cherchait quand elle était enfant, à s'approprier ces mots qu'elle admirait et qui l'attiraient. "C'était tout artificiel, un système de mots de passe pour entrer dans un autre milieu" (*Armoires* 78). Plus tard, mais cette fois grâce à l'écriture, l'adulte va essayer de faire coïncider ces mots magiques avec la réalité qui, au lieu d'être vécue, sera imaginée. A la réalité vécue qui finit toujours par être une déception, Annie Ernaux substitue donc l'écriture, qui lui permet finalement de surmonter sa double aliénation langagière.

Notes

[1] Pour une discussion de ces problèmes, je vous renvoie au volume intitulé *Writing and Sexual Difference*, ed. Elizabeth Abel (University of Chicago Press, 1980), tout particulièrement à l'article de Judith Kegan Gardiner: "On Female Identity and Writing by Women" (177-91).

[2] Pour ces remarques, je me base sur la communication présentée par Annie Ernaux elle-même le 17 mai 1990 lors du *Tenth Cincinnati Conference on Romance Languages and Literatures*.

Oeuvres citées

Abel, Elizabeth, ed. *Writing and Sexual Difference*. Chicago: U of Chicago P, 1980.

Albitur, Maïté et Daniel Armogathe. *Histoire du féminisme français*. 2 vols. Paris: des Femmes, 1977.

Cardinal, Marie. *Une vie pour deux*. Paris: Grasset, 1978.

Ernaux, Annie. *Les armoires vides*. Paris: Gallimard, 1974.

——. *La femme gelée*. Paris: Gallimard, 1981.

——. *La Place*. Paris: Gallimard, 1984.

——. *Une femme*. Paris: Gallimard, 1988.

Light, Alison. "'Returning to Mandelay.' Romance Fiction, Female Sexuality and Class." *Feminist Review* 16 (1984); 7-25.

Yaguello, Marina. *Les mots et les femmes*. Paris: Payot, 1978.

Une autre oubliée: Marcelle Tinayre, 1877-1948

Marie-France Hilgar
University of Nevada - Las Vegas

Marcelle Tinayre est née à Tulle en 1877. Sa mère, Louise Chasteau a elle-même été une romancière de renom et sa grand-mère, poétesse, correspondait avec Lamartine. Mariée très jeune à un graveur parisien, Marcelle fait la connaissance de la directrice de la *Nouvelle revue*, Juliette Adam, qui accepte de publier *Avant l'amour*, son premier roman. Marcelle n'a guère alors que dix-neuf ans. Elle continuera à produire jusqu'à sa mort, survenue en 1948, outre ses articles, ses nouvelles, ses essais et ses conférences, environ un roman par an.

Elle s'est d'abord fait connaître comme une romancière de la passion. Ses premières oeuvres, *La rançon, La maison du péché, La Rebelle,* sont des romans d'amour féminin. Ses héroïnes sont des femmes dont l'amour détermine toute la conduite ou, pour mieux dire, commande toute la vie. Ensuite dans *La vie amoureuse de François Barbazanges* et *Le bouclier d'Alexandre*, Marcelle Tinayre se plaît à transposer des aventures sentimentales dans un cadre héroïque. Puis un renouvellement plus marqué de son inspiration se manifeste dans un récit d'une originalité singulière, *Priscille Séverac*, où elle trace le portrait et raconte les aventures d'une illuminée, sans autre culture que la Bible. Priscille est devenue une sorte de prophétesse qui se croit porteuse d'un message et doit le faire parvenir à sa destination; elle sait que le tsar n'est pas mort et c'est à elle qu'il appartient de le retrouver. Avec elle, nous sommes sur les frontières de la psychologie et de la pathologie.

Renaude Vipreux, dans *L'ennemie intime*, est elle aussi un sujet intermédiaire entre la personnalité normale et la personnalité morbide. Sa passion dominante, exclusive, est la haine, et quand on étudie de près le personnage on n'a pas de peine à reconnaître un cas de refoulement. Renaude a été appelée à titre de gouvernante dans la maison de Villefarge pour soigner le vieux Capdenat auquel sa fille Geneviève, mariée à Paris, ne peut suffisamment se consacrer. De même origine que Geneviève, Renaude a été forcée par la dureté des temps, cruels aux petits rentiers, de descendre à un rang de semi-domestique tandis que Geneviève, grâce à sa beauté, est devenue une dame, l'épouse du riche architecte Alquier.
Dès la première rencontre des deux femmes, Renaude inquiète par

l'humilité orgueilleuse qu'elle met à affirmer son état subalterne, et par le dur regard de ses yeux gris qui, sous les cils roussâtres, sont "comme deux petits canifs luisants" (53). Malgré le grossier accueil de Capdenat, la vieille fille et lui s'entendent bientôt pour haïr Geneviève. Capdenat accuse sa fille d'être une enfant dénaturée qui l'abandonne dans un trou de province. En réalité il est incapable de tendresse. Il n'aime ni les autres, ni lui-même, et s'il finit par s'entendre avec sa gouvernante c'est parce qu'elle lui sert d'instrument de vengeance. Quant à Renaude, elle a détesté Geneviève dès le moment où elle l'a vue, rayonnante, à son réveil: "qu'une femme pût être belle comme une belle statue, et porter des chemises plus luxueuses que des robes de bal, Renaude Vipreux ne s'en doutait pas et la révélation la bouleversait" (51). Marcelle Tinayre a trouvé pour peindre cette demi-nudité de Geneviève devant la fenêtre ensoleillée des mots de chaleur, de lumière et de volupté. C'est cet éblouissement que Renaude ne pardonnera jamais à la femme jeune, belle, entourée de luxe. C'est là le supplice de l'envieuse et la cause de sa haine.

Renaude apprend, par une lettre dont elle est chargée pour Geneviève que celle-ci est aimée, d'un amour coupable. Elle tient une nouvelle raison de détester la jeune femme, elle, vieille fille desséchée, et aussi un nouveau moyen de se venger. Ainsi que le fait Marie de France dans ses *Lais*, Marcelle Tinayre considère que la femme mal mariée a le droit de trouver le bonheur en dehors du mariage. Nous devinons Alquier, qui a vingt ans de plus que Geneviève, profondément dépravé. L'auteur en a indiqué, d'une plume très discrète, les vices et la cruauté: "Certains mouvements du poignet laissaient voir sous la manchette le ruban d'or d'un bracelet souple, insolent et furtif comme un aveu ..." (138) et plus loin, comme Geneviève, triste et lasse, a les yeux humides: "Vous n'allez pas pleurer. Prenez garde! les larmes, m'excitent" (140). Geneviève se rappelle alors le temps où il la faisait pleurer *exprès*, où il la confrontait aux pires dépravations, "toutes ces fêtes secrètes qui appelaient le feu du ciel et la pluie de soufre, tout ce qu'elle avait subi, tout ce qu'elle voulait oublier" (140).

Livrée à un pareil homme, Geneviève a eu la chance de rencontrer un garçon au coeur droit quelques années après son mariage. Roland d'Espitalès possède un petit domaine non loin de Villefarge. Laissant la gouvernante installée au côté du vieux Capdenat, Geneviève va rejoindre son amant, vivre une nuit sur sa poitrine avant de regagner Paris et son triste foyer. Marcelle Tinayre retrouve la plume voluptueuse, dont elle ne se sert que très rarement, avec laquelle elle a dépeint Geneviève au réveil pour évoquer la passion des amants, leur chambre: "La lampe se ralluma, près du rideau qui versait au lit dévasté son ombre ardente. Des feux pourpres coururent sur le damas des tentures" (111). Ils doivent pourtant s'en arracher: "Chacun de leurs pas défaisaient une maille du filet enchanté où leurs corps s'étaient pris, là-haut..." (113). "J'ai eu cela, se dit Geneviève dans le sombre éblouissement du souvenir. Rien ne peut faire que je n'aie eu cela. Mais l'angoisse la prit, l'angoisse panique de ceux qui ont osé dire: je suis heureux" (103).

Geneviève avait raison de craindre. A Paris, elle demeure sans nouvelles de son amant qui, sans doute, l'aimait moins qu'elle ne l'aimait. Au cours d'un séjour de Geneviève chez son père, Renaude se charge de la renseigner. Elle lui apporte le journal local, *Le petit écho du Rouergue.* Elle sait bien ce que la jeune femme va y lire: l'annonce du mariage de son amant avec une voisine.

Pendant le délire qui, à la suite de ce choc, s'empare de Geneviève, Renaude déploie un dévouement dont tout le monde est dupe. Elle se dupe elle-même en se persuadant: "Ce n'est pas cette femme que je hais, c'est son péché" (260). Renaude parvient à dérober une lettre d'amour de Geneviève, à modifier les dispositions testamentaires du vieux Capdenat et à se faire octroyer l'héritage de ses enfants, y compris la vieille maison de famille que Geneviève aime tant parce qu'elle renferme les souvenirs des êtres qu'elle a le plus aimés, sa mère et son frère. Or Renaude tient moins à l'argent qu'à sa vengeance. Sans doute serait-elle déçue si Alquier ne contestait pas la succession, s'il ne lui offrait pas une occasion de lutte, un prétexte à se servir de son arme. Ce qu'elle veut, c'est sa revanche sur Geneviève. Elle apprend à la malheureuse que si elle n'empêche pas son mari d'attaquer le testament, or elle sait que la jeune femme est sans influence sur son mari, elle usera de la lettre qu'elle détient.

Terrifiée, Geneviève part en auto, de nuit, par des routes dangereuses. Dans l'ébranlement de ses nerfs, ayant perdu tout sang-froid, elle se tue. Suicide ou accident? Le lecteur est libre d'interpréter le fait à sa manière mais Renaude, d'une manière ou d'une autre, n'en est pas moins coupable. En fait, elle n'avait pas prévu la fin brutale de sa victime. Elle-même mourra d'un arrêt cardiaque dû à l'épouvante, au cours d'une scène magnifique où le frère de Geneviève, curieuse figure de raté communiste, essaie de lui reprendre les papiers dérobés et de sauver ainsi la mémoire de sa chère disparue.

Ce roman est remarquablement charpenté. L'auteur dévoile le caractère de ses héros sans jamais recourir au langage abstrait de l'analyse. Marcelle Tinayre ne démontre pas. Elle fait parler, elle fait agir. Elle trouve le geste, le mot qui trahit toute la nature du personnage.

Après l'illuminée et la refoulée, Marcelle Tinayre a présenté la mythomane dans *Château en Limousin* (1934). En reprenant l'affaire Lafarge, elle l'a portée sur son véritable terrain qui est non pas d'ordre judiciaire seulement mais aussi d'ordre psychologique. Mme Lafarge a-t-elle empoisonné son mari? Après les audiences de la cour d'assises, les dépositions des témoins, les déclarations des experts, les réquisitoires et les plaidoiries, des doutes subsistent. Aussi n'est-ce point à ces sources d'informations que l'auteur a demandé l'éclaircissement du mystère. Le procès n'est que l'épilogue de son livre. Ce que Marcelle Tinayre s'est proposé, c'est de nous faire connaître et de nous faire comprendre Mme Lafarge, d'évoquer sa vie et d'en pénétrer les secrets, de la replacer dans le cadre et dans l'atmosphère où elle s'est trouvée, de reconstituer le drame avec ses éléments essentiels, le milieu, les personnages et l'action, tel qu'il s'est préparé dans la froide et sombre demeure du Glandier, si différente de ce qu'avait imaginé Marie Cappelle quand elle avait imprudemment accepté d'épouser Charles Lafarge quinze jours à peine après avoir fait sa connaissance.

Elégante et raffinée, Marie Cappelle a vécu jusqu'à vingt-trois ans dans le luxe et parmi la société mondaine parisienne. Elle sait qu'un peu de sang princier coule dans ses veines: elle est probablement l'arrière petite-fille de Philippe-Egalité et de Mme de Genlis. Elle vient de faire un mariage absurde, par dépit, par coup de tête, parce qu'elle se rend bien compte que les prétendants ne font pas la queue à sa porte. Charles Lafarge n'a que vingt-huit ans mais il n'a rien de la jeunesse, rien pour plaire à sa femme: à la fois brutal et faible, mal tenu, grossier, rustre, il a vite fait de la décevoir, de lui déplaire, et de se rendre odieux.

La scène de l'arrivée au Glandier, le 15 août 1839, est saisissante. Il est clair que Marie Cappelle entre dans une atmosphère irrespirable. Il suffit de la voir dans ce manoir délabré, avec un tel mari, une belle-mère hostile, un entourage assorti pour comprendre que ce château en Limousin, qui a été pendant les quelques jours d'illusion de ses fiançailles son château en Espagne, lui apparaisse aussitôt comme une prison inhabitable où elle ne pourra qu'étouffer. Voilà les origines psychologiques du drame.

Jeune fille, Marie Cappelle souffrait déjà d'une imagination débordante et inventait des intrigues qui risquaient de compromettre des innocents. Condamnée à vivre avec Charles Lafarge, la jeune femme s'évade de la réalité et superpose à sa misérable vie réelle une vie fictive et romanesque, et le mensonge, qui ne lui était déjà que trop familier, va désormais dominer sa conduite. L'énigme judiciaire cède la place au mystère psychologique. Au lieu de partir des caractères pour les engager dans une action, Marcelle Tinayre va de l'action aux caractères qui déterminent cette action par leurs conflits. Comme dans tout roman "classique," nous voyons l'apparence physique, l'allure, les habitudes et les manières des personnages, leur réalité extérieure ainsi que leur vie intérieure. Il y a en effet tout un petit monde provincial rassemblé autour de Marie Cappelle: Charles Lafarge et sa mère, demi-bourgeoise demi-paysanne, qui depuis quarante ans n'est pas sortie du Glandier, une soeur et un beau-frère installés aussi dans la maison, l'oncle Pontier, d'Uzerche, avec sa fille Emma, l'un et l'autre séduits par le charme de Marie, Clémentine, sa femme de chambre qui, toujours aux côtés de sa maîtresse et lui ayant vu manier les paquets d'arsenic lui est restée fidèle jusque dans sa prison et a fini ses jours beaucoup plus tard en proie à une folie douce pendant laquelle elle ne prononçait que ces trois mots: "Elle est innocente." Il y a aussi Melle Brun, vieille fille pauvre qui est venue faire le portrait de la jeune épouse et qui, embusquée dans la maison y devient une observatrice aux aguets. Tous, hommes et femmes, sont dominés dans le récit par la figure attirante, inquiétante, mystérieuse de Marie Lafarge.

> L'explication de Marie Cappelle, [dit l'auteur dans l'avant-propos,] je l'ai demandée aux gens et aux choses qui l'entourèrent, à ce petit monde provincial qu'elle détesta, faute de le comprendre, à ce mari qu'elle essaya d'aimer et ne sut que haïr, à leur vie conjugale dont le secret contient tout le secret du drame qui en fut l'horrible dénouement. Et je l'ai demandée surtout à Marie elle-même, à cette âme trouble de mythomane, à cette féminité souffrante et viciée . . . Expliquer un être par ses tares et ses monstruosités mêmes, ce n'est pas l'innocenter; c'est l'excuser, peut-être....

Ces lignes si lucides contiennent en substance le livre tout entier et en indiquent la richesse.

Marcelle Tinayre s'est plu à continuer à nous révéler les secrets de l'âme et du coeur féminin dans *La femme et son secret.* Ce qui l'intéresse, c'est, dit-elle dans sa Préface, "sous les aspects nouveaux de l'Eve moderne, le fonds essentiel et permanent du féminin" et ce qu'elle essaie, c'est "une tentative d'explication de la femme, l'histoire de son imagination et de sa sensibilité, l'aventure de son coeur, de l'enfance à la vieillesse." Elle sait combien les modes sont superficielles et changeantes, mais tout en les suivant, les femmes ne changent pas leurs âmes. Elle les considère donc dans leurs éléments les plus stables, telles qu'elles sont, telles qu'elles étaient, telles qu'elles seront. Il y a une logique intérieure dans tout ce développement de l'aventure féminine, telle que nous la content, en la suivant à travers ses diverses phases, les sept chapitres de *La femme et son secret.* Tour à tour défilent devant nos yeux et s'offrent à notre attention et à notre réflexion: la petite enfance, l'âge ingrat, l'âge de l'ingratitude, le bonheur conjugal, le démon de midi, l'héroïsme féminin, et le chemin de la sagesse qui mène à la vie apaisée.

Marcelle Tinayre perçoit dès l'enfance un contraste entre le petit garçon et la petite fille, contraste qui n'est que l'opposition de deux tendances correspondant à deux fins opposées. La part respective de l'homme et de la femme dans l'humaine destinée est mise en lumière: "Il veut comprendre. Elle veut vivre. Il explique la vie. La femme la donne, la maintient, la défend selon sa loi . . . Elle a besoin qu'on ait besoin d'elle." Là est le principe de ce que Marcelle Tinayre appelle l'héroïsme féminin. Ce qui est héroïque, c'est la direction que prend l'amour et ce sont surtout les actes qu'il fait accomplir. L'auteur écrit à propos de la Pauline de *Polyeucte* et de *La princesse de Clèves*, "une honnête femme chrétienne, fille de Racine et qui est allée à l'école chez Corneille," des pages exquises et profondes, d'une justesse de psychologie indéniable. Elle éclaire le caractère de l'héroïne par l'histoire de l'auteur et l'impossible amour de Mme de Lafayette pour La Rochefoucauld. Selon elle, le coeur féminin de la Princesse de Clèves ne trouvait pas son besoin d'absolu dans celui du duc de Nemours. L'histoire de Juliette Drouet et de Victor Hugo lui apparaît, au contraire, comme la réalisation totale, parfaite, de l'amour féminin, cet amour à l'état pur. Là, toutes les conditions se sont trouvées réunies pour qu'il atteigne son plein épanouissement, qui est, chez la femme, un don total à l'homme qu'elle peut admirer.

Marcelle Tinayre ne se borne point à faire agir ses personnages; elle se livre à des commentaires et par là se révèle autant moraliste que romancière. *Est-ce un miracle*? est l'histoire non de la conversion d'une femme, restée fille, mais de son évolution vers la sainteté. Pieuse certes, mais retenue à la terre par son énergie, son intérêt pour les choses pratiques, elle atteint au désintéressement à la suite du désespoir que son frère, qu'elle chérissait comme un enfant, lui a causé en se montrant diabolique. Elle croyait avoir obtenu du Ciel un miracle en faveur du malheureux, à deux doigts de la mort. Mais c'est en fait sur elle qu'elle attire la grâce divine. Autour de ce personnage central, fortement campé, se détachant en relief sur le paysage de la haute Corrèze, Marcelle Tinayre a dressé la naïve figure d'un curé-artiste, un pittoresque collectionneur entiché de Balzac, un bourgeois de campagne, une jeune fille sensuelle, et le pervers Jean-Claude qui fait le mal gratuitement. L'auteur a mis au service d'une très chrétienne inspiration, ses meilleurs dons de psychologie et d'observatrice réaliste.

Malgré tous ses talents, Marcelle Tinayre est bien oubliée de nos jours et il est quasi impossible de trouver en France des critiques qui s'intéressent à son oeuvre. Pourtant, outre-Atlantique, et dès 1915, alors que Marcelle n'avait publié "que" quinze livres, Winifred (Whale) Stephens lui consacrait un chapitre de quarante-neuf pages dans son *French Novelists of Today* et n'hésitait pas à la placer aux côtés de Romain Rolland. C'est à elle que nous empruntons notre conclusion:

> Madame Tinayre is a writer, the clear mirror of whose delicate art reflects the dawn of the new French spirit. She possesses, united to the average Frenchwoman's wake-mindedness and faculty for observation, the idealist's poetic soul—No one interested in contemporary French fiction can afford to ignore [her novels]. For in every one of them she appears as a consummate artist, a perfect mistress of the literary craft... That lightness and grace, that harmony and sense of proportion, so typically French, are never absent from a single page of her work.[1]

Note

[1] Winifred (Whale) Stephens, *French Novelists of Today*. New York: Books for Libraries Press, 1915. Reprint 1968. 45-46.

Œuvres de Marcelle Tinayre (1877–1948)

Romans:

1897 *Avant l'amour*. Paris: Mercure de France.

1898 *La rançon*. Paris: Calmann-Lévy.

1899 *Hellé*. Paris: Mercure de France.

1901 *L'oiseau d'orage*. Paris: Calmann-Lévy.

1902 *La maison du péché*. Paris: Calmann-Lévy.

1904 *La vie amoureuse de François Barbazanges*. Paris: Calmann-Lévy.

1905 *La rebelle*. Paris: Calmann-Lévy.

1907 *La consolatrie*. Paris: L'Illustration.

1908 *L'amour qui pleure*. Paris: Calmann-Lévy.

1909 *Notes d'une voyageuse en Turquie*. Paris: Calmann-Lévy.

1909 *L'ombre de l'amour*. Paris: Calmann-Lévy.

1910 *Une journée de Port Royal*. Paris: Calmann-Lévy.

1911 *La douceur de vivre*. Paris: Calmann-Lévy.

1913 *Madeleine au miroir*. Paris: Calmann-Lévy.

1915 *La veillée des armes. Le départ: août 1914*. Paris: Calmann-Lévy.

1920 *Perséphone*. Paris: Calmann-Lévy.

1921 *Les lampes voilées*. Paris: Calmann-Lévy.

1922 *Priscille Séverac*. Paris: Calmann-Lévy.

1922 *Le bouclier d'Alexandre*. Paris: L'Illustration.

1922 *Châteaux disparus*. Paris: Firmin Didot.

1923 *La légende de Duccio et d'Orsette*. Paris: L'Illustration.

1924 *Madame de Pompadour*. Paris: Flammarion.

1925 *Un drame de famille*. Paris: Calmann-Lévy.

1926 *Saint Jean libérateur*. Paris: L'Illustration.

1926 Figures dans la nuit. Paris: Calmann-Lévy.

1928 *Terres étrangères*. Paris: Flammarion.

1930 *Une provinciale*, Paris: P. Lafitte.

1931 *L'ennemie intime.* Paris: Flammarion.

1933 *La femme et son secret.* Paris: Flammarion.

1934 *Château en Limousin.* Paris: Flammarion.

1935 *Histoire de l'amour.* Paris: Flammarion.

1936 *Gérard et Delphine: la porte rouge.* Paris: Flammarion.

1939 *Est-ce un miracle?* Paris: Flammarion.

"L'Enfermement dans l'île": la femme corse dans l'oeuvre de Marie Susini

à la mémoire de Marie Susini

Georgiana M. M. Colvile
University of Colorado, Boulder

Romancière trés cotée en France, traduite dans la plupart des langues occidentales, puis en russe, en tchèque et en japonais, Marie Susini demeure néanmoins presque inconnue aux Etats-Unis. Née en Corse, dans un village de montagne, près d'Ajaccio, elle a fait ses études secondaires chez les religieuses, en Corse puis à Marseille, comme l'exigeait la tradition de son pays. De la génération qui a eu vingt ans sous l'Occupation à Paris, Marie Susini avait choisi la capitale pour y entreprendre des études supérieures: Licence de Philosophie, Licence de Lettres Classiques, Diplôme d'Etudes supérieures sur Bergson et la philosophie indienne. Elle a commencé une thèse sur la méditation bouddhique et a suivi des cours à l'école du Louvre (en particulier sur l'art contemporain), à l'Ecole Pratique des Hautes Etudes, ainsi qu'au Collège de France.

Auteur de sept romans, tous en "poche," d'une pièce de théâtre et d'un album illustré sur la Corse, Marie Susini est devenue Présidente du Jury du Prix Fémina, dont elle était membre depuis 1971, membre de l'Académie des Sciences Humaines de Bruxelles, membre du Jury France-Canada, nommée Officier dans l'Ordre des Arts et Lettres, en 1984, par Jack Lang. Paris demeura son port d'attache: Elle habitait Saint-Germain des Prés, ce qui ne l'empêchait pas de retourner régulièrement en Corse et de séjourner souvent aux Indes. Elle est morte le 22 août 1993 en Italie.

La renfermée, la Corse, titre du dernier ouvrage de la romancière, essai poétique sur son pays d'origine, pourrait aussi bien désigner l'auteur. Paradoxalement, Marie Susini, toujours si secrète, se révèle soudain dans ce livre, à travers une Corse où se mirent ses "paysages intérieurs" (90). *La renfermée* apporte à ses lecteurs comme le métatexte de toute son oeuvre. Les illustrations, photographies sobres et émouvantes de Chris Marker, restent sans titres. Texte et images fixent à jamais les traces de la Corse d'avant les années 60, lorsque commença l'invasion destructrice et irréversible des touristes et des promoteurs étrangers. La Corse, telle que Marie Susini l'a vécue et écrite, "tourne résolument le dos à l'Histoire" (29), alors qu'aujourd'hui "le temps de l'Histoire a tout à coup remplacé le temps des légendes" (39). Marie Susini n'a plus écrit sur la Corse, qu'elle perçevait comme "une femme en deuil" (90).

Dans son écriture, Marie Susini recherchait la dimension mythique. Sa propre relation avec la Corse tenait du mythe de Perséphone: installée à Paris, chaque année au printemps ou en été elle retournait vers la Corse ensoleillée, Démeter qui lui inspirait un amour et une haine d'égale violence:

> Je n'ai jamais eu le mal du pays. Dès que l'avion approche de la Corse et que brutalement elle est là, âpre, sinistre, ma gorge se serre, j'ai envie de fuir sur-le-champ, avant même d'avoir posé le pied sur le sol. Dans le temps de ce regard, elle émerge comme le dernier reste de l'immense chaos qui déchira la nuit du monde. (30-31)

Le paysage corse évoque une légende grecque: la création achevée, il ne restait plus rien à Dieu qu'une poignée de rochers, qu'il jeta dans la mer. Pour compenser l'aridité de ce dernier pays, il lui fit don du plus beau climat du monde. Ainsi naquit la Grèce, avec toutes ses îles, dont les Ioniennes, soeurs de la Corse et de la Sardaigne, de l'autre côté de la presqu'île italienne, brûlées par le même soleil, pétries des mêmes contradictions: sécheresse du sol et végetation luxuriante sur la côte, âpreté et bonhomie des habitants. Entre la mer et la montagne, comme entre Charybde et Scylla.

Qui n'a jamais ressenti la nissonostalgie ou nostalgie de l'île, le désir de faire un voyage à Cythère, à la découverte de l'exotisme et de la magie d'un microcosme secret? (voir Moles et Rohmer 47-66). Dans le monde entier, écrivains et artistes recherchent la paix utérine et l'isolement des petites îles. Par contre, ceux qui comme Marie Susini y sont nés, redoutent cette iléité étroite, où ils étouffent, cernés par la mer. C'est ce que Marie Susini appelle "l'enfermement dans l'île" (*La renfermée* 34).

A la difficulté d'être corse vient s'ajouter "le malheur d'être née fille" (82). L'iléité dans l'oeuvre de Marie Susini ne se limite pas à la Corse, toutes ses protagonistes souffrent de "l'elléité" de leur condition de femmes méditerranéennes, marquées dès la petite enfance. La romancière évoque ainsi la sienne:

> J'ai été comme un oiseau en cage dans mon enfance, emmurée dans ma condition de fille, prise à l'intérieur

> de cette cellule aux règles rigides qu'est la famille corse, prise elle aussi dans l'îlot du village, le village bouclé sur lui-même dans un pays tout naturellement isolé, barricadé par la mer. (87)

On notera la force de la métaphore filée et emboîtée de l'incarcération. Le désir d'évasion que provoque l'île chez l'écrivain est le même que celui de la femme corse, piégée par les traditions primitives:

> Le père et la mère offraient à l'enfant l'image de l'amour absolu et qui durait toute la vie. Engagée dans une voie, la femme y restait envers et contre tout. Dans sa vie, au départ, tout était déjà accepté et pour ainsi dire vécu. Même si elle se rendait compte que l'homme qu'elle avait épousé était un homme méprisable et qu'on lui avait fait prendre un chemin qui n'aurait pas dû être le sien. . . . Devant Dieu et devant les hommes elle était liée à son mari pour la vie. (83)

Esclave, vierge ou madone, mère avant tout, aimant ses fils jusqu'à la folie, la femme corse telle que la peint Marie Susini a longtemps incarné ce rôle désigné à la femme par la mythologie, dont parle Luce Irigaray: on lui accordait un certain pouvoir social, à condition qu'elle soit réduite, avec sa propre complicité, à l'impuissance sexuelle. Ainsi l'amour et le désir féminin dans les romans de Marie Susini s'attachent-ils par excellence à l'objet tabou: père, frère, fils. La féminité se vit en tant que faute tragique (*hamartia* en grec) dans le sens d'Aristote. Dans la tragédie il ne peut y avoir de quête, tout étant décidé d'avance.

Deux moyens d'échapper à un tel carcan: le départ et l'écriture. Malgré sa claustrophobie par rapport à la mer et à l'île-mère, c'est dans son amour chargé d'angoisse pour la Corse de son enfance que Marie Susini a puisé l'essence de ses écrits: "L'oeuvre d'art nous impose la même présence solitaire et insolente, qui affirme avec une certitude absolue que l'immobilité et le mouvement, l'amour et la haine, la vie et la mort, c'est tout un" (30).

En 1986 a eu lieu en Grèce un colloque-prise-de-conscience de femmes méditerranéennes (*Canadian Women's Studies* 82). Un numéro de la revue canadienne *Les Cahiers de la Femme* a pour thème "Les femmes méditerranéennes"; on peut y lire que les femmes corses remettent en question leur rôle traditionnel (*Canadian Women's Studies* 118-19). Ce rôle, Marie Susini ne fait que l'exposer. Incapable de vivre avec, elle a besoin de l'écrire.

N'étant pas féministe militante, elle ne cherche nullement à changer les traditions qu'elle fuit et qui la poursuivent.

L'écriture de Marie Susini effectue un retour aux sources. Par la voie/voix de sa Corse natale, elle remonte vers l'Antiquité grecque et plus loin encore, jusqu'au *no man's land* du mythe. Ses personnages romanesques, poussés par leur destin, évoluent dans une dimension mythique qui éclipse le temps et l'espace de l'h/Histoire. Lorsqu'elle écrit, Marie Susini part d'une musique, d'un rythme en elle. Le mouvement, le regard et le non-dit refoulent souvent une intrigue floue ou fragmentée: mariage insolite entre la littérature classique et le nouveau roman. Quant aux lieux, le seul qui prend de l'importance, hormis la Corse des premiers livres, c'est un certain Paris de la liberté (loin de l'île), de la Libération et des vingt ans de l'auteur, revécu l'espace de quelques heures, en mai 1968, par Fabia, l'héroïne de *C'était cela notre amour*, figée depuis longtemps dans un mariage de raison.

Analeptique, la structure de ce dernier roman évoque celle d'*Hiroshima, mon amour*. Marie Susini admire d'ailleurs beaucoup Marguerite Duras et, comme l'auteur de *Moderato cantabile* et du *Ravissement de Lol V. Stein*, elle crée des personnages dont la vie quotidienne oscille entre le désespoir et le vide. Seuls l'amour, toujours violent, éphémère et destructeur, l'exaltation de la guerre (le souvenir le plus vivant de Fabia) ou la mort savent interrompre cette monotonie.

Les trois premiers livres: deux romans, *Plein soleil* (1953) et *La fiera* (1954), suivis d'une pièce de théâtre, *Corvara* (1955), forment une trilogie corse. *Plein soleil*, souvenirs d'enfance autobiographiques, écrits sur le conseil de Camus, est le seul texte de Susini entièrement à la première personne. Vanina, la narratrice de dix ans, évoque avec tendresse la vie de son village. Par contre, la triste initiation à la vie au couvent, où l'enfant pensionnaire découvre le mensonge, la maladie et l'amour malheureux qui entraînent la mort d'une jeune femme, annonce la matière des romans suivants. La petite Vanina porte déjà la marque fatale de la féminité.

Les protagonistes de Marie Susini sont toutes des femmes, sauf l'enfant de douze ans du *Premier regard* (1960), et toutes méditerranéennes. Ce sont les soeurs d'Andromaque, d'Antigone et de Cassandre. Susini ne croit pas à l'écriture féminine, mais elle écrit *la* femme. Les thèmes que lui renvoie la Corse: "le tragique de la vie, l'absolu de l'amour, la toute-puissance du destin" (*La renfermée* 89), sont les indices des chaînes qu'aucune de ses héroïnes ne brisera impunément. Celles qui se sont libérées par la fuite (Fabia: *C'était cela notre amour*), par les amours successives (Sefarad: *Les yeux fermés*, 1960) ou qui se jettent à corps perdu dans l'inceste (Sefarad avec son frère, Anna Livia avec son père) sont aussi irrémédiablement malheureuses que celles qui restent fidèles à la tradition. L'amour demeure le domaine fatal de la femme, dont l'homme fuit la passion dévoratrice (Serge dans *Un pas d'homme*, 1957, entre autres). A la fin de *La fiera*, Sylvie l'étrangère expire, brebis galeuse du village de son mari Matteo, entourée d'un choeur de femmes infortunées, une fille délaissée par sa mère, une mère qui a perdu son fils, une toute jeune fille, déjà meurtrie par l'amour. Le texte le plus fort et le plus dépouillé, c'est sans doute la tragédie *Corvara*, sous-titrée *La malédiction*. Bien que l'être maudit soit un homme, prêtre renégat, il ne paraît jamais et c'est sa femme, Corvara, qui se fait la voix du malheur: "Quand on est marqué, on l'est dès qu'on sort du ventre de sa mère et déjà le cri qu'on pousse en naissant est celui du désespoir" (128).

Si certaines critiques féministes ont réinterprété la théorie déjà fumeuse de Freud sur l'oedipe des filles, jamais tout à fait achevé, en tant qu'aperture et que possibilité d'échapper à la clôture rigide des structures patriarcales (Kaplan 34-35), dans l'oeuvre de Marie Susini, par contre, aucune ouverture n'est accordée aux femmes. On y retrouve cependant des traces de liberté chez l'enfant. Comme Saint-Exupéry, Marie Susini est de son enfance comme d'un pays et, dans ce domaine, à contrario de Marguerite Duras, qui a parlé de "l'horreur de l'enfance" (Lejeune 123). Pour ses protagonistes, l'enfance, même déjà menacée par l'avenir, est le seul moment relativement heureux de la vie, dont la remémoration représente un refuge. La narratrice des *Yeux fermés*, par exemple, ayant perdu le goût de la vie, s'accroche au souvenir de son enfance: "Il y avait . . . Il n'y a plus que les voix de l'enfance perdue" (12). On notera pourtant chez Marie Susini que la petite fille, quoique plus libre que la femme qu'elle deviendra, ressent déjà cruellement son infériorité par rapport au garçon. Le souvenir cuisant de cette injustice s'exprime dans *La renfermée:*

> Lui [le garçon], il avait tous les droits. Le droit de vivre. D'aller dehors quand bon lui semblait, de siffler et de grimper aux arbres, d'entrer dans les autres maisons et de fréquenter tous les autres enfants du village sans distinction sociale. Une petite fille s'y aventurait-elle et elle était considérée aussitôt comme une effrontée. (83-84)

Le visage de la petite fille du *Premier regard*, pourtant si vive, dans le train, lorsqu'elle doit se séparer du petit garçon, pourtant si balourd: "déjà exprimait de façon si pathétique cette antique, cette éternelle soumission des femmes" (150).

Chez Susini, l'enfance va de pair avec la beauté de la nature méditerranéenne, complice de l'enfant, alors que cadre ironique ou indifférent du destin tragique de l'adulte, dont elle devient l'ennemie. Deux éléments surtout ponctuent abondamment les textes de Marie Susini, à l'exception des deux romans parisiens, *Un pas d'homme* et *C'était cela notre amour*: le soleil et la mer, parents archétypaux de l'enfant méditerranéen. Ce schéma s'inscrit clairement dans *Plein soleil*. La petite Vanina adore également son père:

> Il y avait une longue route qui menait au couvent et moi sur le cheval de mon père, tout contre lui sur le cheval, bien prise entre les rênes partagées sur lesquelles jouaient les mains de mon père. (9)

et le soleil: "C'était la même joie que celle qui m'entraînait sur les chemins, avec le soleil, à la recherche du soleil" (55). Or sa mère et les vieilles femmes du village interdisent à l'enfant de rester au soleil, d'où la discussion suivante avec une vieille Italienne:

> —Oh, Vanina, sors du soleil.
> Je répondais:
> —J'ai un chapeau.
> —Si ta mère te voyait!
> —Mais il ne fait pas de mal, le soleil.
> —Il rend fou, criait l'Italienne. (19)

Vanina, encore innocente, transgresse le tabou du soleil, comme plus tard Anna Livia celui de l'inceste avec le père.

La mer demeure mystérieuse pour Vanina: "On parlait souvent de la mer. On n'y allait jamais" (60). Sa mère lui dit: "On ne peut pas dire que ce soit un endroit chrétien, la plage" (70). Au couvent, Vanina interroge inlassablement Blanchette, la petite Marseillaise, au sujet de la mer. La jeune protagoniste éprouve la même fascination mystérieuse vis-à-vis de sa propre mère, avec qui l'intimité est impossible: "Je n'avais jamais vu les bras nus de ma mère" (90). La vieille zia Francesca de *La Fiera*, tout à la douleur d'avoir perdu son fils, ignore jusqu'à l'existence de sa fille dévouée. Anna Livia vit le retour de sa mère disparue comme une intrusion.

Le soleil continue d'éclairer le paysage méditerranéen avant, pendant et après les pires tragédies. Comme le père et la mère de la famille corse, l'eau et la lumière demeurent unis devant l'éternité. Ainsi, à la fin de *Je m'appelle Anne Livia* (1979): "La pluie qui était tombée toute la nuit . . . avait lavé la campagne, si paisiblement lisse au matin, si brillante, toute neuve, et donné plus de force au soleil" (177). Cela a un très beau nom, cela s'appelle l'aurore, ou bien, comme l'ultime souvenir des *Yeux fermés*, le crépuscule: "Le soleil qui bascule dans la mer, nous en avions peur" (124). "Soleil cou coupé" (Apollinaire 14), la mort n'est jamais loin.

La langue de Marie Susini va s'épurant du premier livre au dernier. Dans la trilogie corse, on trouve quelques expressions dans la langue du pays, mais toujours isolées, en italiques: la censure du couvent de Vanina prévaut: "Il était défendu de parler corse au pensionnat" (*Plein Soleil* 39). La vraie langue de Marie Susini, c'est le français. Son perfectionnisme tend vers l'azur mallarméen. Elle n'a cessé de rechercher des formes nouvelles. Au montage alterné de *La Fiera*, des groupes de personnages qui s'acheminent, tels des pélerins médiévaux, un jour de fête religieuse, vers leur prise de conscience collective, viennent s'opposer, par exemple, le travail individuel de la mémoire qu'exprime le long monologue intérieur des *Yeux fermés*, l'intensité au ralenti du moment de la rupture entrecoupé d'analepses d'*Un pas d'homme* ou le pas de deux symétrique entre passé et présent de *C'était cela notre amour*.

Contrairement au ressassement durassien, le désir de Marie Susini aurait été de n'écrire qu'un seul livre. Cet ouvrage unique et parfait, ç'aurait presque pu être son roman préféré, le dernier, *Je m'appelle Anna Livia*. L'histoire existe à peine, comme la fin nous l'indique: "Mais s'était-il passé quelque chose?" (176). Anna Livia grandit dans la nuit des temps, dans une Italie mythique, qui a pour seul indice une rangée de cyprès, symboles de la mort et objets de fascination des enfants. Sa mère a abandonné la protagoniste toute petite. Francesco, fils des gardiens, seul compagon de jeux d'Anna Livia, est mort. Son chien sera tué par son père. Anna Livia n'a désormais plus que ce père. Séductrice instinctive, elle le prend. Il se pend. Elle suit aveuglément un mendiant sur la route, perpétuant le mythe d'Oedipe au féminin. L'errance la ramène au domaine paternel, où elle meurt seule dans la poussière. Sa mère, revenue avant son départ, rejetée par sa fille, demeure en périphérie, tandis que le vieux Joséphino lui raconte par bribes l'histoire d'Anna Livia. Il/elle ne sont pas toujours identifiables, mais *ça* se dit. Anna Livia vit dans le temps du mythe. Ses parents ne sont pas nommés, elle se nomme seule (sa mère l'avait appelée Elisabeta). Elle découvre seule ses premières règles, choisit seule le geste tabou qui *le* tue et *la* tue. Existentielle, elle assume son acte. Elle est la solitude et la douleur faites femme. Marie Susini a réussi une rare prouesse: tout en dévoilant les secrets les plus insoutenables, le murmure du bas-fond de l'âme humaine, elle préserve la pudeur d'une langue châtiée et classique. Dans ce passage de *La renfermée*, elle définit ainsi sa propre écriture:

> Qu'est-ce que l'écriture sinon une solitude et une ascèse, une métaphysique aussi, peut-être celles entrevues vaguement ou pressenties dans les années d'enfance. Quand le silence était plus important que la parole. Quand le temps était à la fois instant et éternité. Le temps du mythe. (90)

Oeuvres citeés

Apollinaire, Guillaume. "Zone". *Alcools.* Paris: Gallimard-NRF, 1920.

Cobanogly-Padley, Poppy. "Women of the Mediterranean." *Canadian Women's Studies* (Summer 1987): 118-19.

Colvile, Georgiana. Interview non-publiée de Marie Susini, 1985.

Duras, Marguerite. *Hiroshima, mon amour*, scénario et dialogue. Paris: Gallimard, 1960.

________. *Moderato cantabile.* Paris: Minuit, 1958.

________. *Le ravissement de Lol V. Stein.* Paris: Gallimard, 1964.

Kaplan, Ann. "Is the Gaze Male?" *Women and Film.* New York: Methuen, 1983.

Lejeune, Paule. *Le cinéma des femmes.* Paris: Atlas, 1987.

Moles, Abraham, et Elisabeth Rohmer. *Labyrinthes du vécu.* Paris: Librairie des Méridiens, 1982.

Susini, Marie. *C'était cela notre amour.* Paris: Le Seuil, 1970.

________. *Corvara.* Paris: Le Seuil, 1955.

________. *La fiera.* Paris: Le Seuil, 1954.

_______. *Je m'appelle Anna Livia.* Paris: Grasset, 1979.

_______. *Un pas d'homme.* Paris: Le Seuil, 1957.

_______. *Plein soleil.* Paris: Le Seuil, 1953.

_______. *Le premier regard.* Paris: Le Seuil, 1960.

_______. *La renfermée, la Corse.* Paris: Le Seuil, 1981.

_______. *Les yeux fermés.* Paris: Le Seuil, 1964.

Topographie de la maison dans *Propriété privée* de Paule Constant

Claudine G. Fisher
Portland State University

Un nouvel écrivain se fait remarquer depuis 1980 sur la scène littéraire française. Elle se nomme Paule Constant. Quatre de ses romans, *Ouregano* (Prix Valéry Larbaud 1980), *Propriété privée, Balta* et *White spirit* (Prix 1990 de l'Académie française), forment le quadruple volet de la saga réelle et mythique de Tiffany, de l'enfance à l'âge adulte, dans un mouvement de pendule entre la France et l'Afrique.

Propriété privée reprend en France la vie de Tiffany où *Ouregano* l'avait laissée rentrant d'Afrique, c'est-à-dire au moment où la petite fille vomissait sur le parquet de l'école religieuse au nom évocateur de Pension des Sanguinaires. Si la ville africaine d'Ouregano inscrit le thème essentiel de l'ailleurs et de l'absence avec pour sous-motif le thème du "dedans" psychique, *Propriété privée* (1981) inverse ces données. L'exploration du "dedans" prend la place centrale tandis que l'ailleurs, l'absence et le "dehors" en deviennent les sous-motifs. La petite Tiffany d'*Ouregano* se voit ailleurs et absente de la maison bien qu'elle se soit appropriée le violet de la carte africaine avec sa terre et son eau. La Tiffany de la demeure française s'approprie la maison du Sud-Ouest de la France, avec la grand-mère comme point de focalisation. Dans la propriété et près de la grand-mère, la fillette se sent protégée du non-sens et du "nulle part" qui convergent à la pension des Dames Sanguinaires.

La projection de la maison dans le livre de Paule Constant relève du mythe et de la réalité, de la dimension physique et du topos psychique. La mise en abyme de la demeure marque des bornes spécifiques, temporelles aussi bien que spatiales. Le vocable "privé" du titre du roman définit les limites de cette topographie dans le conscient et l'inconscient de la jeune Tiffany et renforce les données émotionelles de l'enfant par rapport à ses proches, au moment du passage à la puberté. La maison réelle et onirique crée les tensions de ce roman qui part à la recherche des limites extérieures entraînant leurs reflets intérieurs, pierres de touche de la conscience de Tiffany. En tant qu'Alice au Pays des Merveilles, la petite fille se trouve parfois dans un monde heureux, "dedans," et parfois comme Alice de l'Autre Côté du Miroir, elle se situe "dehors" mais ne cesse d'apprendre à vivre et à mourir et de passer d'un monde à l'autre. De la propriété à la pension, le monde s'inscrit en blanc et noir, pour découvrir les nuances du gris, au milieu du vert des feuillages de la propriété.

Les Soeurs en noir retiennent les jeunes filles dans un monde clos qui aspire au blanc et à la pureté. Le corps étant nié, on pourrait supposer que l'âme prend son essor. Mais dans ce lieu sec, c'est le sans-corps-sans-âme qui prime dans une harmonie superficielle de blanc et de noir. Les Dames en noir (21) prient avec leurs chapelets noirs (12). Les carreaux en damiers noirs et blancs de la chapelle (16) rythment le chemin de croix de Tiffany sur l'échiquier géant d'un puzzle, comme à l'inverse d'une Alice au Pays des Merveilles: "L'élégance suprême était d'avoir éliminé toute coquetterie, d'être noire pour paraître plus blanche, abstraite" (23).

Les Dames, "mariées noires", "veuves absolues" et "gisantes," portent le mystérieux message de la mort. Si elles sont noires, elles évoquent aussi le sang par le nom d'origine du lieu des abattoirs, "Les Sanguinaires." La Dame du dortoir à la peau blanche et aux "cheveux infinis," qui fait ses ablutions nocturnes avec "plus de fiole et de sang que de seau et de broc" (22) épouvante Tiffany. La Soeur se transforme en vampire et l'enfant devine où se situe le lieu de l'exclusion. Paule Constant se sert de l'image frappante du pubis imberbe de l'enfant associé à un visage de nonne: ". . . elle pouvait voir au centre de son corps, lieu ignoré de sa féminité, l'amande pâle, son sexe de petite fille, un visage de nonne" (25).

Tiffany, l'étrangère, ne connaît pas les règles du jeu. Elle ressent cette inquiétante étrangeté ou angst qui la place dans l'exclusion. Freud dans son *Au delà du principe de plaisir* et dans son *Unheimliche* analyse cette angoisse de l'être. Symboliquement, Tiffany est cataloguée comme la petite fille qui a besoin de rattraper ses manques scolaires et de maîtriser son corps. Paule Constant ironise sur le double sens des mots du travail de Tiffany: "Le travail de Tiffany était double. Alors que les autres se contentaient de progresser ou de piétiner, Tiffany devait faire front en comblant ses LACUNES et en bouchant ses TROUS" (43).

"Trous" et "lacunes" apparaissent dans le texte en lettres majuscules pour souligner son destin de mal aimée et la tragédie de sa différence, en rapport direct avec ses trous. Ses "manques" au niveau affectif se concrétisent stylistiquement dans sa vie de pension par la sensation de noyade, par la porte fermée et par l'identité de son nom. Toujours en attente, hors d'elle-même temporellement, Tiffany a l'impresssion de couler dans un "flot bleu noir" (13) et de se noyer dans la marée des autres enfants.

Elle paraît tout faire à contre-courant et chacune de ses actions lui tend un piège. Elle est prisonnière par le masque qu'elle se crée et par les portes qui l'enferment: "Les portes se refermaient les unes après les autres comme des trappes dont elle n'avait pas le chiffre" (38).

A la pension, Tiffany est dépouillée de son prénom, d'où de son identité, puisqu'on l'appelle maintenant Marie-Françoise. Dans le nulle part de sa non-identité et dans l'attente du "là-bas" de la propriété, la petite fille souhaite un état d'inconscience ou d'anesthésie. L'importance du prénom par rapport au nom du père, par exemple, a très bien été analysé dans les essais de Cixous. Le prénom demeure encore l'identité première du sexe féminin. Or, Tiffany n'a aucun rapport d'attachement avec son propre nom de baptême, non utilisé jusqu'alors. Le nom de Tiffany tombant en désuétude, la petite fille se retrouve non-identifiée par elle-même.

Sous la plume de Paule Constant, l'angoisse de Tiffany se métaphorise par la bête sauvage qui ronge le coeur (20) de la petite fille, représentant le passé africain et ses rapports de mal aimée envers ses parents, particulièrement envers la mère. Quant à l'avenir, il s'assombrit déjà par la réalisation de la vieillesse de sa grand-mère, d'où l'attente anxieuse de la petite fille face à la maladie et à la mort. L'attente prémonitoire et le silence tiennent une grande place dans la réalité du moment présent et projette le présent onirique, source de bonheur grâce au lieu propre de la propriété. Le bonheur présent est un lieu et non une personne, même si la propriété ne se dissocie jamais de la vision de la grand-mère. C'est bien l'endroit qui a la primauté, en tant que source de bonheur du temps présent: "Pour la première fois, Tiffany eut l'idée du bonheur. Il n'était pas une personne mais un lieu. Ce n'était qu'une image que le temps avait décoloré" (64).

Au début, la maison est hors du temps, de l'espace et de la mort, puisque Tiffany retrouve instantanément dans ses fibres la sensation de la maison qui l'a fait vibrer et qui est celle de la maison à la Tour qu'elle reconnaît des photos de la jeunesse des vieillards qui entourent ses grands-parents. Pour la première fois à la propriété (élément de terre), Tiffany peut vraiment jouer dans le bassin au jet d'eau avec les têtards (eau comme élément, naissance et jeunesse du monde par les têtards) (74), près de la Tour (jeunesse) et du chêne d'Amérique (force et sécurité). Quand elle est à la pension, Tiffany ne peut par contraste que mimer le jeu pour passer inaperçue. L'oeuvre de Constant s'articule sur le concept très proustien de la quête du passé, capable d'expliciter le présent et d'anticiper les répercussions prémonitoires de l'avenir.

Comme la tour de la propriété symbolise l'enfance de la maison (63), Tiffany se met en quête de l'enfance de Gabrielle-Emilie, sa grand-mère, pour toucher à une pérennité intérieure; elle essaye d'en faire une amie d'âme qui, comme elle, va à l'école (108). Jeunesse et vieillesse, passé et présent se rejoignent en sautant une génération, par l'expérience de Tiffany et pour en faire la dépositaire de la mémoire familiale, "gardienne des souvenirs" (193).

Le bonheur de Tiffany dans la propriété a une corrélation directe avec le langage de son corps. Sans nom, sans langage, hors-jeu, dehors, dans le monde clos de la pension, elle entre "dedans" quand elle vit dans la propriété, au coeur de la fontaine et de l'origine (quête de l'origine identifiée par Cixous comme essentielle à la conscience féminine). Tiffany trouve alors son ailleurs et son identité dans ce vrai dedans. Elle devient "animal sauvage" à la vue de sa grand-mère et jappe comme un petit chien en la léchant et la respirant (21). C'est par le toucher et l'odorat que Tiffany part à la découverte de son monde, alors qu'à la pension il était interdit d'utiliser ses mains (141). *Propriété privée* rappelle par l'utilisation des sons et des sens qui se répondent le poème de Baudelaire *Correspondances*. Les fils de correspondance des sens rejoignent, par odorat et toucher, la réalité tangible de l'amour pour la grand-mère et de la grand-mère. La respiration de Tiffany se trouve toujours en harmonie avec celle de sa grand-mère, que se soit quand la grand-mère se repose dans la chambre, ou lors d'une promenade dans le parc. Le souffle de la grand-mère et l'air de la propriété se mêlent pour ne former qu'un élément unique:

> Qui des mots ou des lieux menait le jeu de cette alliance subtile et ravissante (entre propriété et mots de la grand-mère) dont les sens enchevêtrés éclataient en tant de fragments mobiles qu'il était impossible d'arrêter ce qui appartenait déjà à l'une et ce qui était encore à l'autre? Au bout des doigts de Madame Désarmoise, il y avait des rameaux et dans sa bouche un silence de pierre mais les arbres respiraient la nuit et se "retenaient" le jour. Une grande inspiration de soleil, une longue expiration de nuit. Et de voir les arbres si hauts Tiffany imaginait qu'ils étaient comme de grands poumons qui prenaient au ciel une vie plus claire et plus pure, les poumons mêmes de sa grand-mère, une aide respiratoire, instruments merveilleux qui se substituaient au souffle court, à la gorge enrouée. (116)

Les doigts de la grand-mère sont des rameaux, associés au chêne d'Amérique, sa bouche se lie au silence des pierres de la propriété et prend le rythme de l'inspiration diurne et de l'expiration nocturne: vie et mort, soleil et nuit, mots de la grand-mère et messages de la propriété se rejoignent pour donner à Tiffany sa cadence respiratoire et à Paule Constant son inspiration dans l'écriture, faisant passer la grand-mère au stade d'une aïeule mythique.

Y aurait-il identification totale ou au moins partielle de Tiffany avec la grand-mère? Cette conjecture est certaine sur plusieurs points, comme le fait que la grand-mère ait perdu son père à peu près au même âge où Tiffany perdra sa grand-mère. Un autre exemple serait l'arrivée des règles de Tiffany, signalant que son sang devient la prolongation du sang dont la grand-mère marquait ses mouchoirs: "La réincarnation était accomplie. Madame Désarmoise était entrée en Tiffany jusqu'à la mort" (200).

Dans ce roman, la mère n'apparaît qu'à la fin de l'histoire et scelle d'une manière permanente la destruction du monde de la propriété. L'arbre d'Amérique est détruit, l'aïeule a disparu; le grand-père ne semble que fantôme vu une dernière fois dans le reflet du miroir des escaliers, lieu intermédiaire ou "lieu d'absence" (199) d'où Tiffany observe le déménagement. C'est encore au miroir de la chambre de sa grand-mère que Tiffany pense, envahie de panique, quand elle voit les déménageurs s'attaquer aux meubles de la chambre à coucher sacrée. Ce miroir a une frise de feuilles de lierre (210), symbolisant la fidélité, comme l'illustre la devise: "Je meurs où je m'attache." Tiffany attache à ce lierre une valeur sentimentale extrême. Elle fait l'inventaire dans sa tête de tout le mobilier pour toujours s'en souvenir. Au contraire, sa mère Matilde se débarrasse de tous les souvenirs en faisant le vide du grenier. On pourrait croire que la mère veut tout effacer de sa jeunesse mais ses souvenirs aussi renaissent quand elle admire les chaussures de lézard vert du temps jadis de Madame Désarmoise. Puis, comme une petite fille, la mère se met à serrer dans les bras son petit ours beige Titi. Elle aussi n'est pas dénuée de mémoire: "La petite fille ce n'était plus Tiffany à la porte, mais elle (Matilde) devant les chaussures" (212).

Quand tout est jeté par la fenêtre, Matilde bat des mains, encore comme une enfant. Les rôles sont alors inversés. Tiffany, elle, est devenue adulte et voit sa mère en petite fille, vision horrible, touchante et déchirante à la fois. Même Matilde, tout comme Tiffany le faisait, souhaite être ailleurs (207). Tiffany a choisi la mémoire et le silence devant la destruction de sa vie. Mais son choix a été accompli en toute conscience. L'inscription du silence se transforme en une véritable inscription de son identité toute neuve par le geste ultime de l'écriture: "Sur la tapisserie, très petit, au crayon, elle inscrivit la date. Elle confiait à la chambre ses souvenirs" (211).

Le titre n'a-t-il pas englobé pour le lecteur averti une double lecture dès la page de garde? L'auteur joue sur les connotations en double miroir du titre. Les deux mots *propriété privée* indiquent l'absorption complète par la possession, excluant le monde extérieur par le "privé" ou le non-public. En d'autres termes, la petite fille possède au même titre non seulement sa grand-mère mais aussi la propriété bien gardée aux yeux du monde.

En second lieu, le sens inverse, inscrit en filigrane dans l'expression "privée de propriété" met l'emphase sur l'appropriation qui se dérobe à l'absorption et mène à la menace de mort. Dans le roman, la perte est illustrée par l'arbre d'Amérique déraciné par l'orage, par la mort de la grand-mère, par la vente de la propriété, par le retour de la mère et par son obsession de se débarrasser de tout souvenir.

Dans un troisième temps, le titre fait appel à l'empire du propre comme on peut le voir illustré dans la dialectique de Hegel. Propriété physique et mentale entraîne le meurtre de "l'autre" au niveau familial et social. Ce désir d'appropriation se forme à partir de la peur de l'expropriation ou la crainte de la séparation. Si l'on se sert des définitions cixousiennes sur la différence entre l'économie libidinale masculine et l'économie libidinale féminine, comme elles sont établies par Cixous dans *La jeune née*, Tiffany dans l'enfance suit un modèle d'économie libidinale masculine. Elle s'approprie car elle a peur de la perte et de la mort. Ce modèle de "masculinité" ou d'agressivité, terme naturellement employé ici dans son sens large d'expression d'animus, n'a rien d'étonnant chez les petites filles qui agissent souvent comme des petits garçons avant la puberté.

Propriété privée devient bien plus qu'un livre sur des souvenirs d'enfance puisqu'il démontre l'évolution psychologique de Tiffany de la reconnaissance de son économie libidinale féminine ou encore pour simplifier, de son anima: la convergence de la réalisation de l'animus et de l'anima fait de la petite fille un modèle exemplaire de la cristallisation de l'être en un tout unifié au moment du rite de passage. A la puberté, l'enfance disparaît pour Tiffany. Son animus accepte d'intégrer aussi l'anima dans sa psyché totale. De petite fille, Tiffany a réussi à survivre à la transition et à projeter une personnalité qui se complète à la perfection avec ses animus et anima.

Mais la petite Tiffany a-t-elle fait fuir toutes ses peurs d'enfant de sa mémoire? Pourra-t-elle un jour oublier les paroles "mâles," même dites à travers la voix de Madame de Sainte-Chantal? La terreur d'une bête furieuse, à l'aspect masculin malgré le genre féminin du mot "bête", avait pris possession de Tiffany, comme un viol l'aurait fait:

> La douleur se débandait. Elle était folle de rage et se débattait dans tout le corps de Tiffany, elle lui étreignait la gorge et s'y agrippait de ses pattes griffues, elle pressait, serrait, raclait. Elle descendait dans le ventre et courait en rond, si vite que Tiffany en avait le tournis. Sa peau se décollait et la bête furieuse faisait tant de tapage que Tiffany ramenait ses couvertures qu'elle pressait en boule sur son ventre. Mais la douleur fuyait plus bas dans les cuisses tendues et dures, dans les pieds bleuis et froids. (183)

La topographie de la maison sert bien d'ancrage à la psychologie de Tiffany, autre topos central du roman. Mais il se fait naturellement en la personne de Madame Désarmoise, maîtresse du lieu, en remplacement à la figure de mère. L'ailleurs inscrit la peur et la représentation de la bête. Dans *White spirit*, Paule Constant poursuit avec plus de clarté encore le thème de la lutte avec la bête, qui devient animal physique, psychologique, sexuel et mythique. La symphonie en blanc et noir, venue de France, est représentée dans *Propriété privée* par les Soeurs qui veulent "blanchir" Tiffany. Elle se transforme en un concerto de blanc sur noir, rimant avec Afrique noire et le double blanc du titre qui satirise l'esprit blanc et l'esprit de sel corrosif dans *White spirit*.

Oeuvres citées

Cixous, Hélène, and Catherine Clément. *La jeune née*. Paris: Union Générales d'Editions, 1975.

Dans l'ordre chronologique:

Constant, Paule. *Ouregano*. Collection Folio #1623. Paris: Gallimard, 1980.

______. *Propriété privée*. Paris: Gallimard, 1981.

______. *Balta*. Collection Folio #1783. Paris: Gallimard, 1983.

______. *White spirit*. Paris: Gallimard, 1989.

______. *La fille du Gobernator*. Paris: Gallimard, 1994.

Marriage as Institution and Experience in the Novels of Mariama Bâ

Obioma Nnaemeka
Indiana University

In his article on Mariama Bâ, "Still a Victim? Mariama Bâ's *Une si longue lettre*," Femi Ojo-Ade distinguishes two generations of African female writers: a first generation of traditionalists and a second generation of feminists to which Mariama Bâ belongs. Impressed by the resignation of the traditionalists, who seek refuge in society's idealization of motherhood, and antagonistic to the feminists, Femi Ojo-Ade launches an attack on the latter for their unforgivable deviancy:

> Grace Ogot, Efua Sutherland, Ama Ata Aidoo, Flora Nwapa, women writers all, constitute the "old guard," steeped in the traditions of the land, complaining of their sufferings as subjects of the male master, but seeking solace in a society that has proclaimed woman the mother. That group's conciliatory position has been superseded by a current of revolt. Compromise is replaced by criticism and condemnation. Respect turns into repudiation. Devotion is buried in divorce. Buchi Emecheta, Nafissatou Diallo, Mariama Bâ, those are the voices currently crying out for the liberation of woman, the second-class citizen. Not an easy struggle, that... Hard choices have to be made, and commitment could be destructive. *Une si longue lettre* is a study of those contradictions. (72)

Femi Ojo-Ade's attack is based on the assumption that the African continent is infested by a Western disease called feminism. His condemnation of this unwholesome state of affairs is unequivocably posited in very strong terms:

> Feminism, an occidental phenomenon like many others, has spread ever so slowly but steadily to the forbidden land of Africa... Such "aberrations" as feminism are abhorred by many who are, however, the very purveyors of the bastardization of that culture whose contents remain confusing to their civilized minds.... The war between male and female is now a contemporary constant, and new literary voices from among the once

> silent minority cry out to be heard, even if there is reason to doubt on whose behalf the revolt is being declared. (72)

I must add that feminism is *not* an occidental phenomenon; *western feminism* is. To ignore the decades or even centuries of feminist activism in Africa by *African women* is to distort and deny our history. I agree with Femi Ojo-Ade that there exists some confusion in "their civilized minds" and also that "*Une si longue lettre* is a study of these contradictions." However, we differ in our interpretations of the origin and content of this confusion and these contradictions. While Femi Ojo-Ade sees these contradictions as resulting from the collision between African culture and Western values, I see them deeper and more complex than this binary opposition. The tensions created by the forces of this conflictive encounter constitute part of, but not all, the problem. These contradictions are complicated and exacerbated by the dissonances in the African environment itself. The truth of the matter is that, especially in man-woman relationships, the "modern," urban (but not so urbane!) African man juggles and manipulates different, sometimes conflicting, systems in an attempt to enjoy the best of all possible worlds. In many ways, modernity has intensified the masculinization of the African tradition, thereby deepening the marginalization of women. As African women, we see instances where tradition is progressive and modernity reactionary.

This juggling noted above creates confusion especially for the woman. If the woman is "still a victim,"[1] it is to this confusion that she remains so! This paper will examine the contradictions and discrepancies which exist between theory and practice as they relate to the institution of marriage in the African environment. How does marriage as an institution and as experience affect the lives of women in Mariama Bâ's novels? I argue that it is the practice which distorts and even vulgarizes the institution, thereby leading to the excruciating experiences of the women. I will examine not only the exegesis of the tenets of the institution of marriage in Islam and the African traditional culture but also the transformations the institution has undergone in modern times.

Many critics have identified polygamy as the bone of contention in Mariama Bâ's works. Ojo-Ade argues that:

> Man's basic guilt, the root cause for his vilification, the main element of his vicious behavior, is polygamy. Polygamy, the estate revered by traditionalists as a function of Africanity. Polygamy, once supported and

> even suggested by African women as a socio-economic expediency. That, vows Aïssatou, is a thing of the past. Polygamy is now the bane of society. Polygamy is a vice to be dealt with not by procrastination but by divorce. So, Aïssatou Bâ leaves the beast called Mawdo. (76)

Mariama Bâ states her case less dramatically and more problingly. More than anything else, she exposes how the subversion of the institution of polygamy further complicates women's lives.

Mariama Bâ's protagonists make the distinction between the institution and the current practice of polygamy; often, it is the latter that comes under attack. The protagonists' complaints and protests are often punctuated by three words: deception, betrayal, abandonment; words which are not synonymous with polygamy in Islamic or African traditional culture. It is polygamy as practiced in modern African urban areas by the middle- and upper-middle classes which comes under scrutiny.

In his illuminating study of the rights of women in Islamic Sharia, Rafi Ullah Shehab notes that according to the Holy Koran, polygamy was initially introduced as a means of rehabilitating widows and orphans:

> And if you fear that ye will not deal fairly with orphans, marry of the women, who seem good to you, two two or three three or four four; and if ye fear that you cannot do justice (to many wives) then one only. (Al Quran, Surah Al-Nisa 3)

Furthermore, Islam allows polygamy but with certain restrictions and conditions. A man should marry only when he can afford it: "And let those who cannot afford marriage keep themselves chaste until Allah provides them with means" (Al Quaran, Surah Al-Noor 33).

Shehab explains that under Islamic law, the would-be husband is responsible for all marriage expenses. The custom of dowry (especially as practiced in India and Pakistan) is foreign to Islam as evidenced by the non-existence of the word "dowry" in the Arabic language. Islam considers love an essential ingredient in marriage; consequently, a man should not compel a woman who does not like him to marry him.[2] Marriage is thus a life-long contract requiring a firm agreement, "Messaqan Ghaleezan," between a man and a woman.

Although, in principle, Islamic laws grant equal rights of

separation to both spouses, in practice, these rights are only enjoyed by men. The three important conditions in the Islamic marriage institution are explained by Shehab:

> The main condition mentioned in the Holy Quran for allowing polygamy is to solve the problems of orphans and widows but it has also mentioned three other conditions such as justice between wives, sexual capability and equality in meeting expenses. It may be mentioned here that if a person is not in a position to meet the expenses of even one wife, he, according to Islamic Law, is not allowed to marry. (43)

Shehab concludes by noting that the Islamic institution of marriage has undergone changes due to contact with other systems with the result that certain rights which the institution guarantees women are denied them in practice.

I will now examine what Ojo-Ade calls "polygamy, the estate revered by traditionalists as a function of Africanity"! Patrick Merand (1980) notes that the reasons for contracting a polygamous marriage in the traditional African society range from the superior numerical strength of women, to female infertility, to the desire for change and the acquisition of prestige. Another consideration is the leviratic marriage which aims at caring for and protecting widows and their children.

In the polygamous family in indigenous African society, a particular living arrangement is observed and respected. The man lives in the same compound with all his wives and children. In this compound, the man has his own house and each wife lives in her own house with her children. Sexually and materially, the man seeks to maintain fairness, equity and justice among the wives. The children all grow up together and the man is always there for his family. Arthur Phillips and Henry Morris (1971) note that "the normal position is therefore that, among Africans who are living under their tribal law, polygamy is permitted, and the rights and obligations arising therefrom are legally recognized" (88). The man, or the woman, does not only enjoy the rights but also must execute the obligations. Peace and harmony are maintained through the observance of not only equity but also hierarchy—between the man and his wives and children on one hand and between co-wives on the other. As Patrick Merand rightly observes,

> l'importance du rang parmi les coépouses, appelées aussi, "veudieux," joue un grand rôle. La première femme bénéficie d'une autorité indéniable sur ses

> collègues: c'est par définition la plus âgée; elle seule n'a pas été choisie en "remplacement." (89)

Just as in the Islamic institution of marriage, the traditional African polygamous marriage aims at the maintenance of equity, peace and harmony. What is more important, the man is physically there to ensure this. However, the polygamous arrangement we have in Mariama Bâ's novels is a far cry from what I have noted above.

Patrick Merand correctly states that

> Dans les villages et dans les milieux urbains modestes, le mari vit avec ses coépouses dans une concession regroupant toute la famille. Chaque femme dispose d'une ou plusieurs pièces, la cour demeurant une partie commune. Les enfants logent avec leur mère respective, mais passent toute la journée ensemble. Dans les milieux riches des grandes villes, il s'agit d'une "polygamie géographique." (88)

This "polygamie géographique," which is nothing more than a euphemism for the legitimation of concubinage, is the issue. Vincent Monteil, in his study of the practice of Islam in Dakar, identifies an even more extreme and disruptive variant of polygamy that is practiced in a modern African city:

> La polygamie est, bien entendu, en baisse, dans une grande ville comme Dakar, où il est bien difficile à un fonctionnaire d'entretenir deux ou trois foyers. En pratique, ce qui se passe, c'est plutôt une polygamie "successive," facilité par les divorces hâtifs et l'instabilité conjugale.

It is this vulgarization of the institution of polygamy which constitutes the scandal. The idea of vagrancy—very appropriate, I might add—that Ousmane Sembène links to the man who engages in these urbanized variants of polygamy is antithetical to the image of the polygamous man in the traditional African culture:

> En ville, les familles étant dispersées, les gosses ont peu de contacts avec leur père. Ce dernier, par son mode d'existence, navigue de maison en maison, de villa en villa, n'est présent que le soir pour le lit. Il n'est donc qu'une source de financement quand il a du travail. Quant à l'éducation des enfants, la mère s'en charge. (104)

What emerges from all this is an extreme systemic contradiction which I would call "monogamized polygamy." In this strange marriage of two completely different systems (which goes to support my earlier assertion that the modern African man juggles different systems to his advantage), the man clings to one wife at each point in time and totally ignores the existence of, and his responsibility to, the other wife/wives. It is the confusion resulting from this oxymoronic arrangement of monogamy in polygamy which the women find psychologically and emotionally troubling.

The four women I will study, Ramatoulaye, Aïssatou, Jacqueline and Mireille, are all victims of these variants of urbanized polygamy—"polygamie géographique," "polygamie successive," "monogamized polygamy," or "polygamized monogamy." The other important factor which unites these four women is that they all made huge personal sacrifices to marry their respective spouses; the women alienated themselves, some temporarily and others permanently, from their families in order to contract their marriages.

When Ramatoulaye met and fell in love with Modou, she had a string of suitors but still preferred her "homme à l'éternel complet kaki." She waits for him while he studies in France during which period he writes her eloquently reassuring letters:

> C'est toi que je porte en moi. Tu es ma négresse protectrice. Vite te retrouver rien que pour une pression de mains qui me fera oublier faim et soif et solitude. (25).

When Modou returns to Senegal, Ramatoulaye secretly marries him in spite of her other suitors and strong opposition from her family, especially her mother:

> Daouda Dieng savait aussi forcer les coeurs. Cadeaux utiles pour ma mère.... Mais, je préférais l'homme à l'éternel complet kaki. Notre mariage se fit sans dot, sans faste, sous les regards désapprobateurs de mon père, devant l'indignation douloureuse de ma mère frustrée, sous les sarcasmes de mes soeurs surprises, dans notre ville muette d'étonnement. (28)

After twenty-five years of marriage and twelve childbirths, after a lifetime of hard work to build a family, Ramatoulaye discovers that her husband has abandoned her for her daughter's adolescent classmate, Binetou. An examination of Ramatoulaye's utterances and reactions shows that her feeling of outrage is due not so much to her abhorrence of the institution of polygamy as to the way Modou contracted the second marriage and whom he married. The humiliation and disrespect throw Ramatoulaye into disarray. Ramatoulaye is informed after the fact; not even by Modou, but by emissaries. The day that the marriage is consummated, Modou leaves his matrimonial home informing his wife that he will not be home for lunch. A few hours later, Ramatoulaye is informed that her husband has married a second wife. This is how she recollects the turn of events:

> Et, au crépuscule de ce même dimanche où l'on mariait Binetou, je vis venir dans ma maison, en tenue d'apparat et solennels, Tamsir, le frère de Modou, entre Mawdo Bâ et l'Imam de son quartier.... Je m'assis devant eux en riant aussi. L'Imam attaqua: "Quand Allah tout puissant met côte à côte deux êtres, personne n'y peut rien.... Dans ce monde, rien n'est nouveau.... Oui, Modou Fall, mais heureusement vivant pour toi, pour nous tous, Dieu merci. Il n'a fait qu'épouser une deuxième femme, ce jour. Nous venons de la Mosquée du Grand-Dakar où a eu lieu le mariage. (55-56)

Which woman would not be devastated by such a bombshell? Ramatoulaye now knows the reason for her husband's numerous absences which he explained away as job related and she, the trusting wife, believed him. It is this immense deception which breaks her. Despite her initial shock in learning about this new marriage, Ramatoulaye shows tremendous dignity, restraint and maturity in her comportment:

> Je m'appliquais à endiguer mon remous intérieur. Surtout, ne pas donner à mes visiteurs la satisfaction de raconter mon désarroi.... Enfin seule, pour donner libre cours à ma surprise et jauger ma détresse. Ah! Oui, j'ai oublié de demander le nom de ma rivale et de pouvoir ainsi donner une forme humaine à mon mal. (58-59)

This omission demonstrates that her rival or even polygamy per se is not the issue. What is at stake here is the deception and humiliation which she has come to know.

The polygamous institution in traditional African society is not designed to spring such devastating surprises. Usually, the first wife participates in marriage ceremonies performed on behalf of his co-wife. In spite of her pain and humiliation, Ramatoulaye decides to stay in the marriage and share her man with young Binetou according to Islamic law:

> Je pleurais tous les jours.... Dès lors, ma vie changea. Je m'étais préparée à un partage équitable selon l'Islam, dans le domaine polygamique. Je n'eus rien entre les mains. (69)

Unfortunately, Ramatoulaye does not get the equity and justice that are inscribed in the institution of marriage in Islam:

> Le vide m'entourait. Et Modou me fuyait. Les tentatives amicales ou familiales, pour le ramener au bercail furent vaines.... Il ne vint jamais plus; son nouveau bonheur recouvrit petit à petit notre souvenir. Il nous oublia. (69)

The issue is clearly not polygamy but abandonment. Modou abandons his family and reneges on his moral and financial responsibility to his wife and children. In addition to her responsibilities, Ramatoulaye is compelled to assume the responsibilities which her husband relinquishes: "Je survivais. En plus de mes anciennes charges, j'assumais celles de Modou" (76).

Five years later, Modou dies and it is after the burial and during the period of confinement that Ramatoulaye writes her long letter. During the funeral ceremony, Ramatoulaye is irritated and rightly so, by what she sees as a departure from the traditional custom; —the hierarchy among co-wives which is respected in traditional African polygamous marriage is disregarded in her case:

> Nous, nous avons été méritantes et c'est le choeur de nos louanges chantées à tue-tête.... Nos belles-soeurs traitent avec la même égalité trente et cinq ans de vie conjugale. Elles célèbrent, avec la même aisance et les mêmes mots, douze et trois maternités. J'enregistre, courroucée, cette volonté de nivellement qui réjouit la nouvelle belle-mère de Modou. (11)

Ramatoulaye is confused because of her inability to resolve the contradictions in her married life. First is her husband whose unexplained radical change she tries but fails to understand:

> L'adjonction d'une rivale à ma vie ne lui a pas suffi. En aimant une autre, il a brûlé son passé moralement et matériellement. Il a osé pareil reniement ... pourtant. Et pourtant, que n'a-t-il fait pour que je devienne sa femme! (23)

Secondly, she finds troubling the discrepancies which exist between the institution of marriage in Islamic and traditional

African cultures on one hand, and its practice, especially in her own marriage, on the other. She is guaranteed neither the justice and equity provided for in Islam nor is she the beneficiary of the superior position which the hierarchization of wives in the African traditional marriage encourages.

Aïssatou's marital experience is similar to that of her friend, Ramatoulaye. The major difference is in the solutions which they sought: Ramatoulaye remains in her marriage but Aïssatou seeks divorce. Aïssatou's marriage to Mawdo is equally controversial:

> Puis, ce fut ton mariage avec Mawdo Bâ, fraîchement sorti de l'Ecole Africaine de Médecine et de Pharmacie. Un mariage controversé. J'entends encore les rumeurs coléreuses de la ville. (30)

After several years of a happy marriage and four sons, Mawdo, purportedly influenced by his mother, marries a second wife. It is true that Mawdo's mother never forgave Mawdo for contracting a misalliance with a jeweler's daughter and, consequently, vows to have her only son properly married to a true blueblood. But the question is, why did Mawdo go along with this new marriage? The narrator, Ramatoulaye, provides the subtext: "La petite Nabou était si tentante!" (48) In any case, the arrangements for Mawdo's marriage to "la petite Nabou" are all made without Aïssatou's knowledge. Everyone, except Aïssatou, knew that a co-wife was on the way:

> Je savais, Modou savait. La ville savait. Toi, Aïssatou, tu ne soupçonnais rien et rayonnais toujours. Et parce que sa mère avait pris date pour la nuit nuptiale, Mawdo eut enfin le courage de te dire ce que chaque femme chuchotait: tu avais une co-épouse. (48)

Aïssatou opts for divorce: she leaves with her four sons and lands a good job in Washington, D.C. However, her departure is dramatized by a symbolic gesture; she writes a letter to her husband and leaves it *on their matrimonial bed*:

> Au bonheur qui fut nôtre, je ne peux substituer celui que tu me proposes aujourd'hui. Tu veux dissocier l'amour tout court et l'amour physique. Je te rétorque que la communion charnelle ne peut être sans l'acceptation du coeur, si minime soit-elle. Si tu peux procréer sans aimer, rien que pour assouvir l'orgueil d'une mère déclinante, je te trouve vil. Dès lors, tu dégringoles de l'échelon supérieur, de la respectabilité

> où je t'ai toujours hissé. Ton raisonnement qui scinde est inadmissible.... Je me dépouille de ton amour, de ton nom. Vêtue du seul habit valable de la dignité, je poursuis ma route. (50)

Aïssatou's letter is illuminating. Polygamy or jealousy of her rival is really not the issue. In actuality, she expresses concern for her rival, la petite Nabou, who is brought in to breed children but not to be loved. Aïssatou finds Mawdo's separation of carnal and romantic love abhorrent and unacceptable. She is a respectable and respectful woman; she respects her husband and puts him on a pedestal. She has a tremendous sense of direction and more importantly, has the will and courage, "tu eus le surprenant courage de t'assumer" (50), to follow with dignity the direction which she has chosen for herself.

Some critics, like Femi Ojo-Ade, doubt that Aïssatou is happy with her new life in America. "Is Aïssatou happy in her solitude? How does she survive through the cold wintry New York nights?" (77) We should not tax our minds over such speculations since Mariama Bâ provides the answer in the book. As Ramatoulaye writes to her friend, Aïssatou,

> Tu étais là, débarrassée du masque de la souffrance. Tes fils poussaient bien, contrairement aux prédictions. Tu ne t'inquiétais pas de Mawdo. Oui, tu étais bien là, le passé écrasé sous ton talon. Tu étais la victime innocente d'une injuste cause et pionnière hardie d'une nouvelle vie. (53)

One thing is certain, Aïssatou is better off with her sons and her job in Washington, D.C. than with Mawdo in Senegal.

Now comes Jacqueline. This Christian Ivorian lady met and married the Senegalese Samba Diack while he was a student in the Republic of the Ivory Coast. Jacqueline's family opposed the marriage but she decided to go with Samba. There is no indication in the novel that Jacqueline converted to Islam through marriage; on the contrary, she practiced her Christian religion when she returned to Senegal with her husband at the end of his studies. In Senegal, Samba changed; Jacqueline suddenly became a "gnac" (bush-girl). Samba's flirtations with Senegalese girls are overtly executed with complete disregard of his wife:

> Son mari, qui revenait de loin, passait ses loisirs à pourchasser les Sénégalaises "fines," appréciait-il, et ne prenait pas la peine de cacher ses aventures, ne

> respectant ni sa femme ni ses enfants. Son absence de précautions mettait sous les yeux de Jacqueline les preuves irréfutables de son inconduite: mots d'amour, talons de chèques portant les noms des bénéficiaires, factures de restaurants et de chambre d'hôtel. Jacqueline pleurait, Samba Diack "noçait". Jacqueline maigrissait. Samba Diack "noçait" toujours. (64)

The emotional torture which Jacqueline experiences very far away from home weighs her down: "Ce sont les brimades subies et les perpétuelles contradictions qui s'accumulent quelque part dans le corps et l'étouffent" (67). Again, the woman's maladjustment is due to her inability to cope with the never-ending contradictions in her marriage. Jacqueline suffers a nervous breakdown and is hospitalized. Her doctor's diagnosis reveals the root cause of her problem:

> Madame Diack, je vous garantis la santé de votre tête. Les radios n'ont rien décelé, les analyses de sang non plus. Vous êtes simplement déprimée, c'est-à-dire... pas heureuse. Les conditions de vie que vous souhaitez diffèrent de la réalité voilà pour vous des raisons de tourments. De plus vos accouchements se sont succédés trop rapidement; l'organisme perd ses sucs vitaux qui n'ont pas le temps d'être remplacés. Bref, vous n'avez rien qui compromette votre vie. (68)

Again, the issue is not the institution of polygamy as we know it in Islam and African tradition but rather the practice of concubinage. The point which Aïssatou makes in her letter about carnal and romantic love comes up again. Although she is unhappy and unloved, Jacqueline keeps breeding children in quick succession. However, one positive step she takes at this moment of crisis in her life is that she succeeds in reestablishing ties with her family; ties she broke in her bid to marry Samba Diack.

Mireille's encounter with Ousmane is an extreme and complex case; in this instance, the marital problems noted above are further complicated by race issues: Mireille de La Vallée is a white French girl and Ousmane is black. When Mireille's father, a French diplomat working in Dakar, finds out that his daughter is dating a black man, he puts her on the next available flight back to France. From France, Mireille keeps in touch with Ousmane who eventually goes to study there. In spite of the vehement opposition to her relationship with Ousmane, Mireille chooses to alienate her family and marries Ousmane. In his letter to his family after the wedding, Ousmane admits the immense positive contribution

Mireille has made to his life:

> Si j'ai réussi, si je suis ta fierté comme tu dis, si j'ai comblé tes désirs, si tu es loin de la poussière d'Usine Niari-Talli, si tu vois d'un oeil plus calme les trimestres s'étirer, c'est à elle que tu le dois. Entreprendre est difficile pour un homme seul.... Mireille m'a permis, par un soutien moral constant, de me réaliser. Elle était devant moi, comme un flambeau, illuminant mon chemin. Elle n'est pas l'une de ces vulgaires aventurières qui s'accrochent aux Nègres pour ne pas sombrer. Mireille est une fille d'ancienne noblesse. (99)

The couple returns to Senegal to settle; not too long after, the marriage is blessed with a son. Mireille does all she can to familiarize herself with her new environment and establish close ties with her husband's family but does not get any encouragement. Unknown to Mireille, Ousmane starts dating a young Senegalese girl, Ouleymatou, whom he eventually marries. Another home is rented for Ouleymatou; Ousmane is now the privileged master of two homes! Like the other men who abandon their wives, Ousmane has to find some justification for his action. Like Mawdo before him, Ousmane claims that his action is destined to be. He suddenly discovers his negritude!:

> Ma rencontre avec la Blanche relève du destin car plus que jamais, je me veux Nègre.... Ouleymatou, symbole double dans ma vie! Symbole de la femme noire.... Symbole de l'Afrique.... Reculer à cause des fureurs de ma Blanche qui clame sa colère dans la violence? Reculer à cause de ma conscience quotidienne alertée? Reculer à cause du code universel de l'honneur et de la dignité? Impossible! (225)

Ousmane ignores conscience, honor and dignity. How he has changed!

The shock of the discovery of this immense deception drives Mireille crazy. In a fit of anger and confusion, she pastes Ousmane's love letters to her all over their home; she kills their only child and stabs Ousmane when he comes home, as usual, in the early hours of the morning. Mireille's actions are responses to the contradictions in her married life. These contradictions take a human form in her mulatto son and she kills him—a murder which symbolizes her abhorrence and rejection of these contradictions. Her letters feverishly pasted all over the house contain sentiments—"Je n'aimerai que toi toute ma vie .... Toi ma blanche! Toi ma blonde, comme tu me manques!.... Sans toi, la vie n'a pas de sel" (244)—which contradict Ousmane's current attitude towards her. Ousmane's refusal to "reculer à cause des fureurs de ma Blanche qui clame sa colère dans la violence" (225) provokes that violence. Fortunately for Ousmane, he is left bleeding but not yet declared dead; fortunately for Mireille, the plea of insanity remains a legal recourse.

Mariama Bâ's novels show the extent to which religious and traditional institutions are subverted by "modernity" in Africa's urban areas. The vulgarization of the institution of marriage, or even polygamy, is rampant among the rich middle- and upper-middle-class men whose conception of the best way to use their wealth is to acquire wives and set up homes in different parts of the city. A. B. Diop, in his study of the organization of the African family in Dakar, links affluence to "polygamie géographique."[3] It is ironic that the wealth which the first wife helped to acquire is eventually used against her.

Furthermore, what is at issue is the prevalent distorted, selective, dubious and misleading exegesis of the canon. Even if the institution and institutional literature bestow privileges on a group of people, these privileges come with responsibility. The problem is that often the privileges are appropriated without the responsibility. For example, one of the lead quotes to Femi Ojo-Ade's articles is taken from the Bible: "The head of every man is Christ; the head of every woman is man." This is a part of a longer injunction in St. Paul's epistle to the Ephesians, Chapter 5. The portion which is left out reads:

> Husbands, love your wives, as Christ loved the church and gave himself up for her.... Even so husbands should love their wives as their bodies. He who loves his wife loves himself. For no man ever hates his own flesh, but nourishes and cherishes it, as Christ does the church, because we are members of his body. For this reason a man shall leave his father and mother and be joined to his wife, and the two shall become one flesh. (1421)

The distortion which emanates from this deliberate act of omission sustains the oppressor/oppressed dialectic which constantly privileges the oppressor (the interpreter of the canon).

The issue in the novels is not polygamy as an institution but the practice of it in ways that are disrespectful, deceptive and humiliating to women. It is significant that Mariama Bâ, more than any other African female writer, puts educated middle-aged women on center stage. The women suffer deception at a period in their lives when it is very difficult to pick up the pieces; that explains the intensity of their feeling of outrage. However, through Aïssatou's action, Mariama Bâ demonstrates that a woman can still rebuild her life if she has the will and courage to do so.

The women are not declaring war on men as Ojo Ade claims: "the war between male and female is now a contemporary constant" (72); they are only pursuing happiness,[4] which is normal and should be encouraged. The women are demanding respect and honesty from their spouses; and that is not asking too much! The women are rejecting deception, humiliation and betrayal from their spouses. The women are not enthused about living with enigmas—"Car Mawdo demeurait pour moi une énigme et à travers lui, tous les hommes" (52); and that is quite understandable!

Mariama Bâ's protagonists, at least some of them, still have faith in the cooperation between man and woman. Ramatoulaye ends her long letter in a hopeful, conciliatory note:

> Je reste persuadée de l'inévitable et nécessaire complémentarité de l'homme et de la femme: L'amour, si imparfait soit-il dans son contenu et son expression, demeure le joint naturel entre ces deux êtres. S'aimer! Si chaque partenaire pouvait rendre sincèrement vers l'autre! S'il essayait de se fondre dans l'autre!.... C'est de l'harmonie du couple que naît la réussite familiale, comme l'accord de multiples instruments crée la symphonie agréable. (129-130)

Mariama Bâ, after all, dedicated Ramatoulaye's long letter, *Une si longue lettre*, to men; qualified, however!: "aux hommes de bonne volonté." Are Modou Fall, Mawdo Bâ, Samba Diack and Ousmane among these honorable men? I wonder.

Notes

[1] Part of the title of Femi Ojo-Ade's article.

[2] Rafi Ullah Shehab cites the example of Jamila, wife of Sabit bin Qais. Jamila, dissatisfied with the ugliness of her husband, decided to separate from him. She approached the Holy Prophet who granted the separation without hesitancy but on condition that she return the orchard which Sabit gave her in lieu of dower-money.

[3] A. B. Diop's research shows that polygamy in the urban areas increases as one goes up the economic ladder: "D'autre part, on constate l'augmentation du taux de polygamie avec la montée des chefs de ménage dans la hiérarchie des professions... Ce taux passe de 8,2% chez les domestiques à 10,8% chez les ouvriers, employés, artisans, 17,5% chez les commerçants; elle atteint 19,5% chez les fonctionnaires ... La polygamie ... ne devient fréquente que dans les catégories qui ont les moyens économiques les plus importants."

[4] Edris Markward examines the issue of happiness in his essay that appears in *Ngambika: Studies of Women in African Literature.*

Works Cited

Bâ, Mariama. *Un chant écarlate.* Dakar: Nouvelles Editions Africaines, 1981.

____________. *Scarlet Song.* Trans. Dorothy S. Blair. New York: Longman, 1985.

____________. *So Long a Letter.* Trans. Modupé Bodé-Thomas. London: Heinemann, 1981.

____________. *Une si longue lettre.* Dakar: Nouvelles Editions Africaines, 1980.

Diop, A. B. "L'organisation de la famille africaine." *Dakar en devenir.* Eds. M. Sankale, L. V. Thomas, P. Fougeyrollas. Paris: Présence Africaine, 1968.

Makward, Edris. "Marriage, Tradition and Woman's Pursuit of Happiness in the Novels of Mariama Bâ." *Ngambika: Studies of Women in African Literature.* Eds. Carole Boyce Davies, Anne Adams Graves. Trenton: Africa World Press, 1986.

Merand, Patrick. *La vie quotidienne en Afrique noire â travers la littérature africaine.* Paris: Harmattan, 1980.

Monteil, Vincent. "L'Islam." *Dakar en devenir.* Eds. M. Sankale, L. V. Thomas, P. Fourgeyrollas. Paris: Présence Africaine, 1968.

The New Oxford Annotated Bible. Eds. Herbert G. Mazy, Bruce M. Metzger. New York: Oxford UP, 1973.

Ojo-Ade, Femi. "Still a Victim? Mariama Bâ's *Une si longue lettre.*" *African Literature Today* 12 (1982): 71-87.

Phillips, Arthur, and Henry F. Morris. *Marriage Laws in Africa.* London: Oxford UP, 1971.

Sembène, Ousmane. *Xala* . Paris: Présence Africaine, 1973.

Shehab, Rafi Ullah. *Rights of Women in Islamic Sharia.* Lahore: Indus Publishing House, 1986.

The New Oxford Annotated Bible. Eds. Herbert G. Mazy, Bruce M. Metzger. New York: Oxford UP, 1973.

The Hom(m)osexual Economy in the Fiction of Marguerite Yourcenar

Sally L. Kitch
The Ohio State University

In the author's notes to *Memoirs of Hadrian*, Marguerite Yourcenar wrote:

> Another thing virtually impossible, to take a feminine character as a central figure, to make Plotina, for example, rather than Hadrian, the axis of my narrative. Women's lives are much too limited or else too secret. If a woman does recount her own life she is promptly reproached for being no longer truly feminine. It is already hard enough to give some element of truth to the utterances of a man. (327-28)

Yourcenar further explained that, while "every being who has gone through the adventure of living is myself" (342), she tried "to efface the personal" in writing the novel (342-43).

Comments such as these, seen in conjunction with the nature of her fiction, suggest that Marguerite Yourcenar did not wish to write as a woman, to be judged as a woman writer, or to concentrate on the lives and emotions of women in her work. Among the most compelling pieces of evidence to support that three-pronged conclusion is her exclusive use, in the major novels, of the male narrative voice. Because of that choice, Yourcenar's female characters are routinely presented through a masculine lens which is frequently both misogynistic and hom(m)ophilic.

Other critics who have noted Yourcenar's approach to both her own and her characters' gender identities have responded in varying ways. Pierre Horn believes that concern about Yourcenar's putative misogyny is "unfair" and "incorrect." Horn points out that female characters not only appear in Yourcenar's work but also play "an important supporting role . . . or are essential to the action of the story and the psychology of the participants" (96). (Horn's credibility on the topic of misogyny may be reduced by his failure to see the misogynistic implications of counting as "participants" only the male characters whom the females "support.") Colette Gaudin is somewhat more persuaded of Yourcenar's misogyny. She acknowledges reluctantly that

Yourcenar's "now famous 'humanism'" must be reinterpreted in light of her apparent "self-effacement of the (woman) author" (36).

Critic Linda Stillman offers a psychological explanation for Yourcenar's effacement of both self and other women. She thinks it a sign of the author's repressed female identity. Yourcenar disavowed her sex because she wrote from a "daughter's anguish, elicited by the psychic wound of her imagined matricide and her mother's irrevocable abandonment." The wound Stillman refers to was inflicted by the death of the author's mother ten days after her birth. According to Stillman, Yourcenar inscribed her "desire for her mother's forgiveness and the impossibility of forgiving her mother" through a repressed feminine discourse in which "men sacrifice loving women to the greater and more natural glory of a pederastic relationship" (275-76, 262).

Stillman finds additional proof of Yourcenar's repressed female identity in her name change, from Crayencour to Yourcenar. The initial character of the earlier name, "C," has feminine connotations, according to Stillman, while by Yourcenar's own description, the initial character of the new name resembles a tree—an "ideogram of the friendly phallus," Stillman claims. "The chosen name thus functions like a mask, assuring veiling and transgression . . . endowing its wearer with a new persona . . . the name of the symbolic other" (263-64).

A Fair Appraisal?

One may well ask why this writer, who achieved such acclaim for her brilliance and her extraordinary ability, among other talents, to weave fictional narrative with historical analysis, should be criticized for her treatment of gender. Is it not enough that she was the only woman ever to be elected to the Académie Française since its founding in 1635?

I would suggest several answers to such inquiries. First, Yourcenar's background suggests that, in her early career, she recognized the role of gender in the production, acceptance, and criticism of literature and she was rewarded for her talent as a woman. In the 1920s, she attended the literary salons of the American expatriate, Natalie Barney, who established the Académie des femmes in Paris and was, herself, an outspoken feminist (Shurr 184). In that circle, Yourcenar must have mingled with the likes of Colette, Gertrude Stein, Alice Toklas, Dolly Wilde and others with raised consciousness about sexism and heterosexism. In the late 1920s, Yourcenar was awarded a 500,000 franc award for women writers—the Prix Renée Vivien—sponsored by Barney (Ornstein 488-91). (In later years, Yourcenar never mentioned the recognition of that prize.) In addition, *The Abyss* won the Prix Fémina in 1968 (Shurr 184n). Because Yourcenar received attention and recognition as a woman writer, it seems fair to analyze her work in the context of that fact. Furthermore, although she later resisted the "sexual particularism" she equated with feminism, Yourcenar supported many issues that can be called feminist (*Open Eyes* 221-22).

Second, to understand more fully Yourcenar's literary approach to women and their relationship to men is not equivalent to undermining either her value or her reputation as a writer. Modern critical theory has simply provided the analytical tools for exploring questions of gender in works never before considered from that perspective. This exploration, whether consistent with the stated goals of an author or not, is essential to unmasking the cultural history of gender constructs and to exploring the implications of that history for modern conceptions of gender. In my view, all fictional works can legitimately be analyzed in gender terms because virtually all fictional characters are designated by sex and function at least partly in terms of both cultural and personal gender expectations. More problematic is determining the relationship of an author's sex to that of her characters, but such a project has value insofar as it can illuminate the history of gender constructions which is our cultural heritage.

Finally, Yourcenar's enduring singularity as a woman in the Académie Française is grounds for suspicion rather than complacency. Why was this particular woman, in a culture endowed with so many brilliant women writers, acceptable to the all-male club? Did her obvious preference for the male persona and for suitably public and monumental topics "unsex" her, and thereby render her admissible, in the eyes of the judges?

Theoretical Framework

I have come to understand Yourcenar's literary treatment of women, as well as her ambivalence about her own female identity, according to a theoretical framework that expands Stillman's analysis described above. Without presuming to know what influence her mother's death, her upbringing by her father, or her own lesbian sexual orientation may have had on the process of Yourcenar's psycho-sexual development, I would argue that her experience somehow promoted her complicity in what Luce Irigaray calls the hom(m)osexual economy in Western culture. That economy entails both the psychological and social institutionalization of heterosexuality as a function of a male desire which is actually hom(m)osexual. Even heterosexuality in such an economy is based on men's desire for the Same. Women in this economy essentially reinforce male narcissism and facilitate male-male relationships. Irigaray's analysis parallels Lévi-Strauss' observation of marriage as an institution in which women are exchanged among men in order to cement cross-tribal (or -familial) relationships. Men marry, Lévi-Strauss suggests—and Irigaray echoes—in order to obtain brothers-in-law.

Irigaray also discusses the Freudian concept of penis envy as a male invention that serves primarily to bolster the male ego. "To castrate the woman is to inscribe her in the law of the same desire, of desire for same," she explains in *Ce sexe qui n'en est pas un* (Moi 133). Woman is not merely Other, she is specifically man's Other or mirror image, a non-man, rather than a distinctive human form. Only when masculinized does woman become desirable in a culture that values the masculine and disparages the feminine.

As with other cultural and psychological features in the Lacanian system on which Irigaray bases her work, the use of woman to establish the hom(m)osexual economy is inscribed in language. "Patriarchal discourse situates woman *outside* representation: she is absence, negativity, the dark continent or, at best, a lesser man" (Moi 133-34). The masculine achieves the status of subject by transforming the feminine into an object that remains stable, unexplored, unidimensional. It is against female objectivity that male subjectivity measures itself (Moi 136). Because woman is object rather than subject, "the pleasure of self-representation, of her desire for the same, is denied" her, according to Irigaray (Moi 135). In short, woman cannot be a subject in the economy of male desire for the Same. She cannot speak of or for herself.

The choices given to woman in the hom(m)osexual economy are basically three, according to Irigaray. She can choose to remain silent; she can choose to speak as the Other and, therefore, appear to babble (this may have been Yourcenar's fear); or she can "*enact* the specular representation of herself as a lesser male" (Moi 135). The last appears to be Yourcenar's choice as she presents women through masculine eyes and obscures the subjectivity of women. In the context of Irigaray's work, Yourcenar's fears about making Plotina, rather than Hadrian, the central subject of a work makes perfect sense.

According to Irigaray, Yourcenar's choice to maintain women's status as objective Other is the only one consistent with the system of representation as we know it. The only other alternative within that system is the objectification of the male in support of female subjectivity. What Irigaray proposes, but Yourcenar did not adopt, is that women "not pretend to rival [the male] by constructing a logic of the feminine"; rather they must "try to disentangle this question from the economy of the logos" (Moi 139). Women can also disturb and exceed the logic of the masculine by challenging its formulae for the feminine.

Literary Evidence

I will focus on Yourcenar's treatment of women as an element of her overall literary production in three novels, *Mémoires d'Hadrien* (1951), translated as *Memoirs of Hadrian* (1954), *Le coup de grâce* (1939, translated using the same title in 1957), and *L'oeuvre au noir* (1968), translated as *The Abyss* (1976). In these novels, Yourcenar neither disturbed nor exceeded the male hom(m)osexual economy with the self-representation of the feminine. In fact, although she presented female characters and occasionally praised or admired one, she generally depicted them as opaque, as the "dark continent" the male economy considers them to be. The women are occasionally deuteragonists but more frequently objects in the novels—talked about but not expressive and, therefore, ultimately unfathomable. Few are presented as worthy of male desire in any important sense. In fact, Yourcenar took the male hom(m)osexual economy more literally than many men authors do, by extolling its physical practice as well as its cultural inevitability. Women become valued companions of men only when they are no longer defined as essentially, and sexually, female.

Though not the first of the three novels, *Memoirs of Hadrian* can be seen as Yourcenar's model of the hom(m)osexual economy. This novel alone proves little about Yourcenar's own convictions or sentiments, because her Hadrian is modeled on an historical figure for whom pederasty was a cultural norm. Yet, taken in conjunction with *Coup de grâce* and *The Abyss*, *Memoirs* demonstrates Yourcenar's understanding of, and sympathy with, the ho-(m)osexual economy. In the other two novels, she depicted men who, with much less reason, choose the same route.

Memoirs of Hadrian

Hadrian is technically a bisexual, like many men in his culture. He marries and has love affairs with women, but his deep passions are not for women. He prefers men because of what existentialists call their transcendence; while women are immersed in their immanence, men can rise above their sex to achieve full humanness. Men think like gods; women can think only as women (63). Women's domain is narrow, Hadrian thinks, "their hard practical sense and their horizon turn[s] grey the moment that love has ceased to illumine it." While pleasurable, sex with women never becomes spiritual or deep. He tolerates his marriage because it is harmless: "I could have freed myself by divorce from this unloved woman; had I been a private citizen I should not have hesitated to do so. But she troubled me very little . . . ." (169).

Hadrian's affairs with women, in good Lévi-Straussian manner, procure for him, "almost inevitably, the friendship of the fat or feeble husband." The emperor explains that he "seldom gained pleasure from such a connection, and profited even less" (61). Nevertheless, Hadrian's romantic liaisons with women serve the hom(m)osexual purposes of the economy of the Same.

The empress Plotina, wife of Trajan, is clearly an exception —Hadrian's "sole friend among women" (166). His attraction to Plotina is significant for two reasons, however. First, it is never consummated physically. Second, it is based not on Hadrian's appreciation of Plotina in the context of difference but, rather, on Hadrian's appreciation of the Same. He admires Plotina because of her similarity to himself: "we two were in accord on almost everything," he says (81). He admires her soldierly virtues; he grieves for her death as he would for a male friend.

Hadrian's real passions are reserved for young men, especially for Antonius. Male bodies and souls inspire Hadrian's greatest eloquence. He describes Antonius as a god, and he nearly transforms him into a god by commissioning hundreds of sculptures of the beautiful boy to celebrate his face and body. Hadrian sees male physical beauty as a reflection of male spiritual value: "I see a head bending under its dark mass of hair, eyes which seemed slanting, so long were the lids, a young face broadly formed, as if for repose. This tender body varied all the time, like a plant, and some of its alterations were those of growth." As Antonius aged, "the full chest of the young runner took on the smooth, gleaming curves of a Bacchante's breast; the brooding lips bespoke a bitter ardor, a sad satiety" (155-56).

The essential (and destructive) narcissism underlying the hom(m)osexual economy is also illustrated by Hadrian's relationship with Antonius. Despite his ardor, Hadrian is not always kind to the boy. His power over his lover prevents Hadrian's full empathy with Antonius; Hadrian allows himself to exploit Antonius sexually. Ultimately, Antonius' suffering in the relationship leads to his suicide at the age of twenty. Hadrian's response to the death is blatantly self-indulgent. Though he grieves his loss, he appreciates Antonius' sacrifice. It will prevent the erosion of the couple's passion through habit. Familiarity "would have led us to that inglorious but safe ending which life brings to all who accept its slow dulling from wear," Hadrian thinks (172-73).

While not presented as a contrast to Hadrian's feelings about women, his sentiments about Antonius' death suggest an underlying reason for the greater appeal of a hom(m)osexual love in a misogynist culture. At its core, male love of Same is a love of self. Though it does not prevent some distance from the beloved (as illustrated in Hadrian's abuse of Antonius), the love of self has the potential for arousing the greatest passion. Love for a woman is love of a degraded Other. Such love cannot arouse sufficient passion even to warrant concern that it will diminish over time.

Coup de grâce

The hom(m)osexual theme of the *Memoirs*—that women can never do for men what they can do for each other—is echoed in Yourcenar's earlier novel, *Coup de grâce.* In composing that work, Yourcenar was not restricted by the demands of historical accuracy in her creation of the hom(m)osexual economy. Yet, she chose to create it anyway.

The story involves young people on the fringes of the Bolshevik revolution. Erick and Conrad fight intermittently against the revolutionaries, while Conrad's sister, Sophie, harbors sympathies for them. Sophie suppresses her political views for a while out of love for Erick, but when she realizes her love will be forever unrequited, she abandons Erick and joins the revolutionaries. At the novel's end, she is captured by Erick and his unit. In the line of duty, and at her request, Erick shoots her.

Although homosexual preferences are less explicit in *Coup de grâce* than in the *Memoirs,* they are much in evidence. The novel's male narrator, Erick von Lhomond, not only prefers men for their similarities with himself but also disparages women for their mysterious Otherness. In her introduction to the book, Yourcenar explained Erick's devotion to Conrad as "more than physical or even sentimental." Rather, it is part of "a certain ideal of austerity, born of chivalric dreams of comradeship" that only men can share (n.p.n.). Erick celebrates the "accord between minds and temperaments, and bodies as well, not to mention that unexplained portion of flesh . . . the heart" that exists between himself and Conrad (11). (Perhaps my mind plays dirty tricks, but I hear an allusion to a different "portion of flesh" in that sentence.)

Because they have been friends since childhood, Erick feels bound to Conrad "by a kind of pact" (59). In their youth, Erick and Conrad have known "happiness, the real thing, the inalterable goldpiece exchangeable for whole handfuls of lesser coin" (14). Erick resists Sophie, in part, because he fears that a relationship with her will threaten his intimacy with Conrad: "One does not drop a friend of twenty years standing . . . for a shabby intrigue with his sister," Erick thinks (89). In their prediction of an affectional rivalry between the brother and sister, as well as in their trivialization of a romance with Sophie, Erick's sentiments reinforce the hom(m)osexual economy in the novel.

At times, Erick is fairly explicit about his preference for men. He is scornful of "fancies" with girls (13), and he says he is a man "who has no esteem for sex" (30). He is sorry that Sophie failed to reckon with "one unforeseeable trait" in himself, his disinterest in women (33). "Why is it," he asks, "that women fall in love with the very men who are destined otherwise, and who accordingly must repulse them, or else deny their own nature?" (29). He prefers "friendship" with men to love with a woman because "friendship affords certitude" (19) and because it allows solitude. "Women," Erick explains, "cannot live in solitude" (92). Finally, the suggestion that Sophie has stormed out of Erick's life because she has learned from another soldier that Erick and Conrad are lovers worries Erick more because of Conrad than because of Sophie. Her accusation that Erick has "corrupted" her innocent brother turns the tables on Erick: "The idea that she was defending Conrad against me pricked my guilty conscience at its most vulnerable point," he confesses (103-04).

As with Hadrian, Erick's preference for men rests primarily on his disparagement of women and his failure to comprehend or appreciate their distinctiveness. Erick considers most women to be part of the necessary supplies of a soldier's life, like wine (20). "Nothing is important for women except themselves," he thinks (103). He believes that women's and men's lives are necessarily and essentially different (42-43). Among women there is a "free-masonry," but Erick does not understand or admire it (112). After he has shot Sophie dead, Erick can only fuss: "One is always trapped, somehow, in dealings with women" (151).

The novel's economy of the Same is further illustrated by its depiction of Erick's one moment of physical attraction for Sophie as a moment in which he recognizes their similarity. Erick feels the greatest passion when he sees them "both . . . innocent as beings just resurrected" (76). The feeling passes when the encounter reminds him of a slimy starfish his mother once forced into his hand. Perhaps that image is meant to explain his repulsion for women in general. In any case, he wrenches himself "from Sophie with a violence that must have seemed cruel to a body robbed of defense by felicity itself" (77). In this scene, as throughout the novel, Sophie never defines or describes herself. Her silence is consistent with the hom(m)sexual economy's denial of female subjectivity.

The Abyss

The most recent novel of the three, *The Abyss*, follows a familiar pattern. The major protagonist is male; he is sought by women, but he can seldom work up any passion for them; his passions are reserved for other men and for (in his case) the male world of learning and science. Zeno, an alchemist and physician, wanders Western Europe during the early years of the Reformation, seeking a haven for his research and his values, which please neither the Protestants nor the Catholics. He is ultimately unsuccessful at finding such a haven, since sixteenth-century Europe is a hell-hole of intolerance, corruption, and violence (indeed, these conditions are the main focus of the book). During his travels, Zeno meets many people, men and women, of all classes and persuasions. He both hides and tests his ideas against each of them. He also seeks love, but in love as in ideas, Zeno prefers the Same to the genuine Other. He desires "a body like my own reflecting my pleasure, agreeably dispensing with" women's adornments and coquetry. He finds that intimacy between men "does not try to justify itself . . . by perpetuation of the human race" (117-18).

The novel contains many female characters—historical and fictional. Several burn with love and passion for Zeno, but none is worthy of him. Vivine, Zeno's childhood friend and admirer, is one such character. She is dismissed as "a small wellspring of pure but insipid water" (55). Other women, such as Catherine de Medici (called Queen Catherine), have professional dealings with Zeno, but they too disappoint. Catherine is portrayed as vain and evasive; her nobility is compromised by the vagaries of female marital and reproductive troubles. When Zeno notes that the queen has been somewhat derelict in ensuring his safety at the Sorbonne, he is reminded by another man that, after all, "she is widowed . . . she is considered a Jezebel by the Lutherans and Herodias by our Catholics, and she has five young children on her hands" (144).

Women speak in the novel, but not at length. Their cryptic conversation contributes to the opacity of their characters both to Zeno and to readers. Most responses by the women are passive and muted, if not completely mute. An extreme example is a servant woman who forces herself sexually upon Zeno—another Catherine, who works in the home of Zeno's old friend and master, Jan Meyers of Bruges—and represents "the brute power of sheer flesh." She is contrasted with Zeno's delicate sensibilities about love. Catherine seems "hardly capable . . . of human speech" except when she utters obscenities at the height of her pleasure (154-55).

Zeno disparages such passion and, because, like Erick, he associates it with women, he prefers men. Yet, like Hadrian, Zeno would use female bodies when "chance . . . came in the form of a woman" from time to time (180). Also like Hadrian, Zeno reserves his eloquence for the love of men, even though in Christian Europe, as opposed to the pagan world of Hadrian, those passions "could bring down upon him the fate reserved for heretics . . . burning at the stake" (235-36).

Conclusion

One could argue that these men whom Yourcenar created embody a kind of feminine principle, perhaps even express Yourcenar's own repressed feminine. In many ways, Hadrian is sensitive, thoughtful, and caring. Zeno has delicate sensibilities, sacrifices his health for others, and practices an immanent form of religion that has female connotations. Further, according to such French theorists of "the feminine" as Julia Kristeva, the feminine is simply that which has been repressed in Western culture, and it resides in both males and females.

Such an argument does not really bear scrutiny, however. If Yourcenar's male characters can be said to harbor the feminine—in part consisting of repressed early symbiosis with the maternal body—then why, in their expression of that sensibility, do the men fear and reject women? In addition, if Yourcenar wished to extol the feminine through male characters who somehow embody and/or represent it, why did she simultaneously present such muted and opaque female characters? Why did she not have the courage to associate the feminine with the female? Finally, why did she also allow these "feminine" males to express such misogynist values?

Release of the repressed feminine is not what I see in Yourcenar's fiction. Rather, I suspect that Yourcenar found the fact of her own femaleness in a misogynist world a hindrance to the important work she wanted to do. I suspect that she defined herself as an exception among women—thereby separate from them—rather than as an exceptional woman who resided along the same continuum as others of her sex. I further suspect that the Académie Française rewarded Yourcenar for overcoming the social stigma of femaleness by developing a male authorial voice. Their decision may, in fact, be the clearest illustration of Irigaray's contention that, in Western culture, the male voice will necessarily promote the hom(m)osexual economy.

Works Cited

Gaudin, Colette. "Marguerite Yourcenar's Prefaces: Genesis as Self-Effacement." *Studies in Twentieth Century Literature* 10 (Fall, 1985): 31-55.

Horn, Pierre L. *Marguerite Yourcenar.* Boston: Twayne Publishers, 1985.

Moi, Toril. *Sexual/Textual Politics: Feminist Literary Theory.* London: Methuen, 1985.

Ornstein, Gloria Feman. "The Salon of Natalie Clifford Barney: An Interview with Berthe Cleyrergue." *Signs: Journal of Women in Culture and Society* 4 (Spring 1979): 484-96.

Shurr, Georgia Hooks. "A Reformation Tragedy: Marguerite Yourcenar's *The Abyss.*" *Soundings: An Interdisciplinary Journal* 70 (Spring/Summer 1987): 169-87.

Stillman, Linda K. "Marguerite Yourcenar and the Phallacy of Indifference." *Studies in Twentieth Century Literature* 9 (Spring, 1985): 261-77.

Yourcenar, Marguerite. *The Abyss.* Trans. Grace Frick. New York: Farrar, Straus and Giroux, 1976.

_____. *Coup de grâce.* Trans. Grace Frick. New York: Farrar, Straus and Giroux, 1957.

_____. *Memoirs of Hadrian.* Trans. Grace Frick. New York: Farrar, Straus and Giroux, 1954.

_____. *With Open Eyes: Conversations with Mattieu Galey.* Trans. Arthur Goldhammer. Boston: Beacon Press, 1984.

Le gestuaire de Nathalie Sarraute

Gaëtan Brulotte
University of South Florida

L'existence de l'homme peut être envisagée comme étant d'abord corporelle, puisque toute relation avec le monde implique une médiation par le corps. Mais ce corps quel est-il? Ce n'est certes pas une donnée figée. Des multiples relations que le sujet entretient avec son environnement et les autres, se dégage une typologie des socialités corporelles. En nous inspirant de réflexions récentes de l'anthropologie,[1] il est possible de discerner cinq axes à l'intérieur desquels s'ordonne l'ensemble des manifestations corporelles et des conduites qui ponctuent à chaque instant la vie du sujet. Ces cinq axes sont les suivants:

1) **Les techniques du corps** qui sont le produit d'une somme d'apprentissages centrés sur des habiletés particulières, comme par exemple la marche, l'écriture, la sexualité, les sports, les arts et métiers, etc.;

2) **La gestuelle d'interaction** qui concerne les mises en jeu du corps lors des rencontres avec les autres (comme dans l'échange verbal par exemple), lesquelles rencontres s'accompagnent de multiples signes corporels tels les mimiques, le rire, le regard, les gestes, les postures, la distance d'interaction, etc.;

3) **L'expression des émotions** qui renvoie, dans une société donnée, aux façons d'exprimer l'ensemble des sentiments et des émotions, tels que la jalousie, la pudeur, la colère;

4) **La socialité infracorporelle** qui englobe le domaine de la sensorialité;

5) **La socialité corporelle d'inconduite** qui réfère à tous les gestes associés à l'"anormalité," comme ceux de la folie ou de la maladie.

Ces catégories, appliquées aux œuvres littéraires, nous aident à cerner les diverses facettes du corps que la littérature représente, mais aussi l'image particulière que chaque auteur en élabore. C'est cette image que je voudrais dégager chez Nathalie Sarraute en examinant son gestuaire. Le geste jouit chez cette dernière d'un statut privilégié. D'abord il est omniprésent. Tous ses personnages existent par leurs gestes, à commencer par l'écrivain dont l'activité est pourtant habituellement décrite surtout en termes intellectuels.

Voici le début et le leitmotiv d'*Entre la vie et la mort*, roman d'un romancier en proie aux affres de la création:

> Il étend le bras, il le replie . . . "J'arrache la page." Il serre le poing, puis son bras s'abaisse, sa main s'ouvre . . . "Je jette. Je prends une autre feuille." [. . .] Son bras se déplie et se replie. "J'arrache. Je froisse. Je jette." [. . .] Le geste répété se grave. Encore. Encore et encore. Je reprends une nouvelle feuille. (VM 7s)

Dès le départ, l'écriture pour Sarraute a, en elle-même, un caractère fondamentalement gestuel. En outre, le geste a, pour elle, le pouvoir de résumer et de révéler un être. On connaît bien son opinion sur le sujet: "Un seul geste et tout l'homme est là" (DI 118). Le geste l'intéresse en tant que support de sens. Sa confiance dans la communication non-verbale est à peu près illimitée. ". . . la seule chose qui compte: nos actes" (M 82).

> Le corps ne se trompe jamais: avant la conscience, il enregistre, il amplifie, il rassemble et révèle au-dehors avec une implacable brutalité des multitudes d'impressions infimes, insaisissables, éparses. (Pl 63)

Ce sont ses mouvements, ce sont ses gestes qui rendent ce corps si signifiant. Le geste est pour Sarraute la voie royale d'accès à l'individu et il est aussi une des meilleures portes d'entrée dans son univers imaginaire.

Les techniques du corps

La vie quotidienne se tisse d'une infinité de gestes plus ou moins routiniers codifiés en vue d'une efficacité pratique ou symbolique, gestes associés par exemple aux soins du corps, aux manières de table, aux positions du repos, à l'intimité sexuelle, aux déplacements ou encore à quelque savoir-faire particulier. Ces techniques, produit d'une somme considérable d'apprentissages, sont liées tantôt à des stades de la vie (la marche), tantôt au sexe (l'allaitement), tantôt à une appartenance sociale (moisson et récolte).

Dans l'univers de Sarraute, les gestes routiniers de la vie quotidienne, encore présents dans *Tropismes* ou dans *Portrait d'un inconnu*, deviennent de plus en plus rares après *Martereau*. Les prises de nourriture par exemple, les soins du corps ou le sommeil y font partie des présupposés de l'existence, c'est-à-dire de ce dont on ne parle guère dans la fiction. Ce semble plutôt être le domaine réservé de l'autobiographie, puisque, contrairement à ses romans, il en est largement question dans *Enfance*.

Cependant certains apprentissages corporels bénéficient d'une attention particulière dans ses œuvres romanesques. Ils sont l'apanage d'experts ou de spécialistes. Nombre de personnages sarrautiens sont de fins connaisseurs dans le domaine des antiquités et de l'art. Ils savent comment apprécier ou déprécier les objets. C'est d'ailleurs une situation dans laquelle on les voit souvent. Dans *Le planétarium*, par exemple, ils jaugent avec un œil d'une redoutable précision une statuette d'Alain ou encore ils évaluent une fine amphore de Maine (Pl 238). Tout le roman *Vous les entendez?* porte en bonne partie sur l'analyse d'une sculpture. Dans cette situation pour eux familière, les personnages déploient toute la gamme gestuelle de leur expertise: ils soulèvent l'objet dans les airs à bout de bras, le font pivoter dans la lumière, l'examinent sur toutes ses faces, plissent les paupières pour mieux le scruter; ils le retournent, le caressent, le posent avec précaution, en le replaçant très exactement là où il doit être.

Il ne s'agit pas ici seulement d'une connaissance intellectuelle, mais bien aussi d'un savoir-faire qui met en jeu une technique corporelle: les érudits sarrautiens sont des formes silencieuses ou chuchotantes qui, tout en s'affairant autour des objets qu'ils inspectent avec minutie, ont développé une panoplie de gestes évaluateurs ainsi qu'une habileté exceptionnelle dans le repérage visuel: ils savent palper, apprécier et classer d'une façon sûre tel jeu de lignes d'un décor, tel matériau d'une boiserie, telle miniature. Fins acheteurs aussi, leur passion détermine leurs déplacements et leurs actions: ils fréquentent les galeries, livrés à l'épuisement de longues stations debout (VE 23). Ils ont aiguisé leur goût dans les musées et ont rôdé dans les foires à la ferraille et les marchés aux puces. Ils ont cherché l'objet rare, ont fouiné partout pour le dénicher, ont passé des heures avant d'y apposer leur tampon de garantie, s'en sont emparés, l'ont préservé, etc. Avec tout ce gestuaire d'expert, ils pourraient être de précieuses ressources, mais dans le monde sarrautien ce sont des juges cruels (que l'on compare à l'occasion à des huissiers opérant une saisie—v. VM 133) qui prononcent des sentences impitoyables. Ils excellent à pinailler, à déceler l'invisible faille dans une porcelaine ou à faire résonner un objet pour montrer comme il sonne creux. Ils évoluent dans le système infernal du snobisme, selon lequel on évalue les êtres en fonction, non d'une relation duelle authentique, mais en fonction d'une tierce valeur qui leur est extérieure (ici les objets qu'ils possèdent, indices du goût et de la classe sociale). Ces experts forment "une caste, une secte, une société secrète" (VE 75), écrit Sarraute, groupe fermé, dont le talent, ici décrié, ne sert donc, le plus souvent, qu'une curiosité malveillante.

La composante sadique de l'expertise sarrautienne apparaît encore dans les nombreuses comparaisons qui réfèrent à des techniques du corps liées au savoir médical. Ces comparaisons nous montrent que le narrateur s'y entend dans ce domaine. Sarraute compare, par exemple, la réaction à certains mots à la sensation désagréable que donne un sondage d'estomac au moyen d'un gros tuyau de caoutchouc introduit dans la gorge (FO 105). Elle associe des rires à des anticorps qu'un organisme sain produit pour se défendre contre un microbe nocif (Pl 154). Elle évoque encore une douleur morale par le biais du registre chirurgical: cette douleur devient alors celle qu'on éprouve quand on vous cautérise une plaie ou quand on vous coupe un membre gangrené (Pl 221). Une discussion père-fils couche métaphoriquement le fils sur une table à dissection, tel un cadavre, où il subit les diagnostics de son père (Pl 124). On voit que les techniques du corps auxquelles le narrateur fait référence renvoient déjà à la dimension essentiellement douloureuse, chez Sarraute, des relations humaines.

Dans le rayon du savoir-faire, l'auteur place très haut celui de l'homme de métier: ainsi tels gestes précis et délicats d'ouvriers spécialisés, telle dextérité de déménageurs avec leurs gestes soigneux et prudents, leurs pieds doucement posés sur le parquet (Pl 181), ou tel tapissier qui travaille à la perfection (Pl 40). Le personnage sarrautien est extrêmement exigeant envers les autres. Aussi ne se prive-t-il jamais de relever leurs moindres failles: celles des ébénistes par exemple, dans *Le planétarium*, qui sont l'objet de longs reproches de la part de Berthe: ". . . des abrutis, des brutes, pas un atome d'initiative, d'intétêt pour ce qu'ils font, pas la moindre trace de goût" . . . "incapables de distinguer le beau du laid" . . . "automates insensibles" (Pl 12s). Berthe attribue le ratage d'une porte qui la trouble tant à un certain Renouvier, un "crétin, propre à rien qui ne sait pas faire son métier" (Pl 25). Il faut dire que Berthe, figure de l'oisiveté et de l'argent, est, comme beaucoup de sarrautiens, d'un perfectionnisme maladif. Ce trait de personnalité s'est transformé chez elle en un savoir-faire maniaque. Elle a développé le goût du détail dans la décoration intérieure ainsi que l'obsession de l'ordre et de la propreté (comme Mme Martereau). Et ces soucis s'accompagnent d'une compulsion gestuelle appropriée: elle passe son temps à frotter, à brosser, à astiquer, à pousser des meubles, à ranger, à ravauder, telle une fourmi industrieuse (v. Pl 28). Aucun ludisme dans ces activités: aux yeux de ces maniaques, "la vie est faite de corvées" (M 186) et tout s'y accomplit avec beaucoup de sérieux et de tension, sans que la satisfaction du travail bien accompli ne se manifeste.

Comme le jeu est ici exclu, sont également absents de l'univers de Sarraute la sexualité et les techniques sportives. Dans *Les fruits d'or*, on dit bien de Bréhier, l'auteur, qu'il fait de l'alpinisme, mais qu'il n'est pas fort ni courageux. Dans *Martereau*, un personnage a lâché le tennis et la natation (M 57) et on voit une fois Martereau pêcher à la ligne (réalisant ainsi le rêve du père dans *Portrait d 'un inconnu*—v. P 212), mais cette activité, d'ailleurs infructueuse, ne sert que de prétexte à une conversation (M 238 ss). Dans *Portrait d'un inconnu*, après la manie du plein air qui conduit la fille de ce roman à se fouler un pied, on tente, sans succès, de la convaincre d'apprendre le golf. Voilà à peu près tout ce qu'on trouve dans cette œuvre comme allusion sportive. Quant à la sexualité, elle ne fait son apparition, d'ailleurs mal jugée, que tardivement avec la vieillesse. C'est là le jeu censuré par excellence chez Sarraute. La seule adresse qui semble fasciner l'imaginaire sarrautien, et qui revient d'un roman à l'autre, c'est celle du somnambule à l'extrême bord du vide, c'est-à-dire une adresse qui se déploie dans l'inconscience.

En conclusion, le roman sarrautien évite soigneusement les gestes du quotidien pour privilégier plutôt la dextérité de l'expert ou du maniaque. Mais cette dextérité n'a rien de ludique. Elle est au service du système classificateur du snobisme ou d'un perfectionnisme si inhumain qu'il laisse l'être sarrautien perpétuellement insatisfait.

La gestuelle d'interaction

Contrairement aux techniques du corps, la gestuelle d'interaction relève d'une éducation informelle, impalpable. Son acquisition est liée au mimétisme et à ce savoir diffus et graduel qui circule silencieusement entre les fibres d'une trame sociale.

La rencontre entre les acteurs sociaux et leurs échanges verbaux se ponctue de plusieurs traits gestuels: salutations, poignées de main, accolades, bises, hochements de tête, signes des mains, etc. Comme chaque groupe social, chaque auteur élabore son propre registre de mises en jeu du corps dans l'échange avec autrui.

Dans l'univers sarrautien, de tous les registres de représentation du corps, la gestuelle d'interaction est, de loin, la dimension la plus importante et la plus riche. D'œuvre en œuvre, Sarraute détaille la moindre réaction gestuelle aux paroles échangées. Le signe le plus ténu qui module un propos a ici droit de mention: haussements d'épaules, grimaces, moues, reculs, sursauts, mouvements de tête, de bras, de mains, de doigts (mais rarement des pieds, ce qui signale un déséquilibre du corps, avec un haut surchargé de sens, le bas étant quasi inexistant), accompagnent la palette élaborée et nuancée des regards, des sourires et des airs, ainsi que toute la gamme des tons de voix.

Ces gestes d'interaction sont des signes porteurs de signification. Toujours hyper-qualifiés dans le texte, ils sont plus enracinés dans l'inconscient que la parole et renvoient à la sous-conversation, aux pensées secrètes, aux états d'âme inavouables des interlocuteurs. On y décode leur exaspération, leur dédain, leur haine, leur dégoût, leur impatience, leur dureté, leur indifférence, leur désapprobation, leur colère, leur fierté, leur honte, c'est-à-dire tout ce que la plupart du temps ils ne disent pas pour sauver les apparences.

Entre le gestuaire, mimiques y compris, et les paroles, il y a ici une insurmontable contradiction. C'est autour de cette contradiction que se déploie la majeure partie de l'activité sarrautienne, laquelle consiste, en écoutant parler une personne, à s'appliquer à lire le discours qui s'inscrit sur son visage et dans ses gestes, pendant que ses lèvres en énoncent un autre qui dément le premier. Pour Sarraute, l'humain est déchiré entre le paraître et son émotion profonde. De cette fondamentale inadéquation naît tout le malheur d'être. Le plus souvent la parole est le royaume de l'hypocrisie et la vérité s'inscrit dans le geste. Mais parfois le geste se trouve en retrait par rapport aux ulcérantes blessures causées par la cruauté des mots. Ou parfois encore le geste s'épanouit alors que le cœur n'y est pas, lui donnant ainsi la fausseté d'une convention.

Dans cet enfer, et malgré l'inconfort qu'il vit, le sujet sarrautien parvient tout de même à se donner une contenance corporelle. Il réussit à plus ou moins effacer symboliquement son corps de manière à maintenir l'interaction: il est au cœur d'un drame permanent, il souffre atrocement, mais souvent il ne bronche pas extérieurement. Il refoule ses gestes. Il voudrait bien en fait les produire, mais l'acte s'arrête et reste finalement intérieur: il est bloqué comme dans les cauchemars. L'auto-censure triomphe. “S'il pouvait les prendre par les épaules et les secouer, ces extatiques aux faces béates” (FO 66). Le personnage n'ose pas faire tous les gestes qu'il souhaiterait poser. “Il a envie de mettre sa main sur sa bouche, de lever les épaules peureusement, de rouler les yeux, de trépigner d'excitation joyeuse” (FO 92). Ou il aimerait, comme Berthe, “battre des mains” de contentement (Pl 220), mais il ne peut pas. Ce refoulement n'est pas toujours négatif pour les sarrautiens qui considèrent la retenue comme une qualité quand elle s'associe à la grâce et à la force (Pl 229, 235).

La gestuelle d'interaction est de toute évidence, chez Sarraute, fortement marquée par la violence. L'une des activités favorites des personnages consiste à harponner verbalement l'autre, à le harceler pour voir ses réactions, comme du bout d'un bâton on remue des chairs inertes pour voir si elles vont bouger, et, inversement, à se sentir constamment attaqué. Les assauts sont la plupart du temps méchants et cette méchanceté en arrive à avoir un caractère bestial. Les autres se comportent comme des animaux: ils sont une "meute de loups" (FO 126). "Ils reniflent . . . sont comme des chiens qui flairent dans tous les coins . . ." (Pl 168). Ou devant autrui, on devient soi-même animal: on a l'oreille dressée (Pl 124) ou l'œil bovin (Pl 245). Au sein de ce monde archi-susceptible, émettre une opinion c'est marcher sur la queue des serpents (Fo 123); parler se confond avec aboyer (VE 89; DI 139), bêler (DI 101) ou mordre (Pl 183; DI 139) ou avec quelque intentionalité indomptable: ". . . Je saute et je jappe et je pique et je me gonfle" (DI 139), tel un pou, un chien, un insecte, une grenouille. Les comparaisons animales abondent pour décrire les situations d'interaction où s'affrontent les personnages: de l'oiseau de proie prêt à fondre sur sa victime au taureau résigné devant le matador (Pl 123), la gestuelle d'interaction est très fortement imprégnée d'animalité violente. En cours de conversation, on attaque comme une "bête malfaisante qui s'introduit dans un nid pour prendre un petit" (Pl 137) ou on se défend "comme un vieux sanglier quand il se retourne et s'assied face à sa meute" (Pl 195). A d'autres moments, la conversation apparaît comme une opération de cannibales et de réducteurs de têtes (Pl 53). Et cette méchanceté bestiale se perçoit jusqu'aux bouts des doigts, dont les ongles se redressent comme la queue d'un scorpion (VM 37, 105).

La férocité, voilà bien une des caractéristiques des relations humaines, familière à tout lecteur de Sarraute. Les personnages s'entredéchirent. Ils sont sans cesse sur des charbons ardents ou touchent à des sujets électrisés. Ils éprouvent constamment ce que nous pourrions appeler des "tropismes interactionnels," c'est-à-dire qu'ils connaissent une réaction imaginaire, toujours *à caractère gestuel*, qui s'exprime dans le texte par des relais métaphoriques emphatiques. Par exemple, une parole apparemment anodine provoque chez la personne qui l'écoute un ravage intérieur d'une violence démesurée: ". . . celui qui reçoit cette décharge titube, il tombe, gît à terre, perd son sang" (Pl 95). L'interlocuteur se sent attaqué et mobilise dans son esprit des visions de persécution. Dans l'enfer du soupçon, le simple fait d'isoler quelqu'un du regard revient à l'interpeller comme un coupable, à la prendre sur le fait, à l'arrêter, à lui passer les menottes (FO 48s); le prier d'intervenir dans une discussion équivaut à le saisir par la peau du cou et à le jeter en spectacle aux gens (Pl 20).

Par ces tropismes interactionnels, Sarraute montre la grande fragilité des êtres, si arrogants qu'ils soient en apparence. Une phrase se transforme vite en actions symboliques: "Le coup le fait tituber, il voit des gerbes d'étincelles . . . il s'écroule, assommé, ils lui passent la camisole de force et l'emportent" (FO 97s), il "tombe, il est traîné sur le sol boueux, piétiné" . . . "encore étourdi flageolant, tout meurtri, il se relève, il court" (FO 104), "se laisse gripper, pincer, bourrer de coups" (FO 116). Dans ce monde hypersensible, une parole prend même l'ampleur d'une eau noire dévastatrice: "Ça va déferler sur lui, l'étouffer" (Pl 22); "il va jaillir, les asperger, les inonder—un geyser qui nous fera rouler les uns sur les autres, perdant la face, nos mèches dégoulinantes pendant en désordre sur nos visages, nos vêtements trempés collant à notre peau" (FO 133).

Le tropisme interactionnel à caractère gestuel est la transposition littéraire de ce que les sociologues appellent l'expression corporelle d'outrance, pour désigner les gestes exagérés que produit une personne dans une situation donnée (tel le skieur qui, dans une chute, outre ses effets et les rend volontairement plus spectaculaires).[2] Mais alors que dans la vie quotidienne, cette outrance prête habituellement à rire, chez Sarraute elle est toujours sombre et négative. Elle nous montre que la plus extrême violence habite secrètement la moindre des interactions.

Point donc ici de relation paisible possible. Tout prend forme d'attaque et de défense. Les êtres sarrautiens sont en constant état d'alerte, voire de combat. Le terrorisme règne et la méfiance est généralisée. Il faut être toujours sur le qui-vive. "Impossible de se fier à eux, il sera saisi, happé par eux tout entier, lui, ses guenilles, sa nudité, ils sont sans indulgence, sans pitié" (Pl 167).

Aussi le réflexe du sujet sarrautien est-il souvent celui du recul ou de la retraite. Cette figure majeure de la gestuelle d'interaction touche au degré de distance entre les interlocuteurs. "Aucune familiarité. Pas de contacts," lit-on dans *Les fruits d'or* (81). Les autres sont essentiellement visqueux, gluants. Ils cherchent à se coller, à palper, ils ont des yeux d'affamés (FO 39). D'où, dans ce contexte, le choix souverain de la distanciation et de la solitude: "Toujours un peu à distance" (FO 73). "Seule. Pure" (FO 40). Secouer de soi les autres comme des poussières, les repousser, rompre les ponts avec eux ou ignorer leur présence, cultiver la froideur en dressant contre eux une paroi ignifuge (Pl 143), voilà autant d'attitudes de distanciation. Ultimement, le salut est dans le repli: baisser le rideau de fer du regard, se barricader, boucher toutes issues, s'enfermer à triple tour en soi (FO 68), remblayer sa cache pour se protéger des autres.

Les relations humaines se réduisent ainsi à deux pôles incompatibles: d'un côté, il y a moi et de l'autre, eux. "Vous êtes vous. Ils sont eux" (DI 88). Entre les deux, c'est la guerre permanente.

A d'autres moments, l'isolement apparaît comme une solution tout de même trop hautaine ou douloureuse et représente ce que le personnage sarrautien redoute le plus. Peur de créer une distance à jamais infranchissable avec autrui et angoisse d'abandon (v. Pl 202). D'où des tentatives inverses, mais très prudentes, de rapprochement au cours desquelles on fait l'effort de surmonter ses craintes ou ses répulsions pour aller vers l'autre. Pour faciliter le contact, on aura parfois recours à des intermédiaires, tels des objets d'art ou des livres. Dans l'œuvre de Sarraute, plusieurs scènes, très déterminantes au plan de la gestuelle d'interaction, nous montrent deux personnages en train de feuilleter ensemble un livre ou une revue (par exemple: Pl 134, 150, 156-8, 173; VE, 61). Un livre forme la pierre angulaire de tout le roman *Les fruits d'or* et de toutes les interactions de l'histoire, comme l'œuvre de Michelet est source de conflits entre le père et les enfants dans *Vous les entendez?*[3] Les personnages semblent avoir besoin d'un élément médiateur pour entrer en relation. Sans cette médiation, les rapports ne peuvent s'établir.

Dans les rares moments de complicité qu'il parvient à connaître avec autrui, l'être sarrautien peut côtoyer une autre de ses tentations: "être du même bord" (Pl 134). Car il existe chez Sarraute, de temps à autre, une jouissance réelle du groupe: les personnages sentent la force qui réside dans une collectivité et la puissance de la solidarité. Le coude-à-coude donne confiance et assure une supériorité. On y a envie de "se blottir, comme tout le monde" (FO 67), "de se serrer les uns contre les autres en fermant les yeux, comme s'ils descendaient sur un toboggan" (Pl 195). "Collés l'un à l'autre, ne faisant qu'un seul corps comme le cheval de course et son jockey, ils s'élèvent, ils planent" (FO 104), "soudés en un seul bloc" (FO 132). Plaisir, vertige même, de participer à un mouvement synchrone, unanime et anonyme où *moi* devient *eux*. Mais il y a aussi malheureusement une lâcheté du groupe: lâcheté impardonnable de ceux qui, faute de courage, se rangent du côté de l'opinion commune; veulerie de ceux qui font la queue pour se glisser parmi les bien-pensants; aveuglement débile des fidèles qui obéissent sans se questionner à un culte officiel. En face de cette grégarité moutonne ou dévote et globalement méprisable, s'élève alors toujours la voix dissidente et solitaire de l'authentique paria sarrautien, voix qui suffit à restituer au groupe sa fonction de rejet.

Rares aussi sont les gestes de rapprochement réel avec l'autre qui laissent passer un courant de chaleur ou de tendresse. Les personnages sarrautiens ne se touchent guère. Il y a bien quelques scènes dans cette oeuvre où l'on voit une tape approbatrice ou une main se poser sur la main de l'autre (et ce sont des moments joyeux ou pacifiants (v. P 172; Pl 145; VE 138), mais elles constituent l'exception et c'est le maximum de proximité ou de familiarité qu'on y puisse atteindre. L'intimité heureuse s'arrête là.

Le geste de rapprochement le plus exploité par Sarraute est celui qui consiste à *se pencher* (dont le contraire est *se détourner*). *Se pencher* est un des verbes les plus employés par l'auteur. Mouvement corporel clé, ce "gestogramme" (comme on dit photogramme au cinéma pour l'image isolée d'un film) introduit en général un conciliabule à voix basse. Omniprésent dans son univers, il fait partie du rêve sarrautien (rêve impossible) de complicité duelle: se pencher vers l'autre pour former un couple avec lui. Mais il comporte aussi une bonne dose d'ambivalence: lorsqu'il isole deux êtres d'un groupe, il instaure l'enfer du secret dont les autres sont exclus; il s'associe souvent à la tension ou à l'indiscrétion (voir par exemple P 106); il peut encore signaler une approche menaçante ou répulsive.

Nous sommes ici au cœur même de ce que l'on pourrait appeler le complexe proxémique de Sarraute. Tous les grands problèmes sarrautiens résident dans ce nœud gordien que constitue la proxémie: s'approcher ou non des autres? les laisser s'approcher de soi ou non? accepter ou refuser le contact? jusqu'où et dans quelles conditions?

Dans ce complexe proxémique, le motif particulier de l'introduction et du congé occupe une place privilégiée. Toute l'imagerie de l'escalier et de la porte, si importante chez Sarraute, avec ses contiguïtés émotivement chargées que sont la poignée, la serrure, la clé, la sonnette, le loquet, le seuil, prend son sens ici, dans la kinésique des entrées et des sorties. Ce n'est sans doute pas par hasard que *Le planétarium* et *Les fruits d'or* commencent par le geste de monter un escalier, que beaucoup de transactions de *Tropismes*, de *Portrait d'un inconnu* ou de *Martereau* ont lieu près d'un seuil et que tous les échanges de *Vous les entendez?* passent par une volée de rampes et une porte de chambre qui séparent le monde des enfants de celui des adultes. Manifestement lourdes, chez l'auteur, d'un passé personnel obscur, les marches sont ambivalentes et soutiennent d'innombrables interactions: elles sont un endroit d'exaltation, mais aussi de mésententes, de poursuites, de drames plus ou moins minuscules (VE 86-87, par exemple). L'image de la porte constitue également une obsession majeure de Sarraute. Nombreuses, dans son univers, sont les scènes associées d'une manière ou d'une autre à une porte, comme le sont celles où l'on frappe à l'entrée (on en voit même une dans *Le planétarium* où l'on sonne à la porte pour livrer une porte!) ou dans lesquelles au contraire deux personnages se font face ou se quittent. Dans l'un et l'autre cas, c'est un moment très sensible, imprégné tantôt d'angoisse, tantôt de bien-être. Bonheur d'une poignée de main, d'une accolade tendre, d'un embrassement (Pl 139, 201, 184). Mais aussi malaise des introductions, tristesse des bises de séparation, pathos des doigts qui se desserrent, angoisse de voir une main posée sur le loquet d'une porte prête à s'ouvrir (Pl 178, 234). Le statut idéal de la porte sarrautienne semble être celui de la porte fermée, comme celle qui clôt *Vous les entendez?*: "Tu ne supportes pas les portes qui battent" (VE 55). La porte est un lieu de transaction avec l'extérieur: c'est là où, craintif, encore seul, on se compose un visage avant d'entrer rejoindre les autres (Pl 159), là où l'on cogite quand on rentre chez soi (P 110s); c'est sous la porte qu'on glisse furtivement un message pour éviter la confrontation; dans son entrebâillement qu'un conflit se résout (P 195); c'est encore un lieu fragile par lequel la retraite et l'intimité sont menacées.

Bien que le rapprochement pose des problèmes à l'être sarrautien, il est curieux de constater que prendre congé d'autrui lui semble tout aussi difficile. Quand cette opération s'effectue dans l'harmonie, c'est un véritable événement. En général, il faut du courage pour juger le moment venu de s'excuser, pour oser regarder sa montre, se lever et signaler ainsi son intention de se retirer ou de partir. Certains départs se chargent tellement de sens que les gestes en restent pour toujours dans la mémoire autant familiale qu'individuelle: ainsi le geste à jamais inoubliable d'allumer une cigarette, geste jugé désinvolte et impardonnable, dans un moment d'adieu entre Alain et sa grand-mère (Pl 215-6). Dans *L'usage de la parole*, plus précisément dans un texte intitulé très significativement *A très bientôt*, Sarraute évoque le double sentiment d'inachèvement et d'arrachement lié à la fin d'une rencontre et comment le simple fait de reprendre rendez-vous répare ce manque. Chaque petite séparation, cette "chute dans le vide quand la porte se referme" (M 179), représente une faible image du congé suprême lequel est, bien sûr, la mort, objet d'une exploration poétique dans le texte *Ich Sterbe* (UP 10ss). Nul doute qu'il s'agisse là d'un point psychanalytiquement fort chargé.

La proxémie sarrautienne est ainsi globalement marquée par une vision inquiète des relations humaines. Selon cette vision, tout rapprochement cache au fond d'hypocrites intentions d'agrippement et est finalement suspect, piégé et donc foncièrement dangereux, alors que toute séparation engendre des anxiétés autres. Le sujet sarrautien a beau mesurer avec minutie ses gradients d'approche et d'évitement (comme on dit en psychologie), il n'y a pas d'issues. Le contact est pris dans un cul-de-sac. En bref, entre eux et moi, rien n'est sûr et les rapports sont hautement problématiques. Quelle attitude adopter dans ces circonstances? L'amitié ou l'amour? Non, ce sont des établissements où l'on est enfermé (UP 25) et où ne règne aucune sécurité (voir l'amitié vexée ou trahie dans *Martereau* et dans *Pour un oui et pour un non*). Plutôt que d'entretenir "l'impression de dégradante promiscuité" (FO 76), il est encore préférable de garder ses distances. "La distance, —tout est là" (DI 83).

La socialité infracorporelle

Intimement liée à l'histoire personnelle et socio-culturelle du sujet, la socialité infracorporelle englobe l'immense domaine de la sensorialité. Chaque auteur a un univers sensoriel qui lui est propre.

Chez Sarraute, ce monde est manifestement dominé par le regard et par l'ouïe. Constamment, d'une œuvre à l'autre, les personnages se présentent en situation d'observation active ou subie et se scrutent les uns les autres.

Impitoyable, le regard sarrautien a la puissance d'une loupe, l'indélicatesse de la fouille, la cruauté de l'inquisition, la précision meurtrière d'un viseur de carabine. Il traque ses victimes, les emprisonne, les intimide, les dénude, les inspecte et relève la moindre faille. Son activité favorite consiste à jauger et à juger, ce qui crée une vive insécurité chez quiconque en est l'objet. Perçant, dur, aigu, vorace, féroce, pesant, glacé, voilà autant de qualités que sans cesse on lui prête. Il a une nature fondamentalement gestuelle. Vif et sournois, il glisse, s'insinue, pénètre, roule, s'étale, s'émoustille, se penche, se redresse ou au contraire est immobile, patient, sadique. Il est un poignard qui "pique sa pointe droit dans mes yeux" (FO 26).

Ce regard ennemi, on le compare encore significativement à "la bouche du canon d'un char dans une ville occupée" (FO 33) ou à des miradors fouillant l'obscurité (Pl 153) ou encore à l'œil d'un oiseau de proie.

Pour son plus grand malheur, le personnage sarrautien se retrouve toujours inévitablement dans un cercle d'yeux redoutables. Il sent constamment peser sur lui la menace du regard d'autrui, et ce regard, imaginaire ou réel, n'en finit plus de nourir sa paranoïa. C'est dire qu'il n'y a guère de communication paisible par le regard. Au mieux, quand il ne s'associe pas à quelque active méchanceté, il exprime des sentiments négatifs tels que la fermeture ou le caractère buté d'un être.

L'autre sens qui bénéficie également d'un développement singulier chez Sarraute, c'est l'ouïe. Et parmi tous les phénomènes sonores, seule la voix humaine semble intéresser l'oreille sarrautienne. Les notations vocales y sont omniprésentes et constituent une des caractéristiques des oeuvres de Sarraute. La moindre intonation ou la plus infime inflexion y sont écoutées avec minutie et analysées dans leurs résonnances intérieures les plus profondes et les plus subtiles. Autant que dans les degrés du regard, tout se passe dans les nuances du ton de voix, lesquelles nuances épousent toute la gamme des intentions: de l'hésitation à l'autorité, du détachement à la gêne, de la moquerie à l'hébétude, du chuchotement médisant à l'outrance blessante. La voix ne soutient pas seulement la conversation, elle est aussi commentée en sous-conversation: on la perçoit alors comme un geste d'accompagnement qui prolonge l'énonciation première ou se surimpose à elle. La voix émet des paroles, mais c'est le signifiant qui fait acte plus que le signifié. Au milieu d'une réplique, ce qui attire l'attention du narrateur, c'est la modulation gestuelle de la voix qui parle: en écoutant une personne par exemple, on peut entendre sa voix qui "nasille, et se traîne, comme s'il la tirait, tandis qu'elle résiste pleine de répulsion à travers un orifice étroit" (FO 64). Ou encore, sèche, elle claque (FO 47). Ou bien, sonde flexible qui s'introduit dans l'ouïe, elle violente le sujet. Voilà bien son caractère gestuel: on *brandit* une question (Pl 189) ou les mots résonnent "comme *les coups de pioche* des sauveteurs aux oreilles du mineur enseveli" (Pl 186).

Dans le registre des sens, l'odorat joue également un rôle, mais secondaire par rapport à la vue et à l'ouïe. L'odeur s'associe en général, chez Sarraute, au passé et, d'une manière privilégiée, à l'enfance. Telle cette scène heureuse du Luxembourg dont le souvenir est rappelé dans *Le planétarium* (55s) au cours de laquelle un personnage hume avec délices sur son bras nu sa propre odeur, l'odeur de sa peau d'enfant, de sa manche de coton. Que ce soit la main parfumée de la mère (FO 19) ou l'odeur de tabac et de crème à raser du père (Pl 104), le monde olfactif évoque une tendresse perdue et s'associe comme le regard et l'ouïe à des organes du geste (bras, mains, doigts).

La sensorialité chez Sarraute est donc bien un chapitre de son gestuaire, mais elle se réduit aux sens qui privilégient le contact à distance, évitant soigneusement le toucher et le goût.

L 'expression des émotions

C'est encore le geste avant tout qui exprime les émotions et les sentiments chez Sarraute. L'impatience, par exemple, se manifeste par des doigts qui tapotent sur une table (FO 35); l'admiration par une main caressant amoureusement dans l'air une forme arrondie (FO 35), le snobisme par un long index qui frotte une fine paupière (FO 34) ou l'avarice par des doigts qui choisissent méticuleusement quelques pièces de monnaie à laisser en pourboire (DI 111s). L'amour naît à travers le gestogramme d'un châle posé sur les épaules d'une femme par un homme à ses côtés, geste passionnément discuté par les personnages dans *Les fruits d'or*, tantôt dévalué, tantôt jugé parfait (45-49).

La surface du corps dans ses moindres modifications (à la limite du gestuel) recueille également les signes d'une agitation intérieure. L'envie fait frémir les ailes du nez (Pl 107), la jalousie imprime une ride entre les yeux, la sournoiserie se lit dans le pli d'une bouche ou se glisse le long de la ligne fuyante d'un menton (Pl 177), la répulsion infléchit l'arête du nez (FO 21). Le tropisme s'inscrit instantanément sur cette page si facilement lisible qu'est la peau: l'horreur, par exemple, en hérisse chaque grain (FO 57), les personnages rougissent ou blêmissent aisément, soit de rage, soit de honte.

De toutes les surfaces corporelles, le visage est de loin celle que Sarraute privilégie. C'est le lieu du corps le plus accessible à la lecture, celui où peuvent se décoder tous les registres émotionnels: de l'ennui à la surprise, de la crispation à la détente, de la gêne au triomphe, de la frayeur à la placidité. A cet égard, l'oeuvre de Sarraute constitue une véritable mine pour les physiognomonistes. Les six émotions fondamentales (joie, dégoût, surprise, tristesse, colère, peur) s'y retrouvent et investissent chacune des trois zones du visage: 1) zone du front, des sourcils et des paupières supérieures; 2) zone des yeux, des paupières inférieures et du nez; 3) zone de la bouche et du menton.[4] C'est souvent à son visage que se réduit le personnage sarrautien. C'est là qu'on interprète les apparences et qu'on déchiffre les inscriptions corporelles d'un état d'âme, activité qui, après s'être confirmée dans l'analyse du geste et des mouvements du corps, aboutit d'ailleurs en général à une synthèse finale que Sarraute appelle: l'air.

L'air, voilà sans doute l'un des mots les plus fréquents chez Sarraute. Il revient à chaque page pour résumer un sentiment ou une émotion qu'on repère dans les gestes et les mimiques d'autrui (dans une seule page de *Disent les imbéciles*, il apparaît cinq fois; v. DI 31). L'autre a l'air ennuyé, haineux, satisfait, mauvais, borné, outré, impitoyable, excédé, glacé, rusé, amusé, scandalisé, ulcéré, préoccupé, méprisant, condescendant, désapprobateur, dégoûté, etc. De l'air d'Indien cruel à celui de souris apeurée (M 124, 243), toute la gamme des tropismes y passe. Associé à la voix, à l'accent, au ton, au regard, aux jeux de physionomie, aux mouvements de la tête, des bras, des mains, l'air définit les diverses situations émotives des personnages et circonscrit le climat affectif dans lequel ils évoluent. L'air résume en même temps les efforts d'interprétation d'une conscience en face d'une autre.

L'air se dégage parfois d'un autre produit sonore hautement significatif chez Sarraute: le rire et sa variante visuelle, le sourire. Le rire exprime diverses attitudes psychologiques tels que l'inquiétude, la fausseté, l'idiotie, le mépris, l'ironie, la fatuité, la raillerie, la cruauté, la crispation, la tension. Profondément encariné dans le corps, il s'associe au gestuaire: par exemple, on pouffe de rire la main sur la bouche (VE 132) ou le sourire "tire les joues," fatigue les muscles faciaux et entraîne "la crampe de la politesse" (M 185, 190) ou encore un gros rire cahote et dévale devant un personnage, secoue ses bajoues, se vautre, se roule partout, écorche. Dans *Vous les entendez?*, des rires d'enfants, rires invincibles et dérangeants pour le monde des adultes et des valeurs admises, suffisent à engendrer la plupart des réactions du roman.

Le personnage sarrautien est très conscient des signes à la lisière du gestuel que son visage émet plus ou moins malgré lui. Aussi cherche-t-il à se contrôler en s'efforçant de ne rien laisser paraître aux autres. L'impassibilité, l'immobilité sont ici d'importantes attitudes de salut, mais combien difficiles à adopter. "Tête haute. Visage fermé" (FO 56). Voilà un des idéaux sarrautiens anti-mondains: être inerte, dur, figé, sourd, aveugle, le visage de porcelaine, les yeux de verre; bref atteindre l'indifférence des objets (FO 57). Quand une parole blesse cet écorché vif qu'est le sujet sarrautien, le tropisme interactionnel certes se déchaîne intérieurement et la panique s'empare de l'imagination, mais extérieurement la petite flamme fragile qui pouvait s'être allumée dans son regard vacille et s'éteint. Plus aucune lueur ne brille dans l'œil. Alors la froideur (apparente) arrive à provisoirement triompher, figure ultime du repli protecteur.

De tous les motifs sensoriels que Sarraute exploite pour exprimer les émotions et les sentiments, l'un d'entre eux bénéficie d'une prédilection singulière: c'est celui du gonflement. Ce motif, très fréquent ici, revêt plusieurs significations. Lorsqu'il s'associe à la puissance ou à la fierté (suivant le cliché: gonflé d'orgueil), le personnage a alors l'impression de perdre le sens habituel des proportions et de devenir immense (Pl 165; FO 106, 112) ou de connaître quelque joie aérienne, comme celle de se sentir délivré de la gravité tel un ballon plein d'hélium, ou celle de voir une grosse masse lourde de pachyderme se mettre à danser (v. le père dans VE 150s).

Le gonflement peut encore signifier une maturité atteinte, un état lourd de promesses, d'élans, d'appels (P 88). Il est souvent aussi le fruit d'une extrême tension et exprime alors surtout deux attitudes, la convoitise et la curiosité. Ces variantes du désir ont d'ailleurs une nature aquatique, avec les connotations négatives que l'eau a souvent chez Sarraute. Ce sont les "eaux toujours grossissantes de la convoitise, de la curiosité, cela le remplit . . . cela circule dans tout son corps, dans son allure, son air, dans chacun de ses mouvements" (Pl 162). Le gonflement dit également le plaisir que le sujet sarrautien éprouve à préparer une imminente jouissance de parole (laquelle est le plus souvent jouissance sadique de blesser autrui). "Les mots en moi gonflés, tendus, jaillissent," et après, car c'est d'une véritable jouissance qu'il s'agit, "dans le silence qui suit cet éclat, le calme me revient" (FO 137).

Mais parfois, le gonflement résulte, tout au contraire, d'un blocage et constitue une sorte d'anévrisme existentiel: "On dirait qu'ils sont gonflés à éclater de quelque chose qu'ils cherchent à retenir, à contenir" (FO 22). C'est le versant noir de la retenue, qualité pourtant appréciée dans le monde de Sarraute quand elle s'associe à la grâce et à la force. Ici le gonflement exprime la lourdeur de l'être, la gêne, un étouffement, l'impression d'engorgement, toutes sensations négatives. Ainsi le frère de Berthe, dans *Le planétarium*, qui voudrait prendre congé (avec l'angoisse que ce geste comporte chez Sarraute) et "se lever d'un bond, s'enfuir, mais il est lourd, enflé, hydropique, atteint d'éléphantiasis" (Pl 145). Ainsi encore Alain lorsqu'il perçoit sa compagne non seulement comme encombrante, mais comme doublant son propre volume à lui (Pl 174). Le gonflement exprime donc surtout un état de malaise.

En conclusion, on peut dire que dans l'expression des émotions chez Sarraute, le geste et la visagéité dominent nettement. Les signaux du visage en ce qu'ils ont de plus musculaire sont ici de mini-gestes que l'auteur décode et incorpore aux autres mouvements du corps et résume dans ce qu'elle appelle globalement l'air. Il est finalement intéressant de remarquer que c'est l'émotion qui prime sur le sentiment dans l'œuvre de Sarraute. L'émotion en tant que forme explosive de l'affectivité est, selon les psychologues, une puissance désorganisatrice.[5] La base organique en est plus forte que dans les sentiments et les manifestations corporelles en sont en général plus explicites. Dans l'émotion, l'individu est "désadapté" en présence d'une situation. Au contraire, les sentiments sont des attitudes plus stables, plus tempérées, plus adaptées aux circonstances variées de l'existence. L'émotion, c'est "un désordre de conduite" (Fraisse & Piaget 105) et l'oeuvre de Sarraute, une œuvre habitée, et même essentiellement constituée par le discours émotif.

La socialité corporelle d'inconduite

La socialité corporelle d'inconduite concerne les cas d'anomalie dans la conduite tels qu'ils se manifestent par exemple dans la maladie ou la folie.

Dans l'univers de Sarraute, il n'y a pas d'infirmité ni de maladie physique (lorsqu'elle surgit, on en guérit vite), ce qui donnerait au corps une trop solide existence. Les personnages sarrautiens existent pourtant corporellement, et d'une manière forte, par leurs tropismes d'inconduite. Ils vivent d'abord, nous venons de le voir, l'affolement et le déroutement de leurs émotions d'une manière pour ainsi dire constante. Lorsqu'ils les vivent à ciel ouvert, les tropismes bafouent les bienséances. Les personnages sentent ensuite leur corps plus que jamais dans leurs maladresses gestuelles. Dans *Le planétarium*, Alain a de nombreux mouvements gauches, des gestes brusques et saccadés qui lui imposent une gênante épaisseur et un corps de malaise (Pl 169, 170, 174s). Il en est de même pour le frère de Berthe lorsqu'il retourne par accident un coin de tapis, gaucherie jugée dramatique dans le contexte maniaque dans lequel il se produit.

Beaucoup de gestes chez les personnages sarrautiens affirment aussi une insolence qui scandalise et dérange l'ordre établi. C'est là un des thèmes dominants des œuvres de Sarraute. Il y a toujours chez elle un personnage inconvenant qui commet des entorses plus ou moins graves au savoir-vivre: soit par des gestes impolis, comme celui d'une vendeuse dans un magasin qui lance un manteau dans les bras d'une cliente (Pl 38); soit par des mouvements incongrus comme celui de Berthe qui téléphone tard le soir à son neveu pour se plaindre de sa poignée de porte et qui non seulement le dérange mais l'oblige à venir chez elle (Pl 25); soit par des rires moqueurs comme ceux des enfants dans *Vous les entendez?*; soit par des paroles irrespectueuses. La spontanéité et la sincérité sont des valeurs majeures chez Sarraute, mais celui qui ose les adopter dans le monde si policé et hypocrite qu'elle dénonce fait aussitôt figure de paria.
Ce sont là des situations d'inconduite typiquement sarrautiennes.

"Quelquefois—cela arrive—soudain au milieu de la foule une femme ou un homme s'abat, se tord, se griffe le visage, pousse des clameurs" (FO 147). Vision exagérée de celui qui ose sortir du rang et dire tout haut ou faire ouvertement ce que d'autres pensent tout bas.

Cet impertinent vit aussitôt tous les malaises de l'asynchronie interactionnelle: le groupe s'en désolidarise et il tombe dans la disgrâce. Ce fauteur de troubles est en général vite expulsé (FO 85) ou on s'en éloigne (Pl 35) et l'ordre est rapidement rétabli. Si la sincérité et la spontanéité sont des valeurs positives pour Sarraute, la société mondaine qu'elle met en scène ne les tolère pas. Aux yeux de cette société abhorrée, elles constituent des entorses à la loi. Elles sont à ranger dans les comportements d'inconduite et à mettre au ban. Et nul doute que l'auteur s'identifie jusqu'à un certain point à ce "moi qui sans cesse éveille ce qui veut dormir, excite, suscite, guette, quête, appelle; moi l'impur" (M 72).

Ceux qu'on appelle les fous sont aussi des êtres sincères et spontanés. Le spectre de la folie rôde toujours dans l'univers de Sarraute. Il faut être fou, semble-t-on dire ici en sous–conversation, pour effectuer de telles sorties (gestuelles ou verbales: c'est équivalent, quand parler c'est agir) qui incommodent tout le monde. Et souvent on voit ce corps marginal représenté dans ses efforts piteux et maladroits pour se dégager d'un bourbier où il a mis le pied. Parfois le corps de la folie est directement représenté: tel Montalais dans *Le planétarium*, grand garçon dégingandé qu'on voit assis, balançant son corps simiesque d'avant en arrière, ses mains serrant ses chevilles croisées. Le corps du fou existe davantage que les autres corps. Plus qu'aucun autre personnage, il a droit ici à des descriptions élaborées (Pl 79-81, 147): long corps efflanqué, long visage exsangue, petits yeux très enfoncés, cheveux très noirs, très plats, longues mains osseuses, longs bras, longues dents, nuque malingre (lieu fréquent de la vulnérabilité sarrautienne), épaules étroites et voûtées, robuste poignée de mains. On le compare à un bouffon qui agite ses clochettes et fait des galipettes. Il ose dire ou faire ce qu'il veut, il ose fuir héroïquement le consensus et on envie les libertés qu'il prend. A cet égard, l'écrivain (du moins tel qu'il est représenté dans *Entre la vie et la mort*) lui ressemble beaucoup, parce qu'on le perçoit, lui aussi, comme "inadapté" (VM 33ss).

A d'autres moments, les gestes les plus quotidiens se drapent d'une étrangeté qui s'analyse en un léger décalage par rapport à la "normalité." Voyez Alain Guimier dans *Le planétarium*:

> . . . il y a dans tous ses gestes, quand il accroche

tranquillement son pardessus au portemanteau de l'entrée, quand il lisse ses cheveux devant la glace et s'avance dans la chambre . . . quelque chose de décalé, d'étrange. Les gestes, les paroles des fous donnent aux gens normaux qui les observent cette impression d'être comme désamorcés, vidés de leur substance. (Pl 67)

D'autres dimensions parviennent par moments à marginaliser le corps en lui attribuant des gestes inhabituels: l'alcool (FO 106s), la solitude (Pl 34, 46) et surtout la vieillesse (Pl 32). Le corps de la vieillesse est tout aussi présent, sinon plus, que celui de la folie. *Disent les imbéciles* nous en offre un cas exemplaire. Tout le roman repose sur cette surexistence que le corps acquiert avec l'âge: "mignonne à croquer," la grand-mère de ce livre est un objet auquel les gestes des proches prêtent corps: on la caresse, les doigts des observateurs suivent les contours de son visage; ses replis de chair, ses rides, ses lèvres rentrées, sa joue soyeuse, ses yeux d'émail, ses mèches en désordre (caractéristique sarrautienne du corps déréglé), ses poings noueux, ses mains dodues, ses doigts crochus, ses gestes tremblants dans un ensemble globalement agité, tout cela contribue à lui donner un poids corporel inégalé dans l'univers de Sarraute. Il est d'autant plus présent, ce corps, qu'avec la sénilité qui introduit un désordre gestuel accru (v. DI 118), il accède tardivement à la sexualité, il lâche ses désirs sans contrôle, ce qui en fait cette infamie pour l'ordre sarrautien: un corps "lubrique" (v. DI 22).

Les gestes d'inconduite, chez Sarraute, s'associent ainsi aux valeurs de l'authenticité. Or, la société refuse ces valeurs. Seuls les fous et les vieillards parviennent à les vivre ouvertement, ce qui les marginalise et les rend passibles de rejet. La liberté semble devoir passer ici, pour s'exprimer, par la marginalité sociale.

Conclusion

J'espère avoir réussi à montrer que le gestuaire chez Sarraute est porteur de sens, qu'il mérite attention et qu'il est une bonne voie d'accès à l'œuvre. Le corps est primordial dans cet univers. Ce corps est essentiellement un corps en interaction, défini dans sa relation difficultueuse avec autrui. Corps en général dégagé des situations quotidiennes, toujours assis ou debout avec d'autres (rarement couché), il est un pur produit de la socialité. Les corps sarrautiens ne sont pas des corps ludiques ou jouisseurs: ils ne connaissent guère le plaisir, sinon celui de souffrir et de faire souffrir. Ils ne se touchent pas. Ils vivent tendus, perpétuellement insatisfaits et vulnérables, sans cesse exposés à l'agressivité des autres. Ces corps n'ont qu'une existence mondaine, surinvestis qu'ils sont dans leur moitié supérieure et dans leur frontalité, alors que leur moitié inférieure et postérieure tend à s'absenter. Seule la marginalité de la folie et de la vieillesse réussit à réattribuer aux êtres leur totalité corporelle. Autrement dit, il faut quitter la socialité pour se défaire ici du corps morcelé dit "civilisé" (mais aussi pour parvenir à écrire en toute liberté, loin des censures et des critiques).

Parmi l'ensemble des innombrables gestogrammes que le récit sarrautien nous offre, c'est la gestuelle d'interaction qui domine dans les représentations kinésiques et constitue le filon le plus richement exploité par l'auteur. Au sein de cette gestuelle d'interaction, le complexe proxémique occupe une place centrale et prend une signification particulière, celle, déchirante, d'une soif de contact mêlée d'une répulsion, celle d'un besoin de solitude et d'un besoin d'approbation.

En outre, la forte proportion, dans cette œuvre, de tropismes interactionnels, lesquels cherchent à montrer les effets intérieurs du contact en les illustrant par des évocations d'outrance gestuelle, suffirait à nous convaincre, s'il en était besoin, que l'œuvre de Sarraute est surtout une œuvre d'imagination. Ce que la critique sarrautienne a souvent trop tendance à oublier, Sarraute elle-même nous le rappelle dans un entretien avec Simone Benmussa: "On ne pourrait vivre au niveau de mes livres ni des tropismes. On ne pourrait pas vivre sous le microscope et au ralenti. On deviendrait fou" (Benmussa 71). Nous sommes bien ici dans la fiction et il ne faut pas confondre, insiste Sarraute, la littérature et la vie. Mais, malgré ces préventions trop modestes de l'auteur, l'art pour l'art ne l'intéresse pas: l'art est, pour elle, un instrument de connaissance qui explore la vie et qui lui a tout de même permis de mettre à jour ces dimensions de l'univers mental que sont le tropisme et la sous-conversation. Il serait plus exact de voir dans l'oeuvre de Sarraute une œuvre littéraire certes, animée de sa vie propre et qui s'impose de toute évidence comme telle, mais une œuvre qui rejoint aussi l'expérience commune et nous éclaire sur nous-mêmes, sur notre rapport aux autres et sur l'art difficile d'être soi.

L'attention extrême qu'elle a portée aux gestes et aux relations en public pourrait en faire une romancière behavioriste. Mais elle a dépassé la simple observation de surface: en s'attachant aux moindres gestogrammes qui composent nos relations à autrui, elle en a analysé l'épaisseur sémantique, et, confiante dans leur pouvoir de sommation des êtres, elle a courageusement plongé dans leur profondeur psychologique. Spécialiste de l'interaction des consciences ("Eux. Lui. Moi" (DI 91), tout est là), elle pourrait sans doute résumer son cogito ainsi: "Je communique, donc je suis." Que je le fasse avec certains malaises ou pas, c'est une autre histoire, mais je communique. Donc je suis. Et ne serait-ce pas là également le cogito de l'acte littéraire lui-même? Sarraute semble avoir tout compte fait trouvé dans la littérature (à condition d'ignorer la critique, ce mal nécessaire!) un excellent moyen de régler son conflit proxémique central et de se rapprocher des autres tout en les tenant à distance.

Notes

Liste des abréviations:

P: *Portrait d'un inconnu.*
M: *Martereau.*
Pl: *Le planétarium.*
FO: *Les fruits d'or.*
VM: *Entre la vie et la mort.*
VE: *Vous les entendez?*
DI: *Disent les imbéciles.*
UP: *L'usage de la parole.*
s: et la page suivante
ss: et les pages suivantes
L'édition utilisée est celle de la collection Folio, Gallimard. Sauf pour *Tropismes* et *Portrait d'un inconnu* (coll. 10/18).

[1] David Le Breton, *Corps et Sociétés. Essai de sociologie et d'anthropologie du corps* (Paris, Librairie des Méridiens, 1985).

[2] Cf. Erving Goffman, *La Mise en scène de la vie quotidienne* (Paris: Editions de Minuit). 2:135.

[3] Signalons que le livre a constitué un intermédiaire majeur entre Sarraute et son mari, Raymond. Voir S. Benmussa, *Nathalie Sarraute. Qui êtes-vous?* (Lyon: La Manufacture, 1987), 153.

[4] V. Dubois & Winkin, *Rhétoriques du corps* (Bruxelles: De Boeck-Wesmael, 1988), 79.

[5] Cf. Paul Fraisse et Jean Piaget, *Traité de psychologie expérimentale,* t. V: *Motivation, Emotion et Personnalité* (Paris: PUF, 1975), 103ss; Jean Maisonneuve, *Les sentiments* (Paris: PUF, 1964), 22ss.

From Subjugation to Re-creation: Images of Woman in the Prose and Poetry of Andrée Chedid

Judy Cochran
Denison University

Since the appearance of her first works in the early 50's, Andrée Chedid has received acclaim for her poetry and prose. The Egyptian-born author has been the recipient of numerous literary awards in Europe and the Mediterranean and was recently granted an honorary degree from her alma mater, the American University at Cairo. Chedid has made Paris her home since 1946, and with the exception of her first volume of poetry written in English, French, which is her native language, has been the language of her art. Above all, her work expresses her vision of a united world, where people live peacefully and productively, having overcome the barriers that divide and isolate them from one another. *Fraternité de la parole*, the volume of poetry that won for Chedid the highest prize of the Académie Mallarmé in 1976, illustrates most clearly her global vision. Although Chedid's writing is not "feminist" in a narrow sense, the author focuses at times on issues that specifically concern women within the broad perspective of spiritual emancipation for all. Renée Linkhorn has suggested the term "féminitude" in elucidating this aspect of Chedid's work, for the role of woman is crucial within her poetic universe.[1]

In a first novel, *Le sommeil délivré*, published in 1952, Chedid explores the psychological repression and ultimate release of a young Egyptian woman cloistered in a society governed by antiquated, authoritarian laws and customs. In this first novel Chedid treats in greater detail than elsewhere the subjugation of women in the Middle East. The novel opens with an act of violence—Samya's premeditated murder of her husband Boutros. Bit by bit we piece together the heroine's story. Samya, whose only memory of her mother is a picture of a frightened young girl with lowered eyes, is forced into a marriage of convenience at the age of fifteen by her father and brothers. In her reminiscences of childhood, Samya alludes to the "prison" of her father's house, to feeling "trapped" into lying in her prospective husband's presence, and finally into pronouncing the one word "yes" that "chained" her to Boutros for eternity. Samya describes how a part of her watches in disgust as she submits to Boutros, who suppresses the life force within her, reducing her to a "sleepwalker's" state merely by the sound of his voice. Ironically, Samya was more free in the convent school where she spent her girlhood. There physical confinement, and even her adherence to the vow of silence, had not prevented her from dreaming of marriage: "au vrai mariage... à ce mariage qui était l'amour" (56). She felt rage and shame at the notion that women should be expected to accept material comforts as compensation for solitude in a loveless marriage: "Non, non, cela ne m'arrivera jamais. Moi, je saurai dire non. Saisir ma vie" (57). Samya's sense of isolation is heightened by her social position, and in the convent school she often repressed the desire to weep: "Pourquoi aurais-je pleuré? Parce qu'il y avait des murs entre la vie, entre les êtres? Parce que je me sentais étreinte et que je ne savais pourquoi?" (48). Samya manifests the generous, sensitive nature that will characterize later Chedid heroines. Predisposed to love, she prefigures Athanasia in *Les marches de sable* (1981), who marries for love, sacrifices all for love, and ultimately finds happiness through love of others.

At the same time, Samya reveals an aspiration for the absolute that, in her case, implies a disregard for society's values. Samya's potential for absolutism is realized in the act of violence that alone can set her free. Her brief glimpse of love accompanies the birth of her daughter Mia, which marks her own spiritual rebirth, expressed in imagery of physical unbinding: "Je n'étais plus seule. J'étais comme dénouée" (178). Love of Mia transforms the world for Samya and fills her with hope. When Mia dies of typhus as a result of Boutros' reluctance to call a doctor, all Samya's love for her daughter turns to hatred for her husband. Boutros comes to represent all that threatens life: "Je détestais Boutros. Ma haine s'ajoutait à mon dégoût. Je le voyais, lui, et tous les Boutros du monde, compassés dans leur autorité. Ils réglaient les destinées, ils écrasaient les plantes, les chansons, les couleurs, la vie elle-même; et ils réduisaient tout à la mesure rabougrie de leur coeur" (122). Deprived of the object of her affections, Samya is once again overcome by the "sleepwalker's" torpor. She considers suicide, but fear and apathy prevent her from taking her own life. Finally, she awakens one morning unable to walk. Paralysis has become the physical manifestation of her state of mind.

Despite Samya's "sleepwalker's" state, the memory of Mia's young life remains rooted in her consciousness. She makes an effort to overcome her indifference by encouraging Ammal, a young girl she had come to know before Mia's birth, to continue sculpting figures of clay even though her grandfather discovers and destroys them. All Samya's hopes center on Ammal, who seems to embody what she herself and her own daughter Mia might have been. Samya tells herself that if only Ammal were saved, her life would not have been lived in vain. In fact, she murders Boutros not only to free herself from him, but to set an example for Ammal. The novel closes with the image of Ammal running: "Il faut partir d'ici. Avec des êtres qui naissent de vos doigts, plus semblables aux vivants qu'eux-mêmes ne le seront jamais, on n'est pas seule. Il faut partir. Loin de ce qui étouffe et de cette pourriture qui devient la peur" (226). Samya's violent act arouses her from the "sleepwalker's" state evoked in the title and serves as her affirmation of life. No longer a victim, she takes charge of her own destiny. Only by assuming responsibility for her own destiny can Samya affect the lives of others: "Un poids était tombé de sa poitrine, entraînant sa chambre et l'instant. Cette histoire n'était plus la sienne" (226). At the end, Samya becomes a paradigmatic figure whose story becomes the story of women everywhere.

In Chedid's poetry the first figure that evokes the theme of liberation for women appears in "Première image d'une révolte," belonging to a collection published in 1953, a year after *Le sommeil délivré.*

Première image d'une révolte

La femme sans souvenirs
A quitté pour l'herbe haute
Le triste champ des aïeux

Dans les matins de la colère
Elle court vêtue de robes obscures
Entre les troupeaux dispersés

Il n'y a rien alentour
Seul un village nu
Qui pèse sur la colline. (*Textes pour un poème* 77)

In contrast to her fictional creations, Chedid's poetic figures tend to be archetypal representations indicated by an epithet rather than a name, revealing the author's intent to strip the image to its bare essence. Here, the epithet "sans souvenirs" defines the woman who has taken the first step toward establishing her autonomy by taking leave of her past, and with it her pre-determined role in the patriarchal society of her ancestors. The adjective "triste" applied to the ancestral fields recalls the lifelessness of Samya's existence after her marriage to Boutros. The woman's aspiration toward "l'herbe haute" is the first sign of her desire for self-realization, as is her complete disregard for the scattered flocks. She manifests the sentiments of rebellion Samya felt, as well as her feelings of oppression and isolation, symbolized by the stark village resting heavily on the hill. Like Samya, she takes her initial step toward freedom with an act of revolt against the society that confines her.

Another way of achieving the spiritual liberation that Samya discovered was maternal love, which transformed life. The figure of the mother is significant both literally and symbolically in Chedid's portrayal of woman. In another poem from the early fifties, "Le temps de ma mort," Chedid describes a mother's attempt to explain death to her daughter without making it sound either fearsome or desirable.

Le temps de ma mort

Quand viendra le temps de ma mort
Petite fille que pourras-tu
Comme robe au vent
Sèchent les pleurs

Qu'est-ce que j'emporte
Même pas ton cri
Qui bondissait en moi
Comme un jeune chevreau

Petite fille éloigne-toi
Quand je serai de terre
Cette mère d'absence et d'ivoire
Fuis ce n'est plus moi. (*Textes pour un poème* 70)

This very human scene from daily life illustrates Chedid's gift for elevating the simple and rendering concrete the abstract. In spite of the serious nature of the dialogue between mother and daughter, the mother's tone is almost light-hearted. In her role of giver of life, the mother admonishes her little girl not to linger beside her corpse: "Cette mère d'absence et d'ivoire/Fuis ce n'est plus moi." Like Ammal in *Le sommeil délivré*, her daughter must flee from death to preserve life. Thus, in Chedid's world the mother not only bestows life but affirms it. The author treats the same theme on a more personal level in "Brève invitée," a poem she wrote in 1960 for her daughter Michèle, who learned it by heart and in turn taught it to her own daughter. The poem portrays a mother's love for her child and the legacy she leaves her, which is life itself with all its piquancy and light.

Brève invitée

à ma fille

Ma lande mon enfant ma bruyère
Ma réelle mon flocon mon genêt,
Je te regarde demain t'emporte
Où je ne saurais aller.

Ma bleue mon avril ma filante
Ma vie s'éloigne à reculons,
A toi les oiseaux et la lampe
A toi les torches et le vent.

Mon cygne mon amande ma vermeille
A toi l'impossible que j'aimais
A toi la vie, sel et soleil,
A toi, brève invitée. (*Textes pour un poème* 207)

Chedid's treatment of the maternal role suggests a possible reconciliation between woman's need for human love and her aspiration beyond it. Two poems from *Fraternité de la parole* will illustrate her response to this fundamental human dichotomy.

In the poems of *Fraternité de la parole* two archetypal images complete Chedid's portrayal of the spiritually liberated woman. The first, "La femme des longues patiences," departs from patience, a virtue traditionally attributed to women, to define the woman who has come into her own.

La femme des longues patiences

Dans les sèves
Dans sa fièvre
Ecartant ses voiles
Craquant ses carapaces
Glissant hors de ses peaux

La femme des longues patiences
se met
lentement
au monde

Dans ses volcans
Dans ses vergers

Cherchant cadence et gravitations
Etreignant sa chair la plus tendre
Questionnant ses fibres les plus rabotées

La femme des longues patiences
Se donne
lentement
le jour. (12-13)

The ever-patient woman is sufficient unto herself, creating herself both physically and spiritually. Images of physical actions depicting the baring of the woman's face and body introduce the metaphor of birth. "Ecartant ses voiles" evokes the veils worn by Middle Eastern women today. "Craquant ses carapaces" and "Glissant hors de ses peaux" draw a parallel between the woman who has evolved in society and the reptile who has outgrown its shell or skin. These images tie woman to the earth and generation, comparing her to pre-Christian images of a Goddess-Creator, whose body is identical with the universe. Egyptian mythology projects this image of the woman whose body contains all life in the Goddess Nut, who represents the sphere of the life-enclosing heavens.[2] In Chedid's poem the imagery of the earth and human life—sap, orchards and volcanoes, flesh and fiber—combine in woman, placing her at the source of all creation. The poet employs two symmetrical idiomatic constructions to heighten the link between physical and spiritual birth: "se met lentement au monde," literally, to bring herself into the world, and "se donne lentement le jour," to give herself light. In his discussion of the Goddess, Joseph Campbell has interpreted the virgin birth as the symbol of spiritual awakening, and it is this connotation that Chedid intends. Her ever-patient woman becomes the source of regeneration and illumination, thus overcoming in her totality the opposition that has traditionally existed in Western culture between body and spirit.

A final poem "Femmes de tous les temps," further develops the archetype of a universal woman.

Femmes de tous les temps

Ancestrales et pourtant fraternelles
Lointaines et pourtant proches

Elles viennent à notre rencontre
Ces Femmes d'un autre âge

Dans la pulpe éphémère de leurs corps
Dans la beauté d'un geste périssable
Dans les brefs remous d'un visage neuf ou vieilli

Ces Femmes immémoriales
  à travers argile et pierres
  écartant les écorces du temps
Se frayent passage jusqu'ici

. . . .

Hors du tréfonds des siècles
délivrant l'esprit

Non plus *femmes-objets*
Mais objets devenus Femmes

Elles lèvent échos paroles
et questions d'aujourd'hui. (14-15)

In the image of the woman who is one with the life principle, Chedid has already suggested woman's ability to transcend time and space. In this last poem she demonstrates metaphorically how this is possible. The epithet introduced in the title holds the key to woman's transcendence: each woman since the dawn of time has contained the essence of all women. Chedid's use of adjectives that emphasize contrast—"ancestrales / fraternelles," "lointaines / proches," "neuf / vieilli"—establishes the binary opposition characteristic of Western thought, which she attempts to resolve in the image that concludes the poem. Her choice of images that express the transience of the flesh—"la pulpe éphémère," "un geste périssable," "les brefs remous d'un visage"—heighten the human quality of these women from another age. Once again Chedid employs images of overcoming impediments. The "Femmes immémoriales" have made their way through all the layers of earth and eternity to meet the women of today. These women have set an example of deliverance just as Samya was a model for Ammal. Their concerns are our concerns. In the penultimate stanza Chedid provides the answer to woman's dilemma with a play on the words "femmes-objets" and "objets devenus Femmes." Her choice of the capital letter is important. In the first line "femmes-objets" refers to woman's pre-established role in society. The word "objet" evokes "objet sexuel" and is pejorative. However, in the second line "objets" becomes a metaphor for transcendence, alluding to woman's potential to perfect herself as an individual. In Chedid's view, as women we are what we have made of ourselves, and we are not alone, for each of us is linked to every other.

Chedid's underlying message is that women possess the power to create and affirm life, and that love of this world is not incompatible with our aspirations and dreams. In an interview, the author has described the human desire to fully realize one's destiny as "le désir d'aller au bout de soi-même," a desire reflected both in her life and in her art.[3]

Notes

[1] Renée Linkhorn suggests the term "féminitude" in reference to Andrée Chedid's writing in order to avoid the political connotation of the rubric "féminisme" and the possible implication of gender bias. Although Chedid's art reflects her experience as a woman, the ethic it reveals is humanistic rather than gender-oriented. "Andrée Chedid: quête poétique d'une fraternité." *The French Review* 58.4 (1985): 559-65.

[2] For a more complete development of the image of the mother-goddess, see Joseph Campbell, *The Power of Myth* (New York: Doubleday, 1988) 164-183.

[3] Cited by Evelyne Accad, "Entretien avec Andrée Chedid," *Présence francophone* 24 (1982): 157-74.

Works Cited

Works by Andrée Chedid cited with permission from Flammarion:

Fraternité de la parole. Paris: Flammarion, 1976.

Les marches de sable. Paris: Flammarion, 1981.

Le sommeil délivré. 1952. Paris: Flammarion, 1976.

Textes pour un poème. Paris: Flammarion, 1987.

Rescapée de la bouteille surréaliste: La Poésie de Joyce Mansour et de Robert Desnos

Katharine Conley
Dartmouth College

Joyce Mansour répond à l'appel des voix surréalistes masculines des années 20, avec l'écho déformé de leurs propres images.[1] Sa poésie reprend surtout les thèmes et images oniriques et insolites des poèmes d'André Breton. Mais les poèmes de Mansour brillent aussi des reflets de l'alchimie poétique d'un autre grand poète surréaliste, Robert Desnos.

Cris, le premier recueil de poèmes de Mansour, a paru en 1953, soit huit ans après la mort de Desnos (1945), et vingt-trois ans après l'expulsion/excommunication de celui-ci du groupe surréaliste par son "pape," André Breton. Mais la chaleur intime du lyrisme de Mansour, et son tissage de thèmes entrelaçant la mort et l'écriture avec le désir amoureux, rappellent les vers lyriques de Desnos. Ici, j'examinerai surtout les rapports entre *Carré blanc*,[2] le recueil poétique de Mansour de 1965, et de *A la Mystérieuse* et *Les Ténèbres* (1926, 1927), deux recueils de Desnos, réunis dans *Corps et biens*.[3] Commençons par les différences principales entre les deux, en situant Mansour par rapport à Desnos.

Quand Desnos établit une tension entre la voix narrative, "je," et "tu"—son objet de désir—nous reconnaissons immédiatement l'écart traditionnel entre le poète-serviteur et la femme aimée, qui remonte à la poésie des troubadours. La femme focalisée habite le monde merveilleux des rêves du poète. Dans "Les espaces du sommeil" Desnos précise ce lieu:

> Dans la nuit il y a naturellement les sept merveilles du monde et la grandeur et le tragique et le charme.
> Les forêts s'y heurtent confusément avec des créatures de légende cachées dans les fourrés.
> Il y a toi. (*C & B* 92)

Pour Desnos, le jeu d'amour consiste en un lancement continuel de soi vers l'Autre—une projection qui se répète à perte de conscience pour lui, mais qui, en fin de compte, le laisse toujours seul. Dans "Si tu savais," Desnos démontre son isolement:

> Si tu savais comme le monde m'est soumis.
> Et toi, belle insoumise aussi, comme tu es ma
> prisonnière
> O toi, loin-de-moi, à qui je suis soumis.
> Si tu savais. (*C & B* 97)

Il désigne l'Autre, le "toi" du poème, par "loin de *moi*"; lui-même il se désigne comme "si *tu* savais". Séparés, ils sont néanmoins réunis sur la page, grâce au discours référentiel (Dumas 487).

Desnos se concentre sur l'Autre et la distance qui les sépare. Son identité à lui s'efface derrière cette position de poète qui n'existe que pour écrire sur son amour. Il esquisse la portée de sa passion dans "O Douleurs de l'amour," où l'humour et l'admiration viennent se mêler à l'amour:

> Au réveil vous étiez présentes, ô douleurs de l'amour, ô muses du désert, ô muses exigeantes. Mon rire et ma joie se cristallisent autour de vous. C'est votre fard, c'est votre poudre, c'est votre rouge, c'est votre sac de peau de serpent, c'est vos bas de soie... (*C & B* 89)

En effet, Desnos ne se permet de dépeindre qu'un scénario d'union avec son Autre. Ce n'est qu'en lui, telle une étincelle créatrice, qu'il la ressent près de lui:

> Loin de moi, une étoile filante choit dans la bouteille nocturne du poète. Il met vivement le bouchon et des lors il guette l'étoile enclose dans le verre, il guette les constellations qui naissent sur les parois, loin de moi, tu es loin de moi. (*C & B* 96)

Enclose dans le verre comme une pierre précieuse captive, l'Autre-étoile est parée de descriptions émouvantes. La bouteille de Desnos est un piédestal dans lequel, non pas sur lequel, se trouve l'objet désiré. Ce verre emprisonnant–cristallin et magique–marque effectivement une mesure de distance. La femme-étoile capturée garde le silence. Même en lui, elle et lui restent séparés et isolés. Il souligne l'intensité de son émotion aigre-douce dans les vers suivants:

> Si tu savais comme je t'aime et, bien que tu ne m'aimes pas, comme je suis joyeux, comme je suis robuste et fier de sortir avec ton image en tête, de sortir de l'univers.
>
> Comme je suis joyeux à en mourir. (*C & B* 96-97)

Il semble dire qu'il souffrirait n'importe quoi, même la solitude de la mort pour elle.

Mansour relève ce thème de l'amoureuse seule. Mais son "moi" ne s'élance pas sur son objet de désir de la même manière. Elle se concentre plus sur elle-même que Desnos et par conséquent la personne focalisée est toujours la femme. Dans "Bruit dans la chambre à côté," elle répète le vers, "Combien seule je suis avec ma folle envie" (*CB* 25). "Tu m'as abandonnée nuitamment," démontre comment elle situe sa voix narrative. Les adjectifs *mes* et *mon*, et le pronom *moi* projettent une conscience de soi: "Mes heures coulent impassibles / Au fond du miroir moucheté de bronze . . . Dans la mare profonde où tremble mon visage . . . Quelque part au fond de moi un moule se cristallise" (*CB* 28).

Souvent empreinte de tristesse, sa solitude néanmoins évoque une douleur corporelle, réelle—ce qui introduit une autre différence entre elle et Desnos. Le désir de Mansour se fonde sur une relation explicitement sexuelle. Elle connaît et décrit l'intimité qui lui manque. Ce n'est pas à une union sentimentale qu'elle aspire, mais à la libération de l'esprit par le biais de l'union sexuelle, ce qui fait penser à "L'union libre" de Breton.[4] Pour elle, dit J. H. Matthews, l'érotisme "constitue le geste libérateur par où l'on résiste, à deux, à la menace de l'extinction" (Matthews 33).

Au lieu de voiler son Autre de mystère, elle le dénude sans pudeur: "Votre pénis est plus doux / Que faciès d'une vierge."[5] Et c'est elle-même qu'elle dévoile dans "L'eau des sources" quand elle écrit: "Je ne saurais vivre / Sans brûlant désir / Ni barque / Pour / Mes / Nuits / Blanches" (*CB* 41). Ses rêves sont ancrés dans une réalité de souvenir; ils sont plus réels que les fantaisies arachnéennes de Desnos.

Plus haut, dans "L'eau des sources," Mansour présente une autre image tirée du vocabulaire surréaliste: l'amante-miroir. Desnos, comme Paul Eluard,[6] s'en est servi, le plus directement dans sa pièce, "La place de l'étoile" où le héros affirme: "Tu es ce que je rêve et ce que, chaque matin, je découvre dans ma glace" (356). Mansour insère sa référence entre parenthèses: "(Es-tu réellement en moi / Ou est-ce par réflexion)" (*CB* 41). Elle semble avouer une tendance féminine à servir de reflet aux hommes, répondant à l'appel de Breton pour "la nécessité de reconstitution de l'*Androgyne primordial*"—de rétablir le mythe de l'Androgyne comme principe de base de l'amour.[7]

Pourtant cette réciprocité d'images ressentie par le poète surréaliste masculin n'est pas réalisée pour la femme poète. La femme-miroir évoquée par Eluard et Desnos n'a pas d'équivalent chez Mansour; l'homme-miroir n'existe pas dans *Carré blanc*. Mansour en cherche un dans "Parce que j'ai toute la vie devant moi," mais en vain.[8] Elle transforme le célèbre fragment de Desnos, "J'ai tant rêve de toi" en "J'ai rêve de ton oeil" (*C & B* 91; *CB* 69). Avec cette transformation qui rappelle Bataille, l'emprise du regard masculin n'est pas mise en question.[9] En effet, quand Mansour cherche sa propre image, elle ne voit pas plus clair que quand elle cherchait son reflet dans un homme. Dans "La griffe de l'animal," le premier poème de "Verres fumés"—la troisième section de *Carré blanc*—les miroirs qu'elle cherche s'obscurcissent: "Cette eau qui tel un miroir attire les grimaces et les garde / Si maladroitement enlisées dans la boue" (*CB* 87). Les vers finals du poème suivant reprennent cette image de boue comme miroir de la femme: "Il faut que femme enlace / Son image dans la boue."[10]

Ce reflet boueux va de pair avec ses cris de victime—tels les derniers vers du "Galop du Coquillage de Neige":

> J'ai trop bondi trop rougi
> Trop aiguisé ma rage
> Je ne veux plus être le Goliath
> De ta pierre (*CB* 62)

Le poème suivant développe cette idée de femme-victime sur le plan littéraire aussi bien que sur le plan physique ou sentimental. Elle y dénonce les préjugés des hommes:

> Tu dis que les femmes
> Doivent souffrir se polir et voyager sans perdre
>   haleine
> Réveiller les pierreries embellies par le fard
> Changer ou se taire déchirer la brume
> Hélas je ne saurais danser dans un marais de
>   sang[11]

C'est au piédestal poétique qu'elle s'adresse. Pour elle, la bouteille cristalline de Desnos est brumeuse—une lentille gélatineuse et incorrecte. A l'intérieur de la bouteille, les étoiles ne peuvent survivre; elles doivent réduire cette prison exquise en tessons—une conséquence aussi prevue par Desnos dans "Paroles des rochers." Les derniers vers de ce poème—adressé à des "chevelures" de femme—présagent les sentiments de Mansour: "Les infinis éternels se brisent en tessons ô chevelures! / C'était ce sera une nuit des nuits sans lune ni perle / Sans même de bouteilles brisées" (*C & B* 139). Pour Mansour, la bouteille-piédestal, qui impose la solitude et le silence aux femmes, fonctionne comme le jeu surréaliste du cadavre exquis. Le dessin qui en résulte est fascinant mais néanmoins cadavérique; c'est un objet intéressant mais morcelé. Pour trouver l'Autre désirée, il faut déboucher sinon briser la bouteille.

L'étoile filante à l'intérieur de la bouteille nocturne de Desnos recouvre la parole chez Mansour. Mais sa voix ne chante pas toujours joliment; chez elle, le rêve vire au cauchemar. Avec sa poésie de femme, elle relève le défi que Breton a lancé à la fin de *Nadja*: "La beauté sera CONVULSIVE ou ne sera pas" (190). Elle surprend parfois par son honnêteté. A la fin du dernier poème du recueil elle affirme:

> Je crache sur ceux qui écoutent
> Derrière leurs prunelles limpides
> Leurs braguettes piétinées par trop de cerveaux
> fêlés
> . . .
> Une seule goutte d'urine sur le trottoir
> Tous les museaux s'allongent [12]

Elle s'est déjà désignée comme "Nocturne oiseau de proie" (*CB* 39); pour elle, le mépris est délicieux, un "Amer aphrodisiaque" (*CB* 53); et elle se voit comme une amante/mante: "Comme elle je dévorerai celui qui violera mes flancs . . . Comme elle je grignoterai mon frère / Il faut savoir attendre pour se venger / Imiter les insectes pour plaire" (*CB* 81).

Son poème, "Régions barbares," répond à "Dans les espaces du sommeil" de Desnos. Comme il l'avait imaginé, elle est dans la nuit, mais sa solitude est triste, et elle ne l'a pas choisie. Elle ne se décrit pas comme une merveille du monde, mais: "Blême comme la souffrance de la seule femme au monde" (*CB* 82). Pour elle, les étoiles n'engendrent pas de constellations merveilleuses car les étoiles mansouriennes sont froides. Dans "Des myriades d'autres morts": "La nuit gorgée d'étoiles"—un phénomène naturel, souple—par juxtaposition est comparée au mur rigide de sa chambre. Elle se décrit comme terrestre, non pas céleste: "Je suis l'animal de la nuit" (*CB* 119). Ici, "Les couloirs de l'espace" sont "Peuplés de formes ultimes" et "Pétrissent les somnambules." Pour elle, dans les bouteilles de verre il n'y a pas de vie; elle exhorte son auditeur/auditrice: "Ecoute / Les damnés sont à table dans leurs tristes habitacles de verre" (*CB* 120).

La préoccupation de la mort rapproche Mansour de Desnos. Elle pourrait être "la petite fille" du "Suicidé de nuit" qui "s'en va à l'école en récitant sa leçon"—une leçon qui inclut "une pierre tombale plus transparente que la neige blanche" (*C & B* 125). Sauf que, chez Mansour, les pierres elles-mêmes sont "femmes brisées"; elle avoue qu'elle "pense trop souvent aux cérémonies funèbres"; et, finalement, comme Desnos, elle relie la mort à l'amour: "J'ai peur d'être seule dans ta tombe."[13]

Mansour partage un sens du ludique avec Desnos. Elle n'est jamais trop loin de l'humour, raillant jusqu'à sa propre tendance morbide dans des vers comme: "Seuls les morts n'apprécient guère les finesses de l'autopsie."[14] Mais, aussi comme son précurseur, il y a une chose qu'elle prend absolument au sérieux: "l'alchimie" rimbaldienne de l'écriture. Dans *La liberté ou l'amour*, Desnos parle de l'écriture comme "phénomène magique," alchimique, auquel le poète doit faire appel pour transformer la page blanche en miroir de sa psyché. Car la page risque continuellement de devenir "un cimetière de mots" qui ne peut être sauvé que par "une écriture magique et efficace" capable de la transmuer en matière précieuse (47,58).

L'intensité de Desnos se mire dans l'abandon de la poésie de Mansour: "Ecris signe barre / Je me noie dans l'encrier du moindre mot" (*CB* 122). La page-miroir aussi se retrouve chez Mansour dans le titre, "Papier d'argent"—un poème d'amour joyeux qui anticipe une nuit de rêves.[15] Mansour se réjouit quand son alchimie poétique réussit, comme dans le poème étincelant, (dont le rythme du titre rappelle Mallarmé)[16] "Le Satin / l'opale / la blanche alchimie" où ses images de femme parée de pierres précieuses—"Ah crever comme une bulle dans une mare de diamants"—évoquent l'Autre desnosienne (et rimbaldienne). La clôture de ce poème, "Contrée de mon immense amour," révèle sa perspective sur son titre (*CB* 80). Comme Desnos, c'est avec l'amour de l'alchimie poétique qu'elle transforme la page blanche en poème lyrique.

Justement, pour Mansour comme pour Desnos, l'amour de l'Autre se mêle toujours à l'amour de l'écriture. La différence principale entre les deux se situe dans le caractère de leur voix. La page blanche du titre de Mansour, *Carré blanc*, propose un renversement de l'ordre naturel/culturel des marges et du texte. Quand nous lisons Mansour, ce sont Breton, Eluard et Desnos que nous entendons dans les marges, et c'est la blancheur féminine qui se transforme en matière principale. Echappée de la bouteille, elle se fait spectaculaire dans ses poèmes, d'une manière souvent assez féroce. Car elle n'est pas uniquement échappée, mais véritablement une rescapée du projet surréaliste. Le choc de la venue à l'écriture pour la voix poétique surréaliste féminine résonne à travers les vers de Mansour. Pourtant, malgré l'aspérité d'une grande quantité de ses images personnelles, Mansour garde la conscience de la particularité du spectacle qu'elle fait d'elle-même dans son oeuvre. Elle se réfugie dans son isolation culturelle, et trouve du confort dans les marges, "Dans la forêt hors du gonds de la patrie":

> J'ai envie
> C'est ridicule
> D'une distraction
> D'une mélodie
> De quelque griffonnage
> Ou confiture de dame (78)

En contraste avec la voix muette de l'Autre desnosienne, la voix mansourienne de dedans la bouteille—loin d'être confiture serait plutôt un élixir mystérieux qui devrait porter l'avertissement: attention—capable de déranger autant que d'éblouir.

Notes

[1] Pour une version révisée et en anglais de cet article voir *Paroles gelées* 8 (1990) .

[2] Joyce Mansour, *Carré blanc* (Paris: Soleil Noir, 1965). Ce texte est ci-dessous désigné comme *CB*.

[3] Robert Desnos, *Corps et biens* (1930; Paris: Gallimard, 1968). Ce texte est ci-dessous désigné comme *C & B* .

[4] André Breton, "L'union libre," *Clair de terre* (1931; Paris: Gallimard, 1966) 91-95.

[5] Mansour, "Dans l'obscurité à gauche" 27.

[6] Paul Eluard, "La courbe de tes yeux," *Capitale de la douleur*, ed. Vera J. Daniel (1926; London: Blackwell,1985) 81.

[7] André Breton, "Du surréalisme en ses oeuvres vives," *Manifestes du surréalisme* (1953; Paris: Gallimard, 1963) 184.

[8] "Vainement je cherche un reflet de ma joie / Dans le trou où je pensais trouver ton coeur" (Mansour 83).

[9] Georges Bataille, "L'histoire de l'oeil," *Oeuvres complètes I: Premiers écrits 1922-1940*, ed. Denis Hollier (1928; Paris: Gallimard, 1970) .

[10] Mansour, "En attendant Minuit" 89.

[11] Mansour, "Fleurie comme la luxure" 63.

[12] Mansour, "Sonne n'écoute personne" 132.

[13] Mansour, "Dalle pour trois roues," "La Nuit en forme de bison," "Bronze comme la nuit tombée" 110, 123, 124.

[14] Mansour, "Dans ma chambre" 100.

[15] Le dernier vers, "Bonne nuit Irène," anticipe la continuation de la chanson, en anglais: "Good night, Irene, I'll see you in my dreams."

[16] Stéphane Mallarmé, "Le vierge, le vivace et le bel aujourd'hui," *Poésies* (Paris: Librairie Générale Française, 1977) 75.

Oeuvres Consultées

Bataille, Georges. "L'histoire de l'oeil." *Oeuvres complètes: Premiers écrits 1922-1940.* Ed. Denis Hollier. Paris: Gallimard, 1970.

Breton, André. "Du surréalisme et ses oeuvres vives." *Manifestes du surréalisme.* 1953. Paris: Gallimard, 1963.

______. *Nadja.* 1928. Paris: Gallimard, 1964.

______. "L'Union libre." *Clair de terre.* 1931. Paris: Gallimard, 1966. 91-95.

Desnos, Robert. *Corps et Biens*. 1930. Paris: Gallimard, 1968.

______. *La Liberté ou l'amour! suivi de Deuil pour deuil.* 1927. Paris: Gallimard, 1968.

______. "La Place de l'Etoile." *Nouvelle Hébrides et autres textes 1922-1930*. Ed. Marie-Claire Dumas. 1928. Paris: Gallimard, 1978.

Dumas, Marie-Claire. *Robert Desnos ou l'exploration des limites*. Paris: Klincksieck, 1980.

Eluard, Paul. *Capitale de la douleur*. Ed. Vera J. Daniel. 1926. London: Blackwell, 1985.

Mallarmé, Stéphane. *Poésies*. Paris: Livres de Poche, 1977.

Mansour, Joyce. *Carré blanc*. Paris: Soleil Noir, 1965.

Matthews, J. H. *Joyce Mansour*. Amsterdam: Rodopi, 1985.